SOCIAL WORK

About the Author

LESLIE LEIGHNINGER is currently Associate Professor and Coordi-
nator of the Undergraduate Social Work Program at the School of Social
Work of Western Michigan University. She has published articles in such
periodicals as *Journal of Education for Social Work, Journal of Sociology
and Social Welfare, Social Service Review*, and *Journal of Applied Social
Sciences*.

SOCIAL WORK
Search for Identity

Leslie Leighninger

Studies in Social Welfare Policies and Programs, Number 4

GREENWOOD PRESS
New York • Westport, Connecticut • London

Library of Congress Cataloging-in-Publication Data

Leighninger, Leslie.
  Social work.

  (Studies in social welfare policies and programs,
ISSN 8755-5360 ; no. 4)
  Bibliography: p.
  Includes index.
  1. Social service—United States—History—20th
century. 2. Social workers—United States—History—
20th century. I. Title. II. Series.
HV91.L375 1987   361.3′0973   86-12155
ISBN 0-313-24775-7 (lib. bdg. : alk. paper)

Library of Congress Catalog Card Number: 86-12155
ISBN: 0-313-24775-7
ISSN: 8755-5360

First published in 1987

Greenwood Press, Inc.
88 Post Road West, Westport, Connecticut 06881

Printed in the United States of America

10 9 8 7 6 5 4 3 2 1

amD
3-28-89

To my mother,

Paulette Kahn Hartrich

Contents

Acknowledgments

Many people contributed to this exploration of social work history. I am indebted above all to James Leiby, who directed my
doctoral dissertation at the School of Social Welfare,
University of California/Berkeley. He has provided just the
right combination of support, guidance, and intellectual challenge during my years at Berkeley and in my subsequent career.
While at Berkeley, where I first began work on this study, I
benefited from the advice and intellectual perspectives of
Harry Specht, Harold Wilensky, Milton Chernin, Merle Borrowman,
and Aaron Wildavsky. Harry Specht's ongoing encouragement is
much appreciated. I am also grateful to Charles Guzzetta and
Henry Meyer for the faith they showed in this endeavor. Professor Meyer deserves special thanks for reading and commenting
on the entire manuscript.

During the process of this study, I have learned to appreciate the crucial role of the archivist in the researcher's
task. I have especially enjoyed working with David Klaassen at
the Social Welfare History Archives at the University of
Minnesota. He has been a perceptive guide to the rich
resources of that collection. He is also a key person in the
creation of a network of scholars interested in social work and
social welfare history. I would also like to thank Anna Glover
of the SWHA, Jerry Hess at the National Archives, Laura Gorretta
at the Case Western Reserve University Archives, Archie Motley
of the Chicago Historical Society, Ruth Brooks of the New York
City Chapter of the National Association of Social Workers,
Giustina Ryan and Jayne Parkin of the National Institute for
Social Work, London, and Dean Phillip Fellin and the staff at
the University of Michigan School of Social Work. Interviews
with a number of people expanded my understanding of events in
social work from 1930 to 1960. I am grateful to Henry Meyer,
Mary Burns, Harriett Bartlett, Hasseltine Taylor, Rita Novak,
D. E. Mackelmann, Norman Goroff, Lucille Barber, and Alice
Taylor Davis. Correspondence with Mattie Cal Maxted provided
useful information on the undergraduate movement in social work
education.

I have also benefited from consultation with social work
historians Emelia Martinez-Brawley, Peggy Pittman-Munke, and
Blanche D. Coll. I appreciate the good working atmosphere created by my colleagues at the School of Social Work, Western
Michigan University. I would like particularly to thank David

Joslyn, Marion Wijnberg, Ed Pawlak, Kenneth Reid, and Lethonee Jones for their interest in social work history and their help with various parts of this project. I have received important technical assistance from a number of people, including Jan Rojacki, Jane Vidich, Howard Poole, Lori Krum, Vonceal Lawrence, and Alex Ellingsen and Bill C. Hanson of SSG LaserWorks. James Sabin, Cynthia Harris, and Barbara Howell, of Greenwood Press, provided advice and editorial help.

A major influence in both my choice of career and my pursuit of social work history is my mother, Paulette Kahn Hartrich--a social worker who lived through and contributed to the events described here. I dedicate this book to her.

Finally, for moral support and all those good things that families offer, I thank the Hartrich and Leighninger families. I am especially thankful for the support and editorial assistance given by my son, Matthew, and my mother-in-law, Ruth Leighninger, the cheerful encouragement of my daughter, Margaret, and the ongoing presence and help of Bob, my husband and colleague.

Abbreviations

AAGW	American Association of Group Workers
AAHSW	American Association of Hospital Social Workers
AAMSW	American Association of Medical Social Workers
AAPSW	American Association of Psychiatric Social Workers
AAPWO	American Association of Public Welfare Officials
AASGW	American Association for the Study of Group Work
AASSW	American Association of Schools of Social Work
AASW	American Association of Social Workers
AAVT	American Association of Visiting Teachers
ADC	Aid to Dependent Children
AMA	American Medical Association
APWA	American Public Welfare Association
ASCO	Association for the Study of Community Organization
ASSA	American Social Science Association
BPA	Bureau of Public Assistance
CSWE	Council on Social Work Education
ERA	Emergency Relief Administration
FERA	Federal Emergency Relief Administration
FWAA	Family Welfare Association of America
HEW	(U.S. Department of) Health, Education, and Welfare

NASSA   National Association of Schools of Social
            Administration

NASSW   National Association of School Social Workers

NASW   National Association of Social Workers

NCSW   National Conference of Social Work

NCSWE   National Council on Social Work Educationi

NTL   National Training Laboratory, Bethel, Maine

NYSSW   New York School of Social Work

SASS   School of Applied Social Sciences, Western Reserve
            University

SSSA   School of Social Service Administration,
            University of Chicago

SWHA   Social Welfare History Archives, University of
            Minnesota, Minneapolis, Minnesota

SWRG   Social Work Research Group

TERA   Temporary Emergency Relief Administration

TIAC   Council on Temporary Inter-Association Structure

USPHS   United States Public Health Service

WPA   Works Progress Administration

SOCIAL WORK

1

Introduction

This book describes and analyzes the development of social work as a profession in the United States from the 1930s through the 1950s. Since this period is key to the development of a professional identity in social work, subsequent years are treated more briefly, primarily in terms of their relationship to earlier trends. The historical account is guided by certain ideas about professionalism and the process of professionalization. These ideas help us understand the nature of social work's growth and the impact of a search for professional identity and status upon that growth. In addition, the study of social work leads to greater understanding of general patterns of professional development.

Major changes occurred in social work in the period from 1930 to 1960. These include the creation of a broad professional association, solidification of a system of graduate education, development of an undergraduate training program, and the growth and increased professionalization of public welfare. All of these were affected by social workers' interest in defining a professional identity and their debates about the appropriateness and meaning of that identity. To understand these debates and their effects, it is useful to refer to some general theories about the development of professions.

Studies of professionalism represent two major schools of thought. The first takes a structural approach and examines the attributes of existing professions. It designates as professions those groups which have acquired certain features: a professional association, a code of ethics, a program of scientific training, and the like.(1) The second approach emphasizes process. Members of this school focus on such phenomena as interactions of groups within professions, exchanges between professions and their external environment, and the movement of occupations toward professional status.(2)

The "process model" developed by Rue Bucher and Anselm Strauss is particularly helpful in understanding the growth of social work. Bucher and Strauss reject the notion of professions as homogeneous communities whose members share identity, values, and definitions of role. Stress on homogeneity, they assert, leads the observer to underestimate the effects of opposing interests upon a profession's development. In contrast, their model focuses on diversity and conflict. It pictures professions as "loose amalgamations" of groups, or segments, "pursuing different objectives in different manners and more or less delicately held together under a common name at a particular period in history."(3) Segments often give different interpretations to common professional catchwords, such as "standards" and "scientific approach." Thus even the rhetoric of professionalism varies from group to group.

Competition between segments shapes the organization of the profession. Interaction between interest groups helps define the dominant goals, language, and approaches of a profession at a given point in time. While external forces--socio-economic factors, interaction with other professions and outside interest groups, community sanction or its absence--clearly affect professional development, forces within the profession play a crucial role. Indeed, internal interest groups frequently serve as the channel through which external forces exert their influence. External and internal forces thus interact in a complex way to shape professional growth.

The process model provides an apt description of the social work profession. Diversity and intergroup conflict are important characteristics of social work--a broad field originating in several social movements and encompassing a number of methods and specialized fields of practice. In addition, social work has been subject to strong, often conflicting public expectations and pressures. A continuing theme in social work history is the attempt to unify various segments in the field and thus, it is hoped, to increase the profession's strength. Yet movements toward unity have been affected, and often offset, by intergroup tensions and debate.

These tensions surface in a variety of areas of professional development. Harold Wilensky, in a discussion of the phases in a "natural history of professionalism," pinpoints a number of these areas. Those most relevant to the study of social work are: cultivation of a knowledge base, development of professional training, creation of professional standards and an exclusive professional association, and the attempt to win public recognition and support for the profession's area of expertise. Each area provides an arena for interaction and debate between professional subgroups.(4)

Creation of a distinctive body of knowledge is a major task in professional development. Possession of such knowledge appears to be crucial in public sanction of a profession's activities. Eliot Freidson stresses the ideological qualities of professional knowledge. He argues that professions consciously structure an esoteric body of knowledge and skills and strive to convince the public that these are necessary for the solution of particular problems. At bottom of this process, Freidson says, is the profession's quest for power. Magali Sarfatti Larson extends Freidson's thesis to describe professions as groups seeking to control a market for their expertise.(5) Such single-factor models overemphasize the degree of internal cohesion in professions. Yet Freidson's and Larson's arguments are useful in an examination of social work's approach to its knowledge-building task. The development of social work knowledge and skills has involved input from a variety of groups attempting to create an exclusive theoretical base which would enhance public recognition of social work as well as improve its practice.

Group interaction and debate are evident in other areas of professional development in social work. Wilensky notes that the process of forming a professional association, for example,

is accompanied by a campaign to separate the competent from the incompetent. This involves further definition of essential professional tasks, [and] the development of internal conflict among practitioners of varying backgrounds.(6)

This conceptualization explains some of the issues involved in attempts within social work to create a single set of professional standards and to unify the various specialties in a single organization. Similarly, the development of professional education and the effort to build a coherent public image have been affected by debates between various groups over how best to achieve these goals.

Existing histories of social work pay little attention to the effects of diversity and conflict upon professional growth. The major work in the field is Roy Lubove's The Professional Altruist: Emergence of Social Work as a Career, 1880-1930. In analyzing social work's early years, Lubove stresses the emergence of a professional subculture preoccupied with developing a unique skill. This skill's emphasis, he posits, was enhanced and shaped by the increasing bureaucratization of social welfare. The notions of a cohesive professional subculture and of professionalism emerging primarily to meet a single function--the bureaucratic imperative of efficiency--ignore the internal conflicts and competing external pressures that seem to me essential for understanding social work's development.(7)

Since diversity and debate have been crucial elements in the shaping of social work, they are the central focus of this book. The influence of external forces, such as socio-economic factors and outside interest groups, receives secondary attention. The conflicts and pressures in social work can be reduced to four major professional issues, which serve as the book's guiding themes: (a) Should social workers put primary stress on profession-building or on public service? (b) How should social work relate to a national system of public welfare? (c) What is the appropriate role of a profession in political activity and social change? (d) Should the profession's intellectual, practice, and membership base be broadly or narrowly construed?

At the heart of these issues is an ongoing controversy over how broadly to define social work's mission and professional identity. As the field took shape from the thirties through the fifties, major segments urged pursuit of professional recognition along selective, traditional lines, with a primary focus on maintaining high personnel standards. At the same time other, less dominant, groups sought a wider membership and a major focus on the public services. The difference between groups was not a simple one of "private agency versus public service" commitments. A number of those promoting high standards were also interested in the creation of a professionalized public welfare system. Yet their overall stress on standards worked against the practical approach necessary for building such a system.

High standards groups did not always have the upper hand, and alternate missions for social work were articulated. Yet the dominant professional identity emerging from intergroup conflict in social work was not one of broad-based involvement in a national public welfare system. It was instead an image of skilled practice by a select group, in a private agency or other nonwelfare setting.

To examine these conflicts and their outcomes, the following chapters are organized around certain critical incidents in social work's history. Each incident involves interaction between groups within social work and external forces. The opening chapter 2 gives an overview of social work in the 1920s. It describes the beginnings of important debates over the merits of public versus private welfare, selective versus broad requirements for membership in the profession, specialized practice versus a generic focus, and social reform versus social services.

Chapter 3 examines the movement to raise membership standards within the major professional organization, the American Association of Social Workers. This movement began in the last years of the 1920s and continued through the early years of the Depression. It represented a broad effort to improve standards in social work. To most social workers of the time this meant increased education. To workers with a union orientation, it meant instead improvement in working conditions. The clash between these two points of view was an important element in the development of social work.

Chapter 3 focuses largely on issues internal to the profession. Chapter 4 explores the effects of external events--the Depression and early New Deal response--on social work. This chapter analyzes the type and degree of political activity carried out by various groups in social work during a period of national crisis. Chapters 3 and 4 cover overlapping time periods. Examination of internal professional issues in Chapter 3 establishes a context for exploring the reaction of social work to broad social change in Chapter 4.

Chapter 5 deals with the events immediately following Franklin Roosevelt's establishment of a permanent federal social welfare system in 1935. It focuses on Jane Hoey's attempts to create a professional public welfare service centered in the Bureau of Public Assistance of the Social Security Administration. The chapter highlights important differences within social work regarding the profession's proper role in public welfare.

Chapters 6 and 7 cover developments in social work in the 1940s. Chapter 6 looks at the impact of World War II on social work and describes important rifts which developed within the profession. These related to the issue of American neutrality, the attempt to democratize the American Association of Social Workers, and the role of social work in postwar social planning. Chapter 7 focuses on a specific conflict within social work education in the mid-1940s. This was a confrontation between undergraduate educators and their allies and the graduate school establishment over the proper setting and length of professional training. In this clash, stress on graduate professional education undercut attempts to train the new public welfare personnel.

Chapter 8 describes the attempts of social work to improve and broaden its knowledge and practice base in the 1950s. It focuses primarily on the profession's relationship to the social sciences. Many social workers saw a dilemma in this relationship. How could the profession borrow theories from other disciplines and yet maintain an autonomous knowledge base?

Chapter 9 depicts the events leading to formation of the National Association of Social Workers in 1955. Creation of a broad professional association was a milestone in movement toward cohesion in the field, yet major areas of tension remained. The concluding chapter traces the continuation of these tensions and analyzes present professional dilemmas in light of past conflicts.

The major sources for this history of social work's search for professional identity are the records of its professional organizations: the National Association of Social Workers and the earlier American Association of Social Workers, and of its educational associations: the Council on Social Work Education and CSWE's predecessor, the American Association of Schools of Social Work. The book also draws on the records of the Chicago Chapter of the AASW, the files in the National Archives on the Bureau of Public Assistance, the papers of social work educator Mattie Cal Maxted on the National Association of Schools of Social Service Administration, and the records of the graduate social work programs at the University of Michigan and Case Western Reserve University. In addition, I have consulted the papers and recorded oral histories of a number of social work leaders, and have augmented the picture presented through my own interviews with a number of social workers active in the period.

A final caution is necessary. Recent historians of professions and social reform have criticized the tendency to describe these movements solely in terms of the goals and activities of their leaders. They suggest that this approach loses the fuller understanding offered by attention to the reactions and behaviors of clients and of the profession's rank and file.(8) This book does not attempt to analyze social work's interaction with its clients. It deals with the values and "occupational culture" of ordinary social workers primarily through discussion of social work unionization in the thirties and through attention to membership as well as executive meetings of the professional associations. Evidence of the goals of the rank and file is often less accessible than that describing the aims of more professionally conscious practitioners and educators. Yet the evidence that is available suggests that social workers as a group have been peculiarly self-conscious about professional issues. By focusing on conflicts over these issues, I hope to have produced a realistic account of the major orientations and tensions within the field, and their effects on the role of social work within a larger social welfare setting.

Notes

1. See, for example, Abraham Flexner, "Is Social Work a Profession?" National Conference of Charities and Corrections, Proceedings (1915), pp. 576-90; Ernest Greenwood, "Attributes of a Profession," Social Work, II: 45-55 (July, 1957); William J. Goode, "The Theoretical Limits of Professionalization," in Amitai Etzioni, The Semi-Professions and Their Organization (New York: Free Press, 1969), pp. 266-313; Wilbert E. Moore, The Professions: Roles and Rules (New York: Russell Sage, 1970).

2. See, for example, Harold Wilensky, "The Professionalization of Everyone?" American Journal of Sociology, LXX: 137-58 (September, 1964); Jeffrey Berlant, Professions and Monopoly (Berkeley: University of California Press, 1975); Eliot Freidson, The Professions and Their Prospects (Beverly Hills, Calif.: Sage, 1973); Terence J. Johnson, Professions and Power (New York: Macmillan, 1972).

3. Rue Bucher and Anselm Strauss, "Professions in Process," American Journal of Sociology, LXVI: 325-34 (January, 1961). See also Bucher and Joan G. Snelling, Becoming Professional (Beverly Hills, Calif.: Sage, 1977), pp. 21-23.

4. Wilensky, p. 146.

5. Freidson, pp. 22-31; Magali Sarfatti Larson, The Rise of Professionalism (Berkeley: University of Calif. Press, 1977); see also Berlant.

6. Wilensky, p. 144.

7. Roy Lubove, The Professional Altruist (New York: Atheneum Press, 1969).

8. See, e.g., Barbara Melosh, "The Physician's Hand:" Work Culture and Conflict in American Nursing (Philadelphia: Temple University Press, 1982); Raymond A. Mohl, "The Main Stream Social Welfare History and its Problems," review of A History of Social Welfare and Social Work in the United States, by James Leiby, Reviews in American History, VII: 469-76 (December, 1979).

2

The 1920s: Diversity and the Beginnings of Professionalism

In May, 1929, social workers and welfare leaders gathered at the annual meeting of the National Conference of Social Work (NCSW) in San Francisco. This meeting beside the Pacific of a conference usually held in the central or eastern states was testimony to the spread of professional social work across the country. Porter R. Lee, director of the New York School of Social Work, welcomed the participants. In his presidential address, Lee praised the achievements of pioneers in the field of social welfare, and heralded a new period about to unfold.

Lee's address, "Social Work as Cause and Function," called attention to a significant shift in social work's development. Having paid tribute to early social workers and reformers dedicated to the cause of social welfare, Lee posited a transition from cause to function in a modern, "well-organized community life." Once the object of social reform had been achieved, ongoing administrative machinery was needed. As the goals of the social welfare movement shifted, so did the role of the social worker within that movement. Zeal would now give way to training and intelligence, "sacrifice and flaming spirits" to standards and methods. Lee summed up his theme:

I am inclined to think that in the capacity of the social worker . . . to administer a routine functional responsibility in the spirit of the servant in a cause lies the explanation of the great service of social work. . . . According the fullest respect to our outstanding leaders of the past and present, we may nevertheless assert that social work never would have achieved its great service . . . without its growing army of less conspicuous men and women who have seen no necessary inconsistency between idealism and efficiency. Its future, moreover, is largely in their hands.(1)

Lee's address must have disappointed some of his listeners. Drawn to the field of Jane Addams, Graham Taylor, and Edward Devine, many were eager to take up their role as bearers of a social conscience. Others were excited by the new theories of psychotherapy and the promise of a psychiatric social work. Perhaps they hoped that Lee would elaborate on the common elements in psychiatry and social case work, as embodied in the Bureau of Children's Guidance set up by the New York School in 1921.(2) Was their primary mission instead to build and solidify a professional field and an organizational structure for social welfare? Yet the "function" of social work, while not as glamorous as "the cause" (or "the method"), carried its own promise and appeal. Perhaps social workers would find a new dignity as members of a legitimate, skilled occupational group, with an accepted role in society.

Social workers in 1929 had reason for optimism. The tumult of progressive politics and war had given way to a decade of relative peace and economic expansion. While social work still seemed new, diverse, and vaguely defined, its practitioners had laid foundations for improved service and growth. Social workers were still few in 1929 and the professionally trained among them only a handful. Yet the federal census then in progress had for the first time classified them as "professional." Their claim to this status might be debated, but certain significant milestones had been passed. An important conference on social work method had concluded that a generic case work method underlay social work in its various settings. Professional schools had increased in number and formed a common educational organization. Professional associations, representing both the specialties and the field as a whole, had begun to provide forums for exchanging ideas and developing standards. As Lee noted, a new era in organized professional development seemed about to unfold.

To understand the new era, we need to know what this nascent profession looked like in 1929. Who, for example, were its practitioners? What did they do and where did they work? What were their interests and values and their ideas for the future? To what degree did they accept the goal of transforming social work into a profession, and what model of professionalism did they follow?

A brief description of social work's development in the 1920s helps to answer these questions. The picture emerging from this review suggests growing cohesion within the field, but a cohesion tempered by ongoing areas of diversity and debate. Change and growth in social work were affected by interactions with other professions and by changes in the social and economic environment.

By the late 1920s, social workers had many roles and functions. They had emerged from three earlier streams of social activity: institutional administration, organized charity, and the social settlements. Another influence on social work's development was the creation of a Home Service Program by the American National Red Cross in the years following World War I. This program used paid workers and volunteers to provide case work services, including relief, to the families of servicemen and disaster victims. Although strongest in urban areas, the Home Services brought a first introduction to modern social work to many rural districts and small towns.(3)

Surveys found most social workers practicing case work in private family welfare agencies, hospitals, child guidance clinics, schools, and children's aid societies. Some worked in public welfare settings. Settlement work, community organizing, and legislative reform activity continued as well, although these had lost strength since the early 1900s.(4)

Postwar prosperity was accompanied, paradoxically, by fears of bolshevism abroad and social unrest at home. Neither encouraged an atmosphere of reform. Conscious social change was seen more and more as the prerogative of the expert or the efficient social engineer. One of the Progressive heroes of the 1920s was Herbert Hoover. In his role as head of relief and reconstruction efforts in Europe after World War I, Hoover appeared as a "practical idealist" who used technical skills and efficient organization to solve social problems.(5)   This context helps explain the growing stress on techniques in social case work and the popularity of Mary Richmond's primer on methodology, Social Diagnosis. Richmond's 1917 text, rein- forced by the writings of Dr. Richard C. Cabot, Mary Jarrett, and others, helped establish a "scientific" case work as the foundation of social work practice.

This practice was concentrated in major cities--New York, Boston, Philadelphia, Cleveland, and Chicago. A 1926 study found that over half of the estimated 25,000 paid professional social workers in the U.S. were located in the thirty-three largest cities. About four-fifths worked in communities of 25,000 and more.(6)   This was a small part of a larger landscape of public and private social services which extended into rural areas; yet social work itself was still largely an invention of the city.(7)

Most national social welfare agencies--the Family Welfare Association of America, the Child Welfare League, the Interna- tional Migration Service, and others--had central offices in New York. Boston was a center for hospital social work. Chicago showed growing strength in the public social agencies; the School of Social Service Administration at the University of Chicago had important ties with the national Children's Bureau in Washington. Certain rivalries developed between these centers of education and practice. When Porter Lee defeated the University of Chicago's Sophonisba Breckinridge as president-elect of the NCSW in 1928, the victory was described as the outcome of a "friendly" contest between the University of Chicago SSSA and the New York School of Social Work."(8)   Such regional conflict, along with social work's primarily urban character, would have important consequences for future devel- opment.

In the major urban centers, the private agency constituted the dominant model for practice. Social workers made their diagnoses and conducted their interviews under the auspices of such agencies as the Children's Aid Society of Cleveland, the Family Society of Philadelphia, St. Louis' Provident Associa- tion, the Jewish Home Finding Service of Chicago, and the Orange, New Jersey, Bureau of Associated Charities.

These practitioners were diverse in background and train- ing. A 1921-22 national study of social workers found that 40 percent of the women surveyed, and 60 percent of the men, were college graduates; about 7 percent also had at least one year in a school of social work. On the other hand, 17 percent of the women and 14 percent of the men had neither college nor pro- fessional training.(9)   A 1928-29 census of social workers in Massachusetts suggested little change in the proportion of college-educated practitioners. The study did indicate an increase in the number holding social work certificates or diplomas. Twenty-one percent of the respondents had cre-

dentials from professional social work training programs.(10)
Diversity persisted even among the professionally trained, however. Not all of them had B.A.'s. Their professional education ranged from several months to several years.
    Jewish and Catholic social services were small but well-
organized exceptions to white Protestant predominance in social
welfare. Jewish social workers operated family service agencies in forty-two cities and had their own training school and
national conference.(11) Yet the editors of the Jewish Social
Service Quarterly worried about its small circulation of 800 in
1929.(12) Catholic social service work was organized in some
fifty central diocesan agencies, generally called Catholic
Charities. While Catholic agencies were generally less professional and prestigious than Jewish ones, Catholic social
work boasted four professional schools and also a journal and a
national conference.(13) Because of its ties to a hierarchical
church, Catholic social work was also more likely to follow a
consistent "line" on social policy issues.(14)
    Black social workers were a rarity. By 1932, the largest
group of Negro social workers was 270 family welfare workers
employed in private societies in sixty-five cities. An additional 600 or so worked in a variety of other settings. Blacks
were hampered by lack of funds for higher education and lack of
access to social science and social work programs in the segregated colleges and universities of the South. Many white agencies, in both North and South, would not hire black social workers or accept them for training. The primary educational
avenues open to blacks consisted of short term institutes,
training in one of a handful of social work programs in black
educational institutions in the South, or enrollment in a graduate school of social work in the North. This was generally
followed by employment either in an agency in which all the clients were black, or, more often, in one serving both races.(15)
    The field of Negro social work produced leaders like
George E. Haynes of Fisk University and Forrester B.
Washington, director of the Atlanta School of Social Work.
Their influence extended to the profession as a whole. A few
blacks sat on the Executive Board of the National Conference of
Social Work and spoke at NCSW programs.(16) Yet the black
social work community as a whole, small in size and limited in
interaction with white social workers by Jim Crow laws and
informal discrimination, found it difficult to make an impact
on general professional development.
    The relationship between men and women in social work was a
complex one. The field was initially identified as a largely
female   occupation. Even   in   the   late   twenties,   some
specialties, like psychiatric social work, consisted almost
entirely of women.(17) Early social work pioneers--Jane
Addams, clinical social worker Bertha Reynolds, and Edith
Abbott and Sophonisba Breckinridge of the Chicago School--saw
social work's potential as a new kind of career and an outlet
for the talents of college-educated women. Yet these same
pioneers felt that custom and public opinion sometimes
necessitated a male presence in leadership roles.
Breckinridge, for example, took a back seat to a male dean of
the Chicago School in the early years of its development. In

the late twenties, both sexes held leadership positions in professional associations and schools of social work.

Within the agency, more traditional male/female roles prevailed. Men headed the agencies; women made up most of the rank
and file. There were large salary differentials between the
sexes. In the agency setting, male dominance seems to have
been accepted with little question.(18) Agency executives
were appointed by community boards or political bodies, rather
than by professionals. Perhaps women saw little chance to
change the situation.

Social work professional leadership in the late twenties
included old-timers Jane Addams, Charity Organization Society
leaders Edward Devine and Mary Richmond, Julia Lathrop of the
Children's Bureau, social settlement pioneers Graham Taylor and
Robert Woods, labor and consumer activist Florence Kelley,
Susan Kingsbury, first director of the Bryn Mawr School of
Social Work, Child Welfare League executive C. C. Carstens, and
Mary Jarrett, proponent of psychiatric and medical social work
and a founder of the American Association of Hospital Social
Workers. These were the pioneers in new welfare fields and new
areas of reform. Most had national reputations and remained
heroic figures to the next generation of social workers.

Some, however, encountered a declining interest in their
contributions to the field. Social work educator Mildred
Mudgett recalls seeing a dejected Mary Richmond waiting for the
elevator in the conference hotel after her 1922 defeat for the
presidency of the NCSW. Richmond's sociologically oriented
case procedures already seemed out of step with a growing interest in the psychological factors in human problems.(19) In
addition, charity work had begun to shift its focus from work
with paupers to family service. Richmond's opponent, Homer
Folks, aligned himself with these modern impulses in charity.
Folks headed the State Charities Aid Association of New York,
which pioneered in foster care for delinquent children. He was
supported in the election by the state agency people, who were
well represented in the NCSW.(20)

In addition to Folks, other leaders, already well-known,
would continue their careers up through, and in some cases past
the 1930s: Grace Abbott at the Children's Bureau in Washington
and later part of an impressive trio with her sister Edith and
colleague Sophonisba Breckinridge at the University of Chicago;
Lillian Wald and Helen Hall of the Henry Street Settlement of
New York; social work philosopher Eduard Lindemann; William
Hodson, New York City Welfare Council executive; "functional
case work" theorist Jesse Taft; and Porter Lee of the New York
School. In addition, new personalities were beginning to
emerge. By and large, those rising to prominence in the thirties and later would have a more limited fame. Well-known in
social work education and practice circles, they would not command familiarity in a broader public arena.(21) Their task
would lie in strengthening the knowledge base, building social
work organizations, forging a group identity from disparate
viewpoints and goals, and developing the methodology of a profession. In short, they focused on function rather than cause.

The change of leadership in the American Association for
Organizing Family Social Work is a good example of the change

from pioneering to development. Francis McLean, first executive director of the association, promoted the cause of family
social welfare in field visits across the U.S. He "exerted
tremendous influence on the development of the family service
field through his advice and counsel to hundreds, even thousands of budding social workers."(22) But after 1925, this
inspired organizer gradually relinquished his position of prominence in the organization to Linton B. Swift, recently named
general director. Swift came to the directorship with a background as a practicing attorney and a United Charities
executive.(23) McLean's "retirement" to staff consultant in
1933 signified the shift from a pioneer leader to one of a more
administrative nature.

In the new era, social work needed a more refined practice
methodology. The existing methodology had recently been
scrutinized by a committee drawn from a yearly conference of
case work organization board members and executives. The
Milford Conference represented almost exclusively New York
City-based case work leaders, with a sprinkling of Boston and
Philadelphia agency figures. Yet the conference attempted a
broad view of social case work practice. While recognizing
that social case work did not represent all of social work, conference participants clearly saw it as the major thrust of the
profession.(24)

In yearly meetings from 1923 to 1925, conference members
struggled to define social case work "so as to distinguish it
from other forms of professional work."(25) They sought to
understand the differences between the separately labeled
fields of case work then being practiced. The case work scene
they looked out upon contained definite demarcations. Hospital social workers had formed the first specialized professional association in 1918, quickly followed by the American
Association of Visiting Teachers (AAVT) (1919) and the Section
of Psychiatric Social Workers of the American Association of
Hospital Social Workers (AAHSW) (1922), which became the American Association of Psychiatric Social Workers (AAPSW) in 1926.
Such organizations reflected a philosophy of distinctive and
specialized practice in a variety of settings: schools, hospitals, family welfare agencies, probation departments, child
guidance clinics, and the like. Were there commonalities in
practice in these fields? Or were the skills demanded by each
fundamentally different? Answers to these questions bore
implications not only for practice, but also for the process of
professionalization and unification. Increasingly, members of
the conference became convinced that a

fundamental conception . . . of . . . 'generic social case work'
was much more . . . significant in its implications for all
forms of social case work than were any of the specific emphases
of the different case work fields."(26)

To explore the notion of generic social case work further,
a special committee spent three years collecting and classify-
ing fundamental principles, values, and skills of social case
work as practiced in various settings. A final committee
report was approved by the Milford Conference in November,

1928. More a taxonomy than an analysis, the report's key contribution was its affirmation that a generic case work did
exist. Its principles and methodologies cut across
specialties and provided a common base for social case work as a
major division of social work practice. Study and research
into the case worker's "equipment" would further the field's
claim to a "scientific and professional" character.(27)
    The Milford report, published by the American Association
of Social Workers, sold 250 copies in the first month.(28)
Case work leader Grace Marcus felt it should give to the practitioner "new perspectives on the potentialities of this young
profession in whose making he is so importantly involved."(29)
The Milford Conference conclusions were more symbolic than
practical. Separate fields of practice continued to grow.
The specialist associations remained active. Some even undertook to review and approve the professional schools' curricula
in their areas. The most powerful organization, the AAHSW, had
a full time executive secretary, a membership of 1,500 in 1930,
and an active Committee on Training.(30)
    Forces for cohesion, however, continued to emerge. One
was the American Association of Social Workers, founded in 1921
by social work educators and national leaders concerned with
establishing professional standards in practice and training.
An outgrowth of a national social work employment service, the
AASW was the first organization to cut across all fields of
practice. Its membership was open, theoretically, to all social
workers. Nevertheless, requirements of education and experience in a "recognized social agency" discriminated against
those involved in group work or settlement work.
    From 750 in 1921, AASW membership grew to 3,512 in 1926.
While it represented only some 14 percent of the professional
social workers then practicing, this was still a greater number
than those belonging to the specialist groups. The AASW's 1930
membership of 5,000 was over twice that of the AAHSW, the AAPSW,
and the AAVT combined.(31) Membership characteristics reflected basic trends in the field. Members were concentrated
in local chapters in the larger cities. Certain states--New
York, Pennsylvania, Ohio, California, Illinois, and Minnesota-
-accounted for most growth of the association in 1924-27. By
contrast, no individuals were admitted in those years from nine
southern and far western states.(32) Men averaged 17 percent
of those admitted in 1924-26, 12 percent in 1930, but Neva
Deardorff, of the New York Welfare Council, was the only woman
to hold the AASW presidency during the twenties.(33)
    Of those admitted in 1930-32, about 40 percent had only a
high school diploma. A little over half had a baccalaureate
degree, sometimes with an additional diploma or certificate
from a professional course of study. Only 9 percent had graduate degrees, generally from a school of social work. The over-
whelming majority worked in private social work agencies.(34)
While the AASW membership represented largely the big-city
case work vanguard, its levels of education were fairly low and
unstandardized.
    Such lack of consistency had been a major impetus in the
formation of the AASW. In executive, membership, and other
committee meetings, and at the annual membership meetings, the

association concerned itself with the problems of defining and
maintaining professional social work standards and convincing
agencies to honor these. Gaining acceptance for such standards
outside of the organization was a major task. One member
reporting in 1923 on the problems of the professional schools
regretted that child welfare agency executives were not
stressing special training requirements for their staff.(35)
It was only with some difficulty that the AASW helped secure
professional classification of social workers in the 1930 census. Overlap with other occupations and problems in creating a
satisfactory definition for the group hampered their efforts.(36)
      Internally, AASW leadership struggled with the question of
how to establish membership requirements broad enough to
include members of a diverse field, yet rigorous enough to foster higher standards. A particularly difficult problem lay in
imposing professional yet feasible standards upon public social
service work.(37) These struggles marked the beginning of
important debates over two types of professional models, one
broadly based, the other focused on high standards and
selectivity.
      While the AASW leadership worried about professional
standard-setting and maintenance of a selective group, membership continued to grow. Less concerned with the technical and
philosophical problems of organizing a profession, rank and
file members of chapters like Chicago attended meetings to hear
speakers on "Social Work and the Community Conscience" and committee reports on professional ethics.(38) The AASW journal,
The Compass, kept members informed on issues in professional
training and credentialling, and reported on the activities of
local chapters. Gradually the organization was promoting a
sense of cohesion and "a spirit of unity and common interest
among social workers."(39)
      A second organization that fostered unity was the National
Conference of Social Work. Established in 1873, by the 1920s it
had changed from an agency of state institutions and boards of
charities with a focus on general problems of dependency and
corrections, to emphasis on professional social work concerns.
While maintaining a broad interest in the institution of social
welfare, the conference became more and more a forum to discuss
social work techniques and professional goals. Speakers exam-
ined such topics as "The Relation of Research to Professional
Standards in Social Work," "Underlying Principles and Common
Practice in Social Work," and "The Contribution of Mental
Hygiene to the Theory and Practice of Case Work," often under
the auspices of a Division on Professional Standards and education.(40) In addition, a number of professional social work
associations, including the AASW, found the annual NCSW meetings a convenient time and place for their own gatherings.
      Many social workers read Paul Kellogg's journal The Sur-
vey. While interested primarily in issues of public policy and
social action, it also reported on developments within the profession. Suggesting a growing split between broad policy considerations and concerns about professional standards, the publication divided into two journals in 1922. The Survey
Midmonthly carried on the professional orientation and

described trends in various fields of social work, while the
Survey Graphic addressed itself to a broader audience interested in social reform.(41)   Although Survey and the NCSW maintained an interest in social problems, changes within them
demonstrated social work's trend toward a technical focus and
attention to administrative function.

A publication which combined a social policy focus with an
interest in professional development was the Social Service
Review, created by Abbott and Breckinridge at the University of
Chicago SSSA. A scholarly enterprise, the SSR devoted itself
to a readership concerned with social welfare policies and
administration, and the role of professional social work within
these areas. A more case work focused journal was The Family,
published by the Family Welfare Association of America.

Movements toward a common methodology and a system of professional associations and journals were accompanied by new
developments in professional education. Though few social
workers had training beyond college, the professional schools
had begun to create a small elite of professionally educated
practitioners. By 1930, thirty-four schools had been added to
the list of already established leaders in professional training: the New York School of Social Work, the SSSA at the
University of Chicago, Simmons College School of Social Work in
Boston, the School of Applied Social Sciences at Western
Reserve University in Cleveland, and the Pennsylvania School of
Health and Social Work in Philadelphia. Rivalries between the
Chicago School and those in the East, particularly the New York
School, were beginning to surface. These involved differences
between a clinical and public welfare focus.

Professional schools exhibited a variety of structures:
two-year graduate programs, totally undergraduate programs,
and combinations of the two. Some had agency rather than
university affiliations.

The American Association of Schools of Social Work, formed
in 1919, did for its organizational members what the AASW did
for practitioners. In 1924, it raised membership standards to
require university affiliation of all new applicant schools.
By 1930, its membership included twenty-eight schools, all but
four of which were university-affiliated.(42) The professional association, AASW, required social work training in
"approved schools," and it relied largely on AASSW criteria for
its basis of approval.

Thus, the professional association and the organization of
schools dovetailed in their emphasis on standards. Philosophically, as well, leaders in the field looked to organized
professional training as one stepping stone to professional
identity. "Social work will never be a profession . . ."
Edith Abbott wrote in 1927, "and . . . social agencies can never
be standardized except through the professional schools."(43)

The schools graduated relatively small numbers, but
enrollments rose steadily. By 1930, AASSW member schools
reported a full-time enrollment of about 1,500. Almost the
same number of students attended part-time. For almost half of
the full-time students, professional training was undergraduate rather than graduate.(44) Sydnor Walker's 1928 study of
schools of social work noted the lack of uniformity in subject

matter from school to school.(45) The pattern was still diversity within a broad framework.

Development of social work professional education often involved examination of social work's relationship to science, more specifically the social sciences, and to the fields of psychiatry and psychotherapy. The appeal of science as a foundation for a bona fide profession was a strong one. Porter Lee, Edith Abbott, and others stressed the development of social work as a profession based on the scientific knowledge and technique gained through special training.(46)

And what a variety of new knowledge and technique seemed open to social workers. Freudian psychology was beginning to emerge in classrooms and clinics, primarily in eastern cities, but slowly in the Midwest as well. Psychiatrist Bernard Glueck lectured on Freud to the Chicago Round Table on Psychiatric Social Work in 1929.(47) Students reportedly fainted with shock in Marion Kenworthy's classes on psychiatry at the New York School.(48) Otto Rank delivered a ten-lecture course in New York City, where social workers lectured to him on their adaptions of his ideas.(49) Virginia Robinson publicized the psychiatric trend in A Changing Psychology in Social Casework, published in 1930.

While some pursued the excitement of psychiatric and psychoanalytic theory and techniques, others promoted greater utilization of the social sciences, particularly sociology. Maurice Karpf, an agency administrator and director of the New York Training School for Jewish Social Work, argued that sociology had the greatest promise for a scientific base for social work.(50) Another proponent contended that "the well trained social worker is potentially the sociologist of the future."(51) Sociologists had been intimately involved in the founding of a number of the professional education programs in social work. A resurgence of interest in mutual work was institutionalized in the forming of a Division of Social Work and Sociology by the American Sociological Society in 1927. In that same year, the AASW joined the Society and other groups on the editorial board of a major reference work then in process: the Encyclopedia of the Social Sciences.(52)

Attempts to utilize new theories and insights brought problems. The work of academic social scientists was often not tailored to immediate application. Social scientists did not always welcome associations with "unscientific" practitioners and social reformers. Even Karpf noted:

The social worker who reads the sociological literature and who sees great promise . . . for a more scientific type of social work . . . finds himself in the condition of a thirsty wanderer in the desert who sees a mirage and expects to drink his fill only to be bitterly disappointed at the frustration of his hopes.(53)

The "new psychiatry" was at times shocking and alien to workers schooled in the more straightforward techniques of social diagnosis. Use of psychiatric methods brought troubling questions about the role differences between social workers, psychiatrists, and psychologists. Finally, frustration with "borrowing" theories rather than producing ones indigenous to social work was beginning to be felt by social work thinkers who stressed creation of a unique knowledge base as one characteristic of a profession.(54)

The "science" available for a professional practice was diverse. Sociological and psychiatric emphases suggested somewhat different conceptions of social work's place in the network, or system, of social welfare institutions. How did this network look to Porter Lee and his audience? What roles had social workers assumed within it?

"System" is a misleading term for what they saw. There was no national aim to hold the many elements together. General public assistance was strictly a local affair. Usually conducted by political appointees, "outdoor relief" was poorly administered and often inadequate to meet needs. Though unemployment insurance proposals were being put forth by groups like the American Association for Labor Legislation, no program of unemployment provisions existed on any governmental level. County-financed old-age assistance was available in only a few states. Most states had mothers' pensions for widows and dependent children, administered through local agencies, such as the courts or county poor relief officials. The only national breakthrough in this area was passage of the 1921 Federal Maternity and Infancy Act (the Sheppard-Towner Act), which promoted federal grants-in-aid to states for programs in child and maternal health and mental hygiene. Even this legislation led a precarious existence. Due largely to opposition by the American Medical Association, President Hoover allowed the act to expire in 1928.(55)

Private charities still gave much material relief. In this realm of private welfare, many communities had only begun to coordinate the work of diverse charitable organizations. Sometimes such organizations overlapped; sometimes they left large gaps in needed services. Increasingly, the private agencies found themselves unable to cope with rising relief needs.

The 1920s represented a paradox concerning social welfare and social reform. On the one hand, welfare services were localized, inadequately financed, and restricted in extent and type of coverage. In part this was so because of a lack of national interest in a more organized commitment to social welfare. To some degree the decade saw a return to earlier notions of individual culpability for poverty and individualized responses to social problems. World War I and its aftermath encouraged a general disillusionment with large-scale political solutions to societal ills. Earlier social reformers lost much of their audience, and social engineers like Herbert Hoover, Gerard Swope, and Frederick Taylor were more in vogue. A national Red Scare, symptomatic of suspicions regarding new political systems and philosophies, further undermined support for social activists and their programs. Jane Addams' wartime pacifism turned her public against her. Her proposals for programs to broaden social democracy were met with cries of radicalism.(56)

At the same time, as historians James Leiby and Clarke Chambers have observed, the prosperity decade was a seedtime for constructive ideas in social welfare. Though these ideas

were realized on only a small scale, "by the end of the decade,
new devices for social reconstruction, devices that anticipated
much of the New Deal, had been elaborated."(57)

To a large degree, political and business leaders in the
1920s emphasized experimentation and organization on the local
level and in the firm. The organization, rather than the
state, was the place for reconstruction and growth. The scientific management and efficiency movements supplied new tools
and goals. From a focus on individual structures, attention
often moved to matters of inter-organizational coordination.

The new rationality, when applied to social welfare, meant
a stress on increasing efficiency and accountability in both
public and private agencies. It entailed development of coordination through community chests and councils of social agencies in the private arena, and executive departments of welfare
in the public realm. The movement was half stabilization and
improvement in social welfare methods and organizations, half
demonstration to the public that these actually worked. Porter
Lee expressed the new flavor of the era:

The slow methodical organized effort needed to make enduring
the achievement of the cause calls for different motives, different skill, different machinery. . . . [Such machinery
includes] statistics, case accounting, case studies, scoring
devices, rating scales, indices of dependency.(58)

Organizational development proceeded on the agency and
inter-agency level. Federal involvement in a more broadly conceived system of social welfare was still largely a dream. The
concept was kept alive by leaders of the Children's Bureau, by
people such as social insurance proponent Isaac Rubinow, and by
groups like the National Consumers' League. The private agencies had already begun to give ominous warnings that they could
no longer handle the general relief aspect of social welfare
work. On the eve of the Depression, Rubinow asked "Can Private
Philanthropy Do It?" and argued that community chests could not
meet the growing demand for relief.(59) Five months earlier,
Linton Swift asserted that private social work did not have and
should not be expected to have the resources to relieve societal
evils like unemployment. Rather, in the words of the annual
report of the Association for Organizing Family Social Work a
decade earlier, family agencies, at least, should focus on case
work with the "disorganized family" in place of relief work with
the destitute.(60)

Thus, major realignments and debates in social welfare
were foreshadowed. The seeds had been planted for federal and
state involvement in a greatly expanded public welfare system
and a beginning program of social insurance in the 1930s.
Private social welfare would shift its commitment from meeting
relief needs to promoting socialization, rehabilitation, and
individual and community well-being. While many social workers would be involved in public welfare and social insurance
developments in the 1930s, others would question the role of
social work in broad social planning. A large part of the profession would return to a private agency stress at the end of
the period. The activities of professional social workers in

the 1920s were in keeping with such a return.

Those activities, in the view of one observer, were "dominated by private agency attitudes, philosophy, and methods."(61) The function of what was coming to be identified as professional social work was seen chiefly as case work in a private agency.

A few professional social workers helped staff public welfare departments. Progressive public welfare leaders like Denver's Gertrude Vaile attempted to enhance the prestige of public assistance work. But the private agency stress and the lack of sustained interest in public welfare issues at forums like the NCSW prompted public welfare officials to create their own organization, the American Association of Public Welfare Officials, 1930.(62)

Similarly, settlement workers often found themselves outside the pale of mainstream social work. A lack of professional education frequently barred them from membership in the AASW. As Judith Trolander notes, they stressed a "neighborly rather than clinical relationship with the people they tried to help" and emphasized social issues over the refinements of method and training.(63)

Stress on training, method, and case work in private agency settings fit certain conceptions social workers had about professionalism. While some social workers did not care about the issue, many wanted to achieve professional status for their work. Often the nature of such professionalism was vague. Social workers and their organizations used terms like "professional standards" more in a rhetorical than a definitive fashion. Still, the concept had strong appeal. Papers on professionalism appeared frequently at national conferences and in the journals. AASW local chapters, as well as the national leadership, asked how to raise standards and define an exclusive function for social work. Leaders in professional schools sought to transform agency-related apprenticeship training into a system of university-affiliated professional education.

Curious about the exact prerequisites for professional standing, social workers sometimes looked to other professions for guidance. Conference addresses such as "The Investigation of Engineering Education" and "The Ways in Which Standards of Professional Training Have Been Raised in Schools of Education" offered ideas for social work's development.(64) Social workers saw the established professions, especially medicine and law, as patterns to emulate.

When the National Conference of Charities and Corrections invited educator Abraham Flexner to consider social work's status as a profession in 1915, the conference was asking the advice of a man nationally known for his expertise in evaluating professional standards. Flexner had earlier helped the medical profession raise standards through a radical weeding out of smaller, less well financed medical schools. Flexner told his social work audience that their lack of a specific competency and a unique set of skills prevented them from being a true profession.(65)

Contemporary social workers were probably not as devastated by Flexner's speech as later social work historians have made out.(66) Instead, they seemed to take his statements

about social work's present shortcomings as a thought-provoking
challenge in their continued development toward professionalism. Devine's   accompanying   address   at   the   conference
confidently affirmed social work's professional standing.(67)
     The message from Flexner and other sources stressed a
variety of factors in the achievement of professionalism.
Systematic   technique   was   one   of   these.   Comprehensive
education based on a foundation of scientific knowledge was
another. Flexner emphasized a separate identity as a service-
giving occupation, rather than a role of mediator between
clients   and   the   services   of   other   professional   groups.
Finally, in a statement foreshadowing Lee's cause and function
theme, Flexner suggested that social workers turn from the easy
confidence   of   the   reformer   to   restraint   and   careful
thought.(68)
     The stress on development of technique, training, and
rationality seemed to fall upon a receptive   audience in
social work. Perhaps because of the larger movement toward
rationality and scientific expertise in the 1920s, many social
workers accepted the professional degree and possession of
specialized skills as sure signs of professional competence.
Case workers hoped that their skills, properly defined, would
provide the basis for a unique professional identity. A
selective, high standards professional model was thus beginning
to be defined. Its shortcomings would not become apparent
until social workers grappled with the economic chaos of the
thirties.
     In the late twenties, then, many case work enthusiasts
supported the idea of a professional social work based on a
science of individualized practice. A dedicated minority
countered that social reform remained social work's true
function. Probably a more general expectation among social
workers was simply that of increased growth and cohesion within
the field. Growth seemed assured. Cohesion may have been
doubtful. As one observer noted in an address on social work
philosophy in 1933:

I have been speaking and thinking of social workers as if they
were a united band like Tammany Hall. Truly there is so much
looseness and difference in the profession that it often seems
as if the opposition between social worker and social worker
out-weighed that between social workers and the rest of the
world.(69)

     At first glance, social work would appear to have achieved
many of the prerequisites for beginning professionalism, and
cohesion, by 1919: a national organization, a growing system
of professional education, and development of a specialized
technique. Yet this is a static conception of professional
growth, ignoring the importance of diversity and dissonance
among varied groups. The history of social work in the 1920s
and subsequent decades is really the story of strains between
different segments and of tensions between forces for cohesion
and pulls for separateness.
     Social workers of the 1920s debated the merits of public
versus private welfare, selective versus broad requirements for

membership in the profession, and specialized practice versus a
generic focus. Different professional schools and different
urban centers presented varied approaches to social work goals
and practice. Proponents of several intellectual and scientific
frameworks argued the merits of their approaches. Yet at the
same time progress toward cohesion was bolstered by social
workers' need to define themselves as a distinct group among a
number of competing professions. A process of accommodation
among diverse segments in social work was beginning to emerge in
the arenas of the Milford Conference, the meetings of a national
organization, and the deliberations of an educational association. This process of accommodation, often the product of
deep-seated conflict, was to characterize social work's professional development in the years to come.

Notes

1. Porter Lee, "Social Work as Cause and Function," National Conference of Social Work, (1929), pp. 3, 20.

2. The term "case work" (rather than "casework") was commonly used until the 1950s. I will employ the older term throughout this study.

3. "Family Welfare Work," Social Work Year Book (1933), pp. 173-74; Phyllis Atwood Watts, "Casework above the Poverty Line: The Influence of the Home Service in W.W.I. on Social Work," Social Service Review, XXXVIII: 303-15 (September, 1964).

4. Ralph G. Hurlin, "Measuring the Demand for Social Workers," NCSW, Proceedings (1926), pp. 587-91; Walter West, "Social Work as a Profession," Social Work Year Book (1933), pp. 493-94.

5. David Burner, Herbert Hoover: A Public Life (New York: Alfred A. Knopf, 1979), pp. 19, 96-118.

6. Hurlin, pp. 587-91.

7. Paul S. Boyer, Urban Masses and Moral Order in America, 1820-1920 (Cambridge, Mass.: Harvard University Press, 1978), p. 86.

8. "Notes and Comments," Social Service Review, II: 323 (June, 1928).

9. Neva Deardorff, "The Objectives of the Professional Organization," NCSW, Proceedings (1925), pp. 636-43.

10. The study was conducted by the Boston chapter of the American Association of Social Workers. "Who and Where is the Social Worker?" The Compass, XI: 5-6 (March, 1930).

11. Samuel A. Goldsmith, "Jewish Social Work," Social Work Year Book (1933), pp. 255-59.

12. S. C. Kohs, "Continuing the Quarterly," Jewish Social Service Quarterly, V: 229-36 (June, 1929).

13. Rose J. McHugh, "Catholic Social Work," Social Work Year Book (1933), pp. 55-60.

14. See also Lela Costin, Two Sisters for Social Justice (Urbana: University of Illinois Press, 1983), pp. 155 and 223.

15. Forrester B. Washington, "Negroes," Social Work Year Book (1933), pp. 313-18; Lawrence E. Gary and Robenia Baker Gary, "The History of Social Work Education for Black People, 1900-1930" (Paper presented at the Social Welfare History Group Symposium, Council on Social Work Education Annual Meetings,

Washington, D.C., 1985), pp. 11-17; "Report on Personnel Practices in Social Work Agencies," American Association of Social Workers, 1928, National Association of Social Workers Records, folder 99, Social Welfare History Archives, University of Minnesota, Minneapolis, Minn.

16. Eugene Kinckle Jones, "Social Work Among Negroes," Annals of American Academy of Political and Social Science, CXXX: 287-93 (November, 1928).

17. Mailing List, 1929-30 and 1930-31, Chicago Round Table on Psychiatric Social Work, National Association of Social Workers, Chicago Chapter Records, Box 1, folder 7, Chicago Historical Society, Chicago, Ill.

18. "Report on Personnel Practices," AASW; Esther Brown, Social Work as a Profession, 2nd ed. (New York: Russell Sage, 1936), pp. 108-10.

19. Mildred Mudgett, "The Four Seasons" (Unpublished autobiography, Mildred Mudgett Papers, Social Welfare History Archives), p. 208; Clarke Chambers, Seedtime of Reform (Ann Arbor, Mich.: Ann Arbor Paperbacks, 1967), p. 98.

20. Conversation with Peggy Pittman-Munke, March 18, 1986; and see Pittman-Munke, "Mary Richmond and the Wider Social Movement: Philadelphia, 1900-1909" (Diss., University of Texas/Austin, 1985); Walter Trattner, Homer Folks: Pioneer in Social Welfare (New York: Columbia University Press, 1968), pp. 226-27.

21. Notable exceptions in the 1930s were Harry Hopkins and his assistant, Aubrey Williams, the Social Security Board's Jane Hoey, and Walter West of the AASW.

22. Ralph Ormsby, A Man of Vision: Francis H. McLean (New York: Family Service Association, 1969), pp. 1-3.

23. "Linton B. Swift," Encyclopedia of Social Work (New York: NASW, 1971), pp. 1501-2.

24. AASW, Social Case Work, Generic and Specific. A Report of the Milford Conference (New York: AASW, 1929), p. 15.

25. Ibid., pp. 3-4.

26. Ibid., p. 3.

27. Ibid., p. 12

28. The Compass, X: 5 (August, 1929).

29. Grace Marcus, "A Challenge to Every Case Worker," The Compass, XI: 5-6 (October, 1929).

30. Meeting, American Association of Hospital Social Workers, 3/30, NASW, Chicago Chapter Records, Box 1, folder 7.

31. Roy Lubove, The Professional Altruist (New York: Atheneum, 1969), p. 127.

32. Frances N. Harrison, The Growth of a Professional Association (New York: AASW, 1935), pp. 15-16, Ephemera, NASW Records.

33. Ibid., p. 12.

34. Ibid., pp. 18-19, 22.

35. James Cutler, Joint Meeting, Association of Training Schools and the Committee on Research and Training, AASW, NASW Records, folder 2.

36. Report on Committee of Census of Social Workers, AASW Annual Meeting, 1927, NASW Records, folder 2.

37. The AASW had a Committee on Personnel Standards in Public Social Work by 1928.

38. Membership Meetings, 3/30/28 and 10/22/29, AASW, Chicago Chapter, NASW, Chicago Chapter Records, Box 21.

39. AASW, Statement of Objectives, 1924, Quoted in Moses Beckelman, "A Protective Organization for Jewish Social Workers," June, 1933, NASW Records, folder 31.

40. Mildred Mudgett, "The Relation of Research to Professional Standards in Social Work," NCSW, Proceedings (1928), pp. 549-55; Mary Antoinette Cannon, "Underlying Principles and Common Practice in Social Work," NCSW, Proceedings, (1928), pp. 564-69; Almena Dawley, "The Contribution of Mental Hygiene to the Theory and Practice of Case Work," NCSW, Proceedings, (1928), pp. 353-60.

41. Clarke Chambers, Paul U. Kellogg and the Survey (Minneapolis: University of Minnesota Press, 1971), pp. 84-101.

42. The overall number of schools of social work was larger, as not all belonged to the Association of Schools.

43. Edith Abbott, "Backgrounds and Foregrounds in Education for Social Work," 1927 address to the AASW, in Abbott, Social Welfare and Professional Education (Chicago: University of Chicago Press, 1942), p. 40.

44. AASSW, "Member Schools--Total Number of Students Enrolled," 12/15/30, Grace Browning/Mary Houk Papers, Social Welfare History Archives.

45. Sydnor Walker, Social Work and the Training of Social Workers (Chapel Hill: University of North Carolina Press, 1928), p. 103.

46. Lubove, p. 154. See also Carel Germaine, "Casework and Science: A Historical Encounter," in Robert W. Roberts and Robert H. Nee, eds., Theories of Social Casework (Chicago: University of Chicago Press, 1970), pp. 3-32.

47. Letter from Helen Totten to Anna Belle Tracy, 2/28/30, NASW, Chicago Chapter Records, Box 1, folder 7.

48. Interview with Helen Perlman in Mary L. Gottesfeld and Mary E. Pharis, Profiles in Social Work (New York: Human Sciences Press, 1977), pp. 111-12. See also Gisela Konopka, Eduard C. Lindemann and Social Work Philosophy (Minneapolis: University of Minnesota Press, 1958), p. 47.

49. Interview with Yonata Feldman in Gottesfeld and Pharis, p. 65.

50. Maurice Karpf, "The Relation between Sociology and Social Work," Journal of Social Forces, III: 419-27 (March, 1925).

51. H. L. Lurie, "Specialized Approaches to Family Case Work," The Family, VIII: 202 (October, 1927).

52. "Notes and Comments," Social Service Review, I: 310-27 (June, 1927).

53. Karpf, p. 421.

54. See, e.g., Edith Abbott, "Some Basic Principles in Professional Education for Social Work," in Abbott, Social Welfare and Professional Education, pp. 66-78; Neva R. Deardorff, "The Relation of Applied Sociology to Social Work," Social Forces, XI: 190-93 (December, 1932).

55. Costin chronicles the fight over extending Sheppard-Towner and the roles played by the Children's Bureau and the AMA in Two Sisters for Social Justice, pp. 166-76.

56. Clarke Chambers, Seedtime of Reform, p. 19; Allen Davis, American Heroine (New York: Oxford University Press, 1973), pp. 212-81.

57. Chambers, Seedtime of Reform, pp. xi-xiv. See also James Leiby, A History of Social Welfare and Social Work in the United States (New York: Columbia University Press, 1978), pp. 163-90.

58. Lee, pp. 4, 16.

59. Isaac Rubinow, "Can Private Philanthropy Do It?" Social Service Review, III: 361-94 (September, 1929).

60. Linton Swift, "The Relief Problem in Family Social Work," The Family, X: 3-11 (March, 1929); AAOFSW Report of Committee on Future Scope and Policy, 1919, quoted in Ormsby, pp. 114-15.

61. Josephine Brown, Public Relief, 1929-1939 (New York: Henry Holt, 1940), p. 55.

62. Leiby, p. 179.

63. Judith Trolander, Settlement Houses and the Great Depression (Detroit: Wayne State University Press, 1975), pp. 48-49.

64. H. P. Hammond, "The Investigation of Engineering Education," and Charles W. Hunt, "Ways in Which Standards of Professional Training Have Been Raised in Schools of Education," NCSW, Proceedings (1926), pp. 613-17, 618-20.

65. Abraham Flexner, "Is Social Work a Profession?," National Conference of Charities and Corrections, Proceedings (1915), pp. 576-90.

66. See, e.g., Frank Bruno, Trends in Social Work (New York: Columbia University Press, 1948), p. 141; Steven J. Diner, "Scholarship in the Quest for Social Welfare: A Fifty-Year History of the Social Service Review," Social Service Review, LI: 3 (March, 1977).

67. "Education for Social Work," National Conference of Charities and Corrections, Proceedings (1915), pp. 606-10. See also Edward Devine, "A Profession in the Making," The Survey, XXXV: 408-10 (January, 1916).

68. Flexner, pp. 578-90.

69. Marie Antoinette Cannon, "Changes in the Philosophy of Social Workers," NCSW, Proceedings (1933), p. 602.

3

In Search of Professional Standards: Changes in the AASW Membership Requirements

At no point is a profession so vulnerable as at that of professional education and in maintaining professional standards; no asset is so jealously to be guarded.(1)

Walter West, 1936

Social workers in the late 1920s showed increasing interest in professional development. They sought to refine their training and technique, and to achieve a professional identity recognized by the public. This interest led to a tightening of professional standards in 1929. There were reservations about the new standards from the beginning, but both the reservations and the call for standards increased when the Depression and resulting federal programs of public relief seemed to change the character of the profession and to challenge the assumptions of its leadership. Public welfare programs in the 1930s brought thousands of new workers, often unfamiliar with social work, into the field. As a result, social workers faced important questions--how exclusive should they be to create a profession, and how exclusive could they afford to be in the face of vast changes in the organization of social welfare?

During the late twenties and early thirties, the American Association of Social Workers came more and more to see its major role as protector of standards for the good of the profession. Such an approach meant lesser attention to protection of working conditions and job security of individual members. Social workers thus faced an additional dilemma: what were the most appropriate goals of a professional organization--standard-keeping or job protection?

The AASW established the new professional standards in July, 1929, when delegates at an annual meeting approved major changes in membership requirements. Experience, apprenticeship training, and general education would no longer suffice. As of July, 1933, specialized professional education would become the primary criterion distinguishing the "professional social worker." The AASW thus moved to tighten requirements for membership just as the field of social work was about to expand.

Social work standards had initially been proposed to cope with diversity and lack of training among practitioners. During the 1920s, social workers spoke of gaining cohesion and changing their public image from that of enthusiastic reformer

or untrained but good-hearted volunteer to skilled provider of
a needed service. Leaders in the push toward professionalism
included officials of the AASW such as Neva Deardorff and Walter
West, social work educators such as Porter Lee, Stuart Queen,
Edith Abbott, and Sophonisba Breckinridge, and important figures in charity organization and family welfare, including
Linton Swift and Joanna Colcord.

These leaders described the need for professionalism in
social work and the necessary elements in that professionalism.
Some, like Neva Deardorff, stressed the importance of a scientific approach to practice. Deardorff served several terms on
the Executive Committee of the AASW and was its president from
1926 to 1928. She directed the Research Bureau of the New York
City Welfare Council. To Deardorff, professionalism in social
work meant both a pragmatic attitude and a scientific spirit.
While professional social workers recognized the need for
immediate responses to problems, they also saw the necessity
for continuous scientific testing of the operation and outcome
of social programs.(2)

Flexner had earlier told social workers that genuine
professions engaged in intellectual activity based on learning
and science.(3) The scientific cast of medicine provided an
appealing role model. In general, scientific expertise was a
powerful legitimator in American society. As one social worker
optimistically noted: "In so far as it gains mastery through
the skilled, wise use of science, [social work] can be the cre-
ator of a new vocation."(4)

To Deardorff, the difference between amateur and professional was a scientific spirit. Others stated the difference in terms of skill. The undisciplined enthusiasm of the
amateur had no place in the "objective social work" of the
twenties. In its stead, as Lee observed, would come technique--
the sifting out of good results from bad, the discovery of which
methods brought the good results, and their repetition and
refinement.(5) Stuart Queen echoed Lee's ideas. Queen, a
sociologist, was an important figure in social work education.
He equated professionalism in social work with "skilled service
in place of or in addition to good intentions and sympathy."(6)

Professional education was seen as crucial in imparting
skill and the scientific approach to social workers. Early
social work training consisted of apprenticeship in social
agencies. Educators like Abbott and Breckinridge of the Chicago
School were determined to move the field beyond the apprenticeship model. They stressed careful preparation in an academic
setting. Such preparation was an important way to legitimize
this new career available to women. As Abbott noted, admission
to the professional association should be based not on what a
person does but rather on "what he knows."(7)

The equation of education with professionalism figured
importantly in the philosophy of Walter West. West was a major
figure in the campaign for professional standards. A former
journalist, he was "inducted into social work" through work
with the Red Cross and later held administrative positions in
several councils of social agencies. In 1927, he became
executive secretary of the AASW. Although he himself lacked
professional training, West became a champion of graduate

social work education as the main criterion distinguishing the social work professional. As head of the one general member- ship organization in the field, West was concerned about devel- oping a unified profession out of a collection of specialties. He saw social work education as a common base for such cohe- sion.(8)

Those pushing for professionalism in the 1920s felt that emphasis on a skilled and scientific approach, acquired through academic training, would help refute the popular notion that "anyone can practice social work." Public confusion between professional social workers and untrained workers employed by social agencies was threatening to those who wished to raise the status of the field.(9) To combat this confusion, social work- ers stressed the development of professional standards. As West explained, a standard was a test of quality, "an identi- fication of the genuine."(10) The AASW, as the professional association with the broadest membership, seemed to many the logical vehicle for developing standards. Its membership requirements could be used to define professionalism for the field as a whole.

AASW members had adopted a minimum set of membership qualifications in 1922. According to these, a full member had to be at least twenty-five years old, with four years practical experience in "social organizations of recognized standing." A member must also possess an educational background "warrant- ing expectation of success . . . in the profession of social work." For those applicants with lengthy experience, educa- tional requirements were thus rather vague. In the early stages of professional development, this vagueness allowed the "grandparenting in" of established workers. Yet even at this point there existed an alternate track of entry, stressing pro- fessional education. In place of four years of experience, applicants could offer two alternatives:

1. Graduation from a two-year course in an approved school of social work and one year of experience
2. One year in an approved school plus three years of experi- ence

Another variation combined graduate work in the social sciences with experience.(11)

A junior membership category, which members could hold for five years, allowed for total reliance on educational qual- ifications. Juniors had to be college graduates with one year of supervised social work experience or a year of training in a school of social work.(12)

The relative importance of experience and professional education in defining professional standards was a difficult issue for social workers in the 1920s. The 1922 AASW member- ship requirements gave no clear answer as to the best path to professional legitimation. Part of the ambivalence stemmed from a practical problem--relatively few social workers had acquired formal training. Yet even so, many felt that "the acceptance of applicants on the basis of experience alone was unfortunate, since it opened the doors to large numbers of social workers who had had only apprenticeship training at the

most."(13) This might reinforce the amateur image which social
workers were trying to avoid.

     Concern with the need to refine and raise the minimum mem-
bership standard surfaced at the 1926 annual meeting of the AASW
and led to establishment of a subcommittee on membership
revisions. In its deliberations, the committee recognized
changes in the field since the early twenties. It saw promising new professionals entering social work by the college
course route. The committee stressed the importance of that
route. It sought to develop revisions based on a balance between
general education, "technical" social work training, and supervised experience. From the beginning, however, committee members grappled with issues of exclusivity and the feasibility of
their proposals. They asked themselves, "If the AASW requires
that future new members be graduates from a school of social
work, will the best social workers still be eligible?"(14)

     Despite such misgivings, in 1928 the committee recommended
increased educational requirements for members and a set amount
of field work experience, to be supervised through an academic
social work program, rather than by an agency. The committee
met with chapter membership chairmen and discussed the recommendations at length. Some chapter representatives objected
that the training requirements would seriously limit applica-
tions for membership. Hesitations led participants at the 1928
annual meeting to postpone action on the recommendations until
the following year.(15)

     A majority of AASW members, however, appeared to support
the committee's attempt to raise standards. Interim reports
were approved with only minor suggestions. Representatives of
national agencies polled by the committee added their sanction
to the proposed changes. The revisions were presented in final
form to participants at the 1929 AASW meeting. Here, despite
opposition "at a number of points," the new requirements were
passed. The existence of opposition was acknowledged in passage of an "escape clause" amendment. This granted the AASW
Executive Committee power to solicit and consider chapter
objections before putting the new requirements into practice.(16)

     What did these new qualifications look like? In place of
the original routes to senior membership--four years of experience plus general educational background or lesser experience
coupled with social work training--the new requirements substituted an educational minimum applicable to all. Though this
minimum, two years of college, seemed slight, it was to be combined with five years of general education, technical training,
or employment in an approved agency. Options included the following:

1. Graduation from college plus one year in an approved school
of social work plus two years of employment in an approved
social agency
2. A combination of: college attendance, attendance at an
approved school of social work, and two years of agency employment. These experiences had to include 20 semester hours of
social/biological sciences, 24 hours of approved social work
courses, and 300 hours of supervised field work

3. Graduation from college plus completion of a two-year graduate course in an approved school of social work(17).
    The complicated permutations spelled out in the new
requirements for senior membership were a tacit recognition of
the continued diversity of education and experience among
social workers. Yet the new requirements marked a definite
move toward a single educational standard. This emphasized a
specific kind of professional training--that received in a
school of social work approved by the American Association of
Schools of Social Work. The third option in the new requirements introduced what by the fifties had become the single
accepted criterion for individual professional standing--
possession of an M.S.W. Even in option two, which presented
alternatives to professional school enrollment, formal professional education was stressed. Social work courses taken
outside of association schools had to be approved by the professional organization (the AASW). The hours of supervised
field work had to be administered through a school, in connection with professional social work courses. Revised recommendations for junior membership were a reduced version of the
qualifications for seniors. Thus the AASW asserted the inadequacy of social work's traditional apprenticeship system of
training and promoted academic education as a mainstay of professionalism.
    Lead time was allowed before the new requirements would
take effect. Application of the requirements for junior members would begin in January, 1930. Requirements for full membership would not be put into place until July, 1933.
    In the period between acceptance of the standards and
their actual enactment, AASW members and officers continued to
debate their merits. Interim polls of chapters brought lively
discussion of the issues, although each time a majority
reaffirmed the decision to raise requirements. Objections to
this decision focused on three matters: the weighting of professional education over expertise, the practicality of educational requirements, particularly in small cities and rural
areas, and the potential mismatch between high standards and
the growing employment needs of public welfare programs during
the Depression.
    Some AASW members felt the stress on professional educa-
tion was excessive and would screen out experienced workers.
They tended to endorse the older "apprenticeship system" of
social work training. Several chapters went on record in support of continuation of supervised field work run by agencies as
well as that conducted by professional schools.(18) This was
in a sense a practitioners' view, stressing practical training
and experience as an important path to professional competence.
    Most of the dissidents, however, were in favor of higher
education requirements, at least in theory. Their hesitations
related to putting the requirements into practice. They
questioned the feasibility of higher educational standards in a
period when social work education was still underdeveloped.
The Northeastern Pennsylvania chapter reported, for example:

The emphasis placed on study in schools of social work seems
ill timed so long as there are not enough schools to train the

people needed in the various fields of social work.(19)
      The new requirements seemed particularly unrealistic to
members in small communities or areas away from the big cities
where most schools of social work were located. Chapters in
Grand Rapids, Michigan, Milwaukee, Scranton, Buffalo, and
Southern Texas pointed out the inaccessibility of professional
education and school-supervised field work for workers in those
areas. They also noted that few graduates of big-city schools
would elect to work in outlying areas. The situation was
aggravated by the lack of effort on the part of urban schools of
social work to train workers for smaller communities.(20)
      Regional differences thus played a role in the debate over
membership requirements. This time the differences were not
between educators and practitioners in particular cities, but
between those in large cities and smaller communities. In a
1929 poll of chapters by the Executive Committee, twenty-two
chapters voted for immediate acceptance of the revised requirements. Eleven chapters disapproved. (Eight did not vote.)
Half of the chapters approving the new requirements were
located in or near large cities with approved schools of social
work. Over two-thirds of those rejecting the changes represented areas without approved schools.(21)
      Probably the strongest argument against the new standards
was their lack of fit with the needs of a rapidly expanding
public social service in the thirties. The effects of
depression were not immediately apparent to Americans in the
months following the stock market crash of 1929. By the winter
of 1931, however, some 200 banks had failed and persistent unemployment was becoming a national concern. Soup kitchens,
breadlines, and Hoovervilles had become commonplace. By 1933,
25 percent of the labor force was out of work. The newly unemployed swelled the ranks of the chronically poor--the aged,
dependent children, sharecroppers and farm laborers--to create
an appalling picture of distress.(22) Private charity
depleted its resources. The need for public relief began to
soar.
      While President Hoover resisted attempts to bring the fed-
eral government into the relief area, local governments
expanded their welfare activity. In New York State, Governor
Franklin D. Roosevelt pioneered a state-run program of general
public relief. Expanded relief work on the state and local
level created a demand for new social work staff. When
Roosevelt became president, he brought with him a belief that
the federal government must take a larger share of the responsibility for alleviating the effects of the depression. As a
start, he created the Federal Emergency Relief Administration,
modeled after the New York system. The FERA brought about further demand for social work employees.
      The early thirties thus witnessed changes and expansion in
the settings in which social work was practiced, and changes in
the number and kinds of people drawn into the field. The count
of those holding social work positions almost doubled between
1930 and 1940. A comprehensive picture of the characteristics
and jobs of individuals entering the field in those years does
not exist. In looking at the years 1930 to 1935, we must piece
together several sets of data to get a sense of the changes tak-

ing place.

A 1932 survey of public and private social work agencies in Chicago gives one of the few cross sections of social workers in a particular region. Based on records of four family welfare and relief agencies, the study found that of the 502 case workers employed by these agencies, 73 percent were college graduates and 68 percent had some professional social work training. The median length of such training was only one and one-half quarters. A small number held a certificate or degree from a school of social work. The average level of professional education varied from agency to agency. While 90 percent of the case workers in one private family agency had attended a school of social work, only 59 percent of those in a county unemployment relief service had done so.(23)

Many of these case workers were new to social work. Forty-four percent had less than two years experience. The group was young. Half were under thirty-one years of age and one-fourth under twenty-six.

Figures on the 523 case aides employed by the two public agencies in the survey shed light on the types of people occupying the first rung of the public welfare occupational ladder. An even larger number of these (79 percent) were college graduates, 29 percent had some graduate education, but only 18 percent had had any professional social work training. Case aides were younger and less experienced than the case workers--70 percent were under thirty, about 40 percent under twenty-five. Eighty-three percent had less than one year's experience in social work. Many of them "fell into" social work jobs when other jobs for B.A.'s vanished during the Depression. One of them recalled:

I graduated in 1933 from the University of Chicago, with majors in English and history. After a year without a job, I went to work as a case aide in the Cook County Bureau of Public Welfare. I took it because it was a job.(24)

While other areas of employment contracted, social work jobs multiplied. A study of private family agencies in eleven cities found a 50 percent increase in nonclerical personnel from 1930 to 1932. The most dramatic growth was in public welfare employment. A census of social work positions in Massachusetts noted a 43 percent increase in the number of public agency social workers from 1928 to 1932. The Joint Vocational Service, a social work job referral service organized by the AASW, found a similar expansion in public welfare employment opportunities. Advertised openings in public welfare increased from less than 1 percent of the total in 1931 to 78 percent in 1934.(25)

These surveys describe a pattern: many new jobs in public welfare, little professional training or identity among their holders, and a continuing range of experience and training among all social workers. The pattern appears in data on AASW members. At this point, AASW membership represented only about a fifth of those in the field. Still, it is helpful to look at the characteristics of new members admitted to the association in the early thirties. A study comparing members admitted in

1924-26 to those admitted in 1930-32 found slightly younger workers entering the AASW in the later period. From 1930 on, the percentage of men admitted to the organization increased. There was a trend toward higher educational attainments among new members, but only 9 percent held post-bachelor-level degrees. Twenty-two percent did have a certificate, diploma, or degree from a social work course of study, compared with 14 percent of the earlier group.(26)

The AASW also experienced an increase in the number of public agency workers in its membership. Between 1930 and 1931, the percentage of new members coming from the public field jumped from 17 percent to 29 percent. These changes were accelerated in the years following the AASW study. A 1936 profile of new AASW members showed 59 percent of them working in public agencies. Two-thirds were under thirty.(27)

Although a number of the newer workers were being accepted into the AASW, it was clear that the new requirements would prevent many more from achieving membership. A study of applicants admitted in 1929, 1930, and 1931 indicated that only 19 percent of those admitted in 1929-30 in the senior category would have been eligible under the new regulations. In 1931, the figure had jumped to 29 percent. In that year, many more new members had completed a two-year graduate course. Some AASW National Membership Committee members considered this a sign that impending new requirements were indeed raising the level of professional training. While they were aware of the influx of new, untrained workers into social work, these members stressed both the desirability and feasibility of maintaining high standards.(28)

Other committee members were less certain. Figures indicating that two-thirds or more of recent applicants would be ineligible under the new rules made them uneasy. They worried that the requirements would keep out "important new people coming into social work in the present emergency." The division between public and private agency workers would be perpetuated if few of the former could qualify for membership in the professional association.(29)

These arguments were echoed by others in the profession. The National Conference of Social Work, for example, realized that newcomers to the field lacked appropriate recognition. In 1933, the conference passed a resolution in praise of "these unsung workers of the ranks who have cheerfully held the first-line trenches."(30) Yet the majority of AASW members and leadership continued to extol the benefits of more rigorous professional standards.

The campaign for adherence to the July, 1929 membership requirement decision stressed the importance of raising standards even in rural areas, as well as the need to defend the nascent profession from an influx of untrained workers. As we have seen, those supporting the requirements included large chapters in the major training centers of Chicago, New York City, and Boston. Yet even some of the more remote areas approved the new standards, seeing them as a spur to further professional training efforts in their own regions. The Denver chapter noted that while their city lacked a school of social work, "we believe that accepting these requirements will act as

an incentive . . . to secure more adequate training for our
workers in the near future."(31)
    The use of membership standards as incentives to work
toward greater professional recognition across the country was
a major selling point for membership reform. In a statement
sent to all chapters, the National Membership Committee warned
against overemphasis on the difficulties the requirements might
cause in particular areas. "Don't think about it sectionally,
think nationally," the committee urged. Ask "Is this going to
raise the repute of my profession?" While it recognized
regional differences and problems, the committee maintained
that professional education could be carried out only under
academic auspices. Only such training offered the uniform
standards necessary for professional recognition on a national
scale.(32) This was a persuasive counter to arguments about
lack of resources in particular regions.
    A more troublesome issue for the National Membership Com-
mittee and AASW members as a whole was the propriety of raising
professional standards in a time of influx of new workers. Here,
concerns for supporting the new public welfare and intensified
private relief endeavors battled with the fear that mass
employment of untrained social workers would undercut the profession's standing. Unfortunately for the broader development
of social work, fears about the new workers won out. A committee of the Chicago chapter warned: "Constant vigilance is necessary to prevent inroads upon the profession by incompetent
workers." Walter West, the AASW executive secretary, found it
worrisome that only a minority of regular positions "for which
professionally-trained [social work] personnel should be
employed are at present filled from professional ranks."(33)
    The AASW carried its concern for maintaining standards
into its policy regarding staffing of the new public welfare
departments. In the late twenties, organization leadership
had agreed that public welfare jobs should be filled by professionally trained workers. During the creation of state
relief programs and the FERA, AASW representatives continued to
push for development of higher personnel standards in public
agencies. The New York City chapter boasted in its 1933-34
Annual Report that chapter influence and representation on the
personnel committee of the state's relief program helped lead
to adoption of "very gratifying standards."(34)
    Despite arguments about the practicality of higher stan-
dards, a final poll of chapters upheld the association's membership policy in 1932. While noting a probable drop in new members, most chapters were convinced that the strength of the
association lay not in members but in quality of professional
leadership. Chapter executives and membership committees did
not ignore the problem of new emergency relief workers, but suggested that rather than lower standards, the AASW should become
involved in developing training facilities. Many of the chapter
responses outlined a position which was to become increasingly
dominant within the AASW. This was the notion that "new workers . . . who desire to become social workers should ultimately
take professional training and come in under the regular
requirements."(35) Essentially, new workers should fit themselves to the standards of the AASW (and thus the profession).

The association's job was to maintain standards, rather than bend them to meet new conditions.

The AASW membership changes were duly put into place in July of 1933. In the following years, increases in public welfare employment continued to bring large numbers of untrained workers into the field. In an attempt to meet the needs of new workers, Walter West suggested provisional and associate membership schemes. A Detroit chapter plan called for a simple register of untrained workers, who could attend chapter meetings on a nonvoting basis. When presented to the national membership, however, such proposals were always defeated.(36)

Dorothy Kahn's presidential speech at the 1935 AASW meeting summarizes the complex fears and ambivalences of the professional group and its ultimate belief in the sanctity of standards. Kahn noted:

The outstanding fact of this year . . . is the attacks on social workers and their clientele, on professional standards from without and . . . within. . . . We have seen social work diluted by the introduction into its ranks of vast numbers of inexperienced and untrained persons, some of whom are becoming members of the profession, others wholly unsuitable to represent it.

She recognized the danger of a professional group isolating itself from beginning practitioners and building "tariff walls about our precious standards." Yet she saw no reason to believe that newer workers required less training and experience to do their jobs than those already established in the field. Appealing to these new workers, she explained:

Eventually we shall be colleagues. . . . Your first professional step will have been taken when you recognize that it is standards of performance to which we must be loyal, not status alone.(37)

AASW standard-raising was matched by a similar move on the part of the American Association of Schools of Social Work. The AASSW sought to bring all social work education up to the graduate level. In 1932, the organization ruled that all schools applying for membership must have at least one year of graduate-level course work. To avoid a double standard, the association also agreed that existing members would have to meet the new standards within three years.(38) The Association of Schools took on a standard-setting role like that of the AASW. The motivations sound familiar: desire to protect "quality education" against pressures to increase enrollments and change programs, and fear of the influx of new, hastily thrown together social work programs in land grant colleges and state universities. Educators like Porter Lee recognized the increased demands put upon schools of social work, but felt that limits on the size of schools were necessary to maintain quality. The New York School accordingly restricted its enrollment in 1930.(39) Even where schools wished to expand, lessened financial resources were a roadblock.

Some educators felt the number of schools should also be limited. Speaking of a college whose social work program had

been rejected for membership in the AASSW, Sophonisba
Breckinridge wrote:

My own thought about the Dominican College is that it is much
easier to keep them out than to get them in and that until we are
clear about a number of points, we can afford not to admit any
institution about which we have doubts.(40)

Breckinridge was president of the AASSW from 1933 to 1935. At
Chicago, she and Edith Abbott stressed a scholarly curriculum
and fought for the autonomy of their school among other professional schools at the university. A Chicago student in the
years 1936-38 recalls the faculty's concern to demonstrate that
social work was indeed a profession "just like medicine and
teaching."(41) A number of Chicago school faculty and former
students were prominent in AASSW higher circles in the thirties. This "Chicago influence" contributed to the stress on
high standards.(42)
     Social work schools in the thirties did make some effort to
accommodate new students. They increased enrollments and
educated a large proportion of students through part-time
courses. The University of Chicago School arranged with the
State Department of Public Welfare "to release all its
untrained workers to carry at least one course at the
University." Yet schools worried about the effects of such
measures on educational quality. The New York School, for
example, discouraged part-time enrollment in the early thirties.(43) Many school people maintained a philosophy heard
also within the AASW: encourage the "best" of the new workers
to join the professional ranks through school of social work
training. Be careful lest the remaining bulk of workers change
the image of social work and its standards of practice.
     AASSW philosophy and the actions of member schools made
the goal of filling all social work positions with professionally trained workers an impossible task. Member schools could
not handle all applicants, even though the number of schools
rose slightly from twenty-eight in 1930 to thirty-three in
1936. Actual enrollments could not meet job demands. Total
enrollments for all students in graduate and undergraduate
courses during these years ranged from 3,000 to almost
7,000.(44) Yet the 1930 census reported about 36,000 persons
in social work jobs. Only a small proportion of social work students completed degrees or diplomas. The M.S.W. recipients
were a drop in the bucket--186, for example, in 1933. Large
numbers of workers had neither the time nor money to attend
schools, even if places had been open for them.(45)
     When AASW membership requirements were raised, members of
the professional association spoke of the obligation to help
increase opportunities for social work training. Yet the
organization did little to carry this out. An Executive Committee request that the Membership Committee help the Association of Schools led simply to a half-hearted attempt to gather
information on the problem.(46) Neither the schools nor the
AASW were prepared to make professional training available to
new recruits in a large-scale, systematic way.
     Despite broad changes in the field as the New Deal

unfolded, the AASW and AASSW chose to follow a path familiar to other American professions--build professional standards on specialized, advanced education. Why did they maintain this stress on graduate professional training? Many social workers sincerely believed that professional training improved one's practice. But two other factors strengthened the appeal of education as a standard for a developing profession. The first was the simplicity of an educational certificate or degree as a basis for distinguishing the professional from the amateur. The second was the powerful legitimizing role of higher education in American society.

In a loosely defined field such as social work, certifying professionals was a difficult task. One appeal of educational criteria was the relative ease with which they could be applied. As Walter West put it:

Schools of social work are one of the major things you can offer as evidence that social work has a meaning in practice. . . . It's a shortcut to a person to whom you can't tell or demonstrate the competence of social workers.(47)

In addition to their simplicity, educational credentials held particular significance for professionals seeking to improve their standing. Observers of professionalism in the American context have commented on the importance of higher education in the legitimizing process.(48) Social workers in the thirties recognized the power of advanced education as an indication of professionalism. They looked to the examples set by other professions. They also quoted A. M. Carr-Saunders and P. A. Wilson to one another. These two English scholars had just produced a major study of the development of professions in Great Britain. Their conclusion that education played an important role in creating professional monopoly was carefully noted.(49)

By stressing professional education, social workers promoted the notion of a specialized body of knowledge. Even before their encounter with Abraham Flexner in 1915, social workers had been aware of the importance of a distinctive knowledge base in defining the boundaries and degree of legitimacy of their field. West summarized this awareness when he noted that "professional development in social work is synonymous with increasing knowledge about social problems."(50) Wayne McMillen, a faculty member at Chicago, listed the major identifying attributes of a profession as "first, the possession of a special body of knowledge, and second, a strong sense of obligation to place this asset at the disposal of the community."(51) West and McMillen stated a common theme: the possession of distinctive understandings, transmitted through specialized education, created social work experts who would be valued by the community at large.

While professional leaders concentrated on creating experts, the continuing limits on training facilities and entry into the professional association helped create the rise of an alternate form of organization for social workers: a professional union movement called the Rank and File. The growth of this movement challenged dominant ideas about social work

professionalism in a variety of ways. One challenge, in the
area of political ideology and social action, will be discussed
in the following chapter. Others, regarding the nature of
standards and the proper role of a professional association,
are pertinent to the present discussion.
     AASW and AASSW actions were of course only one factor in
the rise of unionism in social work. Poor working conditions,
particularly in public welfare, played a significant role. Bad
job conditions were common in the thirties. Workers carried
large case loads. They worked long hours in crowded, ill-
equipped offices. Across-the-board salary cuts frequently
occurred, both in public and in private agencies.(52) Shifts
in federal priorities and concomitant changes in welfare programs caused large numbers of workers to be let go.
     As a result, public relief workers in Chicago, New York,
and other cities began to form protective associations to promote improved working conditions and salaries. These associations followed an industrial union model. Membership was open
to "workers of all categories . . . case workers, case aides,
clerical workers" in social agencies. At the same time that
welfare workers were organizing, professional social workers
were forming two similar types of groups: discussion clubs,
set up by private agency workers as open forums "for the
analysis of basic social problems and their relation to social
work," and practitioner groups, created by younger AASW members
and focusing on employment problems within a professional context. Each group saw broad social reform as more important
than a narrow professionalism. They promoted client welfare as
an important professional concern. By the mid-thirties, protective, discussion, and practitioner groups began to interact
in a national Rank and File Movement. In particular cities,
their memberships overlapped. All three types of organization
emphasized employment conditions rather than professional
standards. They used the word "standards" to refer to conditions of work rather than attributes of employees. The Rank
and File presence constituted a new challenge to the AASW stress
on high personnel standards as the path to professional development.(53)
     The experiences of individual AASW chapters indicate the
seriousness of the Rank and File challenge. In Los Angeles,
for example, an incoming chapter president was warned of the
existence of dissident social work groups, antagonistic to the
chapter's program. The chapter executive set up a committee to
meet with representatives of social work union groups around
common concerns. Yet the president worried:

Shall the standards of the AASW, secured after years of struggle, be tossed to the winds now, to admit to membership the mass
of relief workers who cannot qualify by education or training?(54)

     Members of the Chicago chapter showed a similar ambiv-
alence. Events in the chapter in the early thirties give a good
picture of the clash in social work between a thrust toward professional standard-raising and recognition of the personnel
problems brought by the Depression. The clash was exacerbated

by the presence of a practitioners' group, which challenged a chapter leadership made up primarily of social work administrators and educators.(55)

Chapter records for the early thirties show a growing awareness of the existence of a sizable group of Chicago social workers either unwilling or unable to join the association. Many were workers in public agencies, but the chapter also recognized that a "large number of Junior members of United Charities is presently unable to join." In addition, chapter leadership realized that many younger AASW members felt alienated from chapter activities. The Executive Committee was troubled when members of these various groups formed a Rank and File organization, the Social Workers Discussion Group.(56)

Sophonisba Breckinridge was the chapter chair. As a strong believer in professional standards, she was concerned about the growth of union-type organizations in social work. Although she recognized the problems of those new to the field, she warned her Executive Committee, "This [Discussion] group includes a number of radical workers who are not members of the AASW, nor are they willing to become members." She was particularly incensed about the inclusion of clerical and maintenance workers in groups concerned with social work issues.(57)

Chapter and Executive Committee members had varied reactions to the growth of organizations like the Discussion Group and their possible impact on the push for professional standards. Some felt such groups posed little threat to the chapter or the profession. They believed that maintenance of high membership standards would spur outsiders to get the proper training to join the professional ranks.

Others in the chapter were more ambivalent. They feared the impact of rival social work organizations, particularly union-type groups, on their recently won professional status. But they also sympathized with the difficulties of new, inexperienced workers in getting training. Many were aware that poor working conditions and lack of job security lay behind much of the impulse to practitioner organization. Some sort of accommodation, they concluded, must be made with the "outsiders" and dissidents within the ranks. Yet just how much accommodation should be made remained an open question.

Chapter leadership launched a series of attempts to build relationships with Rank and File groups. The chairs of the chapter's Recruiting and Membership committees met with representatives of the Discussion Group and the Junior Case Workers of the United Charities. Commenting afterward to Breckinridge, they called the meeting "very friendly, very challenging, and very frank." They urged further cooperation between the chapter and the Discussion Group. But since many of the group's members were currently ineligible for AASW membership, it was at the moment questionable "whether efforts should be made to include this group within the AASW."(58)

At Breckinridge's suggestion, the chapter made overtures to the Discussion Group. But when the group asked the national AASW for concessions allowing some of the new workers to join the chapter, the national office refused.(59) This left affiliation as the only tactic which the Chicago chapter could pursue with the Discussion Group. Eventually the Discussion

Group agreed to a joint committee between the two organizations. Many in the Discussion Group were ineligible for chapter membership, but those who did belong to both organizations
formed a special Practitioners Group within the chapter structure, open to all chapter members except agency executives.(60)
     Over the next four years, the chapter maintained a tenuous
relationship with the Discussion Group and the in-house Practitioners Group. At first, chapter leadership was enthusiastic,
though watchful. Breckinridge wrote to the chapter secretary,
"I think that Mr. Levy and Mrs. Hamilton [Practitioner Group
officers] will be all right. After all, it is so nice to have
any of the young ones quite active."(61) The chapter supported
some of the Rank and File recommendations regarding action on
personnel practices and relief issues, including a protest to
the Illinois Emergency Relief Commission over the firing of six
relief workers accused of belonging to the Communist party.(62)
Several leaders of the Practitioners Group became important
chapter members.
     Yet strains between the two groups remained. The Practi-
tioners Group often played the role of critic within the professional organization. Members noted the power of agency
executives within the chapter. They warned of the AASW becoming "another entrenched group, limited in number, [holding]
fast to their control of social work."(63) The Practitioners
Group remained part of the larger Discussion Group, which was
instrumental in founding a social work employees union in
1934.(64) Concerned about these activities, and fearing the
influence of non-AASW members in Practitioners Group meetings,
the chapter sought to control the group by structuring it as a
chapter committee, subject to the supervision of the Executive.
The Practitioners Group protested such restraints. Anxious to
maintain some tie with the dissidents, the chapter compromised
and loosened its attempts at control.(65)
     Finally, in 1937, the Practitioners Group voted to dis-
band. Members attributed this decision to two factors. One
was their feeling that the AASW had indeed become more receptive
to the needs of newer workers. The other, significantly, was
the rise of protective groups in social work, which could provide a more appropriate vehicle for union-type activities.(66)
     The chapter's relationship with the Practitioners Group
was indicative of the ambivalence mainstream social workers
felt toward the new emergency relief workers and the growth of
unions in the field. This ambivalence was mirrored within the
national AASW. Broadening membership requirements to include
the new workers could mean being swamped by people who "have no
real vocation in social work."(67) Once in the AASW, their
activities might be hard to control. However, not catering to
their needs encouraged the formation of separate organizations
which might threaten AASW leadership in the field. For those
who feared the Rank and File Movement, it was hard to decide
which was worse: the potential of strong rival social work
organizations or the danger to professional standards and
organizational policies if these workers were let into the
AASW.
     The growth of social work unions presented one final chal-

lenge to the AASW. This was the question of the degree of
responsibility the profession should assume for the protection
of social workers' job security. Those identifying as professional social workers often felt they had to choose between
protecting individual workers and upholding personnel standards. They saw a basic conflict between a professional
organization's maintenance of personnel standards, and a
union's protection of workers' rights and job conditions. Thus
professional standards issues in the thirties related not only
to questions of who could be called a professional social
worker, but also to arguments about the most appropriate model
for social work organization--that of a union or a professional
association.

An important thrust behind social work union development
was the lack of job security for social workers in both public
and private agencies. Workers involved in union or political
activities were often fired. In addition, social work practitioners had little voice in agency policy decisions. A large-
scale AASW study of working conditions in a variety of agencies
found nonsupervisory professional staff included in policy--
making in only 14 percent of the 394 agencies surveyed.(68)

Lack of a voice in agency decision-making, selective fir-
ings, and large-scale layoffs led to grievances and mass
protests. A cause célèbre was the case of Sidonia Dawson, a New
York City Home Relief Bureau worker. Dawson, who was not a professionally trained social worker, was an officer in a public
relief employees protective organization. In 1934, she took
part in a protest against the use of police to break up a clients' delegation attempting to register complaints with the
Relief Bureau's administrators. At a public meeting, she
called for picketing of bureau offices. The Home Relief Bureau
promptly fired Dawson. The resultant publicity prompted
several AASW members in New York City to ask their chapter to
investigate the situation.(69)

The chapter's investigation sheds light on AASW attitudes
toward grievance situations. The investigating committee consisted mainly of educators and agency representatives, including, ironically, a top administrator in the Home Relief Bureau.
Gordon Hamilton of the New York School was a member. After
examining the case, the committee decided not to deal with the
specific charges. They discussed instead "some major issues,"
including the poor supervisory practices and physical setting
of the agency, the overall insecurity of Home Relief workers,
and the use of police by administrators. Although recognizing
these as problems, the committee justified the use of police in
certain situations and stressed the importance of using regular
channels in protesting agency practices. They agreed that
Dawson's discharge was improperly handled, but affirmed:
"Just as we recognize the place of organized protest, so we also
recognize the place of system, discipline, and orderly authority in administration."(70)

"System" seemed to include higher personnel standards.
The report implied that Dawson's activities were due in part to
the fact "that as standards have been raised, the less well-
equipped have organized themselves against dismissal." In
"such situations" employee protection may be "over-stressed."

Committee members, as professional social workers, were reluctant to put emphasis on protection of workers above considerations of personnel standards or the reasonable and orderly
operation of agency practices. Upon hearing the committee's
report, the chapter voted down a motion from the floor to recommend Dawson's reinstatement.(71)

As the rate of grievances increased and practitioners'
groups pressured the AASW to respond, the association began to
develop more formal machinery for reviewing cases. In 1934,
the association strengthened its rudimentary grievance procedures by establishing a Committee on Personnel Practices. This
was chaired by Lillian Adler and was made up of members of a
similar committee which Adler had headed within the Chicago
chapter. The Chicago committee had developed largely in
response to Practitioners Group pressure. Creation of the committee in the AASW signified acknowledgment that working conditions were a proper concern of a professional association.

The existence of grievance committees on both the chapter
and national levels indicates greater willingness to take on
certain protective functions. This change occurred in part
because of pressures from the Rank and File. Yet the AASW was
unsure about how best to deal with employee problems. This
ambivalence was reflected in the development of procedures and
the handling of actual grievances.

A recurring question was whether the AASW should review
the specific charges and actions in a grievance case or whether
it should explore general principles. Generally, chapter
grievance committees spent more time "studying conditions" and
formulating ideal employment codes than they did handling
actual grievances. This emphasis on basic principles was consistent with the professional organization's preoccupation
with standard-setting. It was also, no doubt, a product of the
influence of agency executives and supervisors within grievance
committees. The AASW Committee on Personnel Practices, for
example, consisted of twelve administrators and supervisors and
seven case workers in 1934. It was not unusual for grieving
employees to find executives of their agencies on the committee
considering their case.(72)

Executive influence was a factor complicating grievance
policy. Yet beyond this lay the broader issue of the appropriate organizational model for a professional association.
Involvement in the grievance process helped AASW members
crystallize certain assumptions about the desired relationship
between a professional organization and its constituents.
Gradually, many professional social workers came to believe
that whereas a union's fundamental responsibility consisted of
protection of individuals, a professional organization's
responsibility lay in protection of personnel standards.

The AASW Committee on Personnel Practices declared the
association's chief function to be protection of the professional character of social work. "In so far as this purpose
serves to protect individuals it is because of their professional competence and not because they have jobs in social
work."(73) Arguing against the "one for all, all for one"
philosophy of a union, AASW officials and membership saw the
organization's major job as protection of the quality of work-

ers, rather than protection of members as members. The over-
riding concern for quality meant that incompetent workers
should not be supported.

Though both the professional association and social work
unions stressed the protection of standards, each defined this
in a different way. To AASW members, standards meant certain
qualifications held by social work personnel, such as professional training and possession of specialized skills. To
union members, standards related to job conditions. Improving
job standards meant making jobs more secure, raising salaries,
and reducing case loads.

The AASW did not completely ignore the importance of
improving working conditions. It recognized that good social
work practice often depended on good employment practices. Yet
in a crucial departure from the union model, association members and officials argued that the best way to assure sound
working conditions and employee security was to strengthen professional standards. "Professional standards are in themselves protective," argued Rachel Childrey, chair of the
Division of Employment Practices in 1935.(74)

Union groups--with good reason--might question this faith
in the utility of professional training or special skills in
safeguarding social work jobs. Employees often put little
stress on professional education as a job qualification. Yet
many professional social workers came to believe, along with
Walter West, that social work's real strength lay in its professional competence.(75)

Thus an important segment within the profession rejected
much of the tenets of unionism. They saw unions as narrow
organizations jeopardizing hard-won personnel standards. Many
AASW leaders feared the use of union tactics and put their faith
in "enlightened employment practices."(76) The idea that
employers could be expected to play an enlightened role in part
reflected the presence of agency executives in the policy-
making circles of the AASW. Yet beyond this employer influence
lay a broadly held belief in the importance of improving social
work's professional standing.

Notes

1. Walter West, "The Purpose and Value of Standards in Case Work," National Conference of Social Work, Proceedings (1936), p. 98.

2. Directory of Members of the American Association of Social Workers (New York: AASW, 1936); Neva Deardorff and Mary C. Jarrett, "Are There Underlying Principles and Policies Basic to Professional Standards in Social Work?" NCSW, Proceedings (1928), pp. 560-64.

3. Abraham Flexner, "Is Social Work a Profession?" National Conference of Charities and Corrections, Proceedings (1915), pp. 581-84.

4. Mary Willcox Glenn, "The Growth of Social Case Work in the U.S.," The Family, IX: 274 (December, 1928).

5. Porter Lee, "Technical Training for Social Work" (1913) and "The Future of Professional Social Work" (1926) in Lee, Social Work as Cause and Function (New York: Columbia University Press, 1937), pp. 29-32 and 131-50.

6. Amos Griswold Warner, Stuart A. Queen, and Ernest Harper, American Charities and Social Work, 4th ed. (New York: Thomas Y. Crowell, 1930), p. 25.

7. Edith Abbott, "Backgrounds and Foregrounds in Education for Social Work," 1927 address to the AASW, in Abbott, Social Welfare and Professional Education (Chicago: University of Chicago Press, 1942), pp. 38-39. Consistent with her times, Abbott used the male pronoun when she wrote.

8. "Walter West," Encyclopedia of Social Work (New York: NASW, 1971), p. 1537; Neva Deardorff, "The New Secretary," The Compass, IX: 2, 5 (October, 1927); Minutes, Executive Committee, AASW, 6/9/35, NASW Records, folder 21, Social Welfare History Archives, University of Minnesota, Minneapolis, Minn.

9. Lee, "The Future of Professional Social Work," p. 138; "Continuing the Membership Discussion," The Compass, X: 3-4 (September, 1928).

10. West, "The Purpose and Value of Standards in Case Work," p. 90.

11. Neva Deardorff, "Social Work as a Profession," Social Work Year Book (1929), pp. 435-38.

12. Ibid. An additional year of experience was required for full membership.

13. Esther Brown, Social Work as a Profession (New York: Russell Sage, 1935), pp. 70-71.

14. Minutes, Ad Interim Committee, AASW, 6/17/27, NASW Records, folder 20; "Will Future Members Have Technical Training?" The Compass, IX: 1 (January, 1928).

15. "The Memphis Meetings," The Compass, IX: 1-4 (May, 1928); Annual Meeting, AASW, 5/7/28, NASW Records, folder 2.

16. "Are You Prepared to Vote on Membership Revision?" The Compass, X: 1-3 (May, 1929); Minutes, Executive Committee, AASW, 4/13/30, NASW Records, folder 21; "The Association Adopts the Proposed Membership Requirements," The Compass, X: 1-4 (August, 1929).

17. "The Association Adopts the Proposed Membership Requirements," p. 3.

18. Margaret Byington and Maurice Karpf, "Chapter and Individual Criticisms and Suggestions on New Membership Requirements," pp. 4-5, AASW, National Membership Committee, 4/1/30, NASW Records, folder 21; see also "The Association Adopts the Proposed Membership Requirements," p. 4.

19. "The Association Adopts the Proposed Membership Requirements," pp. 3-4.

20. Byington and Karpf; "The Ayes Win," The Compass, XI: 1 (December, 1929); "Yes and No on Membership Revision," The Compass, XI: 6-7 (October, 1929); "Yes and No on Membership Revision," The Compass, XI: 6-7 (November, 1929); Minutes, Membership Committee, AASW, 1/22/30, NASW Records, folder 48.

21. "Analyzing the Votes," The Compass, XI: 1 (December, 1929); Minutes, Executive Committee, AASW, 4/12/30, NASW Records, folder 21.

22. James T. Patterson, America's Struggle against Poverty, 1900-1980 (Cambridge, Mass.: Harvard University Press, 1981), pp. 38-42.

23. Helen Jeter, "Salaries and Professional Education of Social Workers in Family and Relief Agencies in Chicago," Social Service Review, VII: 225-253 (June, 1933).

24. Interview with Rita Novak, May 8, 1979.

25. Esther Brown, pp. 93-94; Walter West, "Social Work as a Profession," Social Work Year Book (1935), pp. 479-86.

26. Frances N. Harrison, The Growth of a Professional Association (New York: AASW, 1935), p. 26, Ephemera, NASW Records. Note that professional social work training could be on the graduate or undergraduate level.

27. Harrison, p. 22; "Facts about New Members," The Compass, XVIII: 5-6 (October, 1936).
28. Minutes, National Membership Committee, AASW,

3/12/32, NASW Records, folder 50.

29. Ibid.

30. "Business Sessions of the Conference," NCSW, Proceedings (1933), p. 733.

31. "Yes and No on Chapter Membership," The Compass, XI: 3 (November, 1929).

32. "Continuing the Membership Discussion," The Compass, XI: 3-4 (September, 1929).

33. Chicago Chapter, AASW, "Personnel Practices Committee Statement," 5/3/35, NASW Records, folder 21; West, "Social Work as a Profession" (1935), p. 479; see also "Public Service Personnel," The Compass, XV: 2-3 (July, 1934).

34. Gordon Hamilton of the New York School was the chapter's representative on the committee. Annual Report, 1933-34, N.Y. City Chapter, AASW, NASW Records, folder 147.

35. AASW, National Membership Committee Minutes, 5/15/32 and 3/12/32, NASW Records, folder 50.

36. Walter West, "Provisional Recognition in Social Work," The Compass, XVI: 7-8 (October, 1934); Memo from West to Chapters, 9/4/34, NASW: Chicago Chapter Records, Box 2; "Detroit Plan for Provisional Social Workers," The Compass, XVI: 2 (July, 1935); Lea Taylor, "Preliminary Report of the Conference," The Compass, XVI: 2-5 (March, 1935).

37. Dorothy Kahn, "Professional Standards in Social Work," The Compass, XVI: 1-5 (June, 1935). See also Wayne McMillen, "The Professional Base for Social Action," in American Association of Social Workers, Four Papers on Professional Function (New York: AASW, 1937), pp. 7-21.

38. Minutes, Executive Committee, AASSW, 10/20/34, Council on Social Work Education Records, Record Group I, Box 4, Social Welfare History Archives.

39. Elizabeth G. Meier, The New York School of Social Work (New York: Columbia University Press, 1954), p. 81; Porter Lee, "Report of the Director," Bulletin of the New York School of Social Work, XXIV: 1-6 (October, 1930).

40. Letter from Breckinridge to Mildred Mudgett, 4/10/35, CSWE Records, I-1.

41. Interview with Paulette Hartrich, August 18, 1977.

42. Elizabeth Wisner of Tulane, a Chicago Ph.D., was president of the AASSW, 1935-37. Marion Hathway was executive

secretary, 1938-41; other Chicago faculty and former students served on the Executive and other committees.

   43. Mildred Mudgett, "The Four Seasons" (unpublished autobiography, Mildred Mudgett papers, Social Welfare History Archives), p. 230; Meier, p. 81.

   44. AASSW, "Member Schools--Total Number of Students Enrolled," 12/15/30; "Enrollment of All Students as of Nov. 1, 1936," AASSW files in Grace Browning/Mary Houk Papers, Social Welfare History Archives; Edith Abbott, "Education for Social Work," Social Work Year Book (1933), pp. 143-49. Many of these students were half-time.

   45. Esther Brown, p. 45; Porter Lee, "A Critical Period in Education for Social Work," Bulletin of the New York School of Social Work, XXVIII: 3-9 (October, 1934).

   46. "Operating under the New Membership Requirements," The Compass, XI: 4-5 (March, 1930); Minutes, Executive Committee, AASSW, 2/17/31, CSWE Records, I-4.

   47. Minutes, Executive Committee, AASW, 6/19/37, NASW Records, folder 22.

   48. Corinne Gilb, Hidden Hierarchies (New York: Harper, 1966), p. 57. See also Eliot Freidson, The Professions and Their Prospects (Beverley Hills, Calif.: Sage, 1973).

   49. A. M. Carr-Saunders and P. A. Wilson, The Professions (Oxford: Clarendon Press, 1934); Arlien Johnson, "Implications of Type I and Type II Schools of Social Work," AASSW Newsletter, V: 15, 18-19 (January, 1939), CSWE Records, I-13; letter from Frank Bruno to Joanna Colcord, 10/9/39, NASW Records, folder 233; Herschel Alt to Grace Marcus, 4/21/39, NASW Records, folder 64; Alfred Winters to Lillian Adler, 11/15/34, NASW Records, folder 31.

   50. West, "The Purpose and Value of Standards in Case Work," p. 98.

   51. McMillen, "The Professional Base for Social Action," p. 13.

   52. "Salaries in Private Family Agencies Back at 1929 Level," The Compass, XVIII: 10 (October, 1936); AASW Job Analysis Committee Records, NASW Records, folder 44.

   53. Jacob Fisher, The Rank and File Movement in Social Work, 1931-1936 (New York: New York School of Social Work, 1936), pp. 7-17; Leslie Alexander, "Organizing the Professional Social Worker: Union Development in Voluntary Social Work, 1930-1950" (Diss., Bryn Mawr College, 1977); "The Case for the Practitioners' Movement," The Compass, XIV: 7-8 (July, 1933).

   54. Mary Stanton, "The Road to Chapter Strength," Annual

Report of the President, L.A. County Chapter, 1934-35, The Compass, XVII: 9-13 (September, 1935).

55. Minutes, Executive Committee, Chicago Chapter, AASW, 7/29/32, NASW: Chicago Chapter Records, Box 20, Chicago Historical Society, Chicago, Ill.

56. Minutes, Executive Committee, Chicago Chapter, AASW, 7/29/32, 8/19/32, NASW: Chicago Chapter Records, Box 2 and Box 20.

57. Minutes, Executive Committee, Chicago Chapter, AASW, 7/29/32; letter from Breckinridge to Marion Hamilton, 11/3/33, NASW: Chicago Chapter Records, Boxes 2 and 20.

58. Letter from Lucille M. Smith to Breckinridge, 10/12/32, NASW: Chicago Chapter Records, Box 1.

59. Minutes, Executive Committee, Chicago Chapter, AASW, 8/19/32, 9/12/32, NASW: Chicago Chapter Records, Box 20.

60. Minutes, Executive Committee, Chicago Chapter, AASW, 11/14/32, NASW: Chicago Chapter Records, Box 20. Similar groups developed in the New York City and St. Louis chapters.

61. Letter from Breckinridge to B. Jennings, 5/2/33, NASW: Chicago Chapter Records, Box 2.

62. Minutes, Committee on Standards of Working Conditions, Chicago Chapter, AASW, 11/8/33; letter from Josephine Murphy (Chapter Secretary) to Robert Dunham, 11/28/33, NASW: Chicago Chapter Records, Box 2.

63. Membership Meeting, Chicago Chapter, AASW, 11/9/34, NASW: Chicago Chapter Records, Box 21.

64. This was the first social work union in the thirties.

65. A useful source for insights into the relationship between established social workers and the rank and file is Jacob Fisher, The Response of Social Work to the Depression (Cambridge, Mass.: Schenkman, 1980). Fisher appears to overemphasize the degree of cooperation between the two groups, however.

66. Minutes, Executive Committee, Chicago Chapter, AASW, 7/16/37, NASW: Chicago Chapter Records, Box 20.

67. Statement by Joanna Colcord, of AASW National Membership Committee, Minutes, Membership Meeting, Chicago Chapter, AASW, 10/25/34, NASW: Chicago Chapter Records, Box 21.

68. Report on Personnel Practices in Social Work Agencies, 1928, NASW Records, folder 99.

69. Letter from Winters to Adler, 12/26/34, NASW Records,

folder 31; "The Case of Sidonia Dawson," The Survey, LXXI: 8-
10 (January, 1935).

70. Report from Gordon Hamilton to Walter West, regarding
N.Y.C. Chapter Investigation of Dawson Case, 12/34, NASW
Records, folder 35.

71. Ibid.; Emma S. Schieber, "Open Letter on Dawson
Case," The Compass, XVII: 10 (February, 1935).

72. AASW, N.J. Chapter, "Statement and Recommendations
of the N.J. Chapter Relating to Employment Practice Surrounding
the Discharge of [two workers] from the ERA," 3/21/35, NASW:
Chicago Chapter Records, Box 2, folders 10 and 11; Membership
List, Committee on Personnel Practices, Chicago Chapter, AASW,
12/17/34, NASW Records, folder 31; NASW Records, folders 36 and
37.

73. "Tentative AASW Procedures for Considering
Complaints," 6/3/35, NASW Records, folder 31.

74. Rachel Childrey, "Professional Protection for the
Social Worker," The Compass, XVI: 12-18 (June, 1935).

75. Report on Personnel Practices, 1928; L.A. Chapter,
Report of Subcommittee on Grievance Procedure, Division on
Employment Practices, 2/35, NASW Records, folder 31.

76. Handbook for Delegate Conference, 1940, NASW
Records, folder 76.

77. Proceedings, 1940 Delegate Conference, AASW, pp.
260-94, NASW Records, folder 77.

4

Social Workers and Political Action: AASW Involvement in Social Planning During the Depression

As a social worker profoundly interested in the problems of afflicted humanity and at the same time in the professional integrity of my group, I believe the time has come for social workers to meet existing issues with a comprehensive program of social reform.(1)

Jane Purcell Guild, 1933

During the 1930s, social workers debated the importance of professional standards. Members of the American Association of Social Workers rejected a union model of organizing and reaffirmed the importance of leadership by a professional association with selective membership requirements. Concurrent with the debate over internal standards was a conflict over the profession's proper political role. How should social workers and their membership organizations respond to the crisis of economic depression? What changes in social and economic policy should they suggest, and what part should they play in these changes? A major setting for this debate was the AASW's first delegate conference, a national meeting in 1934 on "Governmental Objectives for Social Work." The more broadly based National Conference on Social Work had discussed New Deal measures one year before. Yet the AASW conference marked the first comprehensive attempt by those identified specifically as professional social workers to deal with the appropriate commitment of the profession to social planning.

In the years following the conference, the association continued to examine this commitment. Social change and social work's role in such change were discussed in meetings of AASW delegates, the Executive Committee, and the special Division on Government and Social Work, created to carry out the organization's social welfare program. Discussion, and subsequent action, were shaped both by internal professional concerns and by external events and political realities.

In 1933, Porter Lee warned a New York social work audience of "the creeping paralysis which has afflicted our civilization and its institutions." In the "wilderness" brought by depression, social workers could be "pioneers again"--joining others in the monumental task of building a sound relief program which would help ensure economic security for all Americans.(2)

Social workers may have felt the pioneer spirit as they traveled to Washington, D.C., for the 1934 AASW delegate

conference. National events were both frightening and
challenging. Some two and one-half million families were on
the welfare rolls. The Federal Emergency Relief
Administration had been established by President Roosevelt,
under fellow social worker Harry Hopkins, to demonstrate the
federal government's commitment to relief. Yet the FERA was an
emergency response, not a permanent federal program. It was
reported that Roosevelt planned to phase out direct relief and
replace it with work relief. The Civil Works Administration
was about to be terminated. In the coming months, national and
state legislators would meet to consider new social and
economic legislation. The time seemed propitious for social
workers to try to influence legislative and administrative
responses to the problems of depression.(3)

Publicizing the upcoming conference, The Compass urged:
"Members of the profession must concentrate their best efforts
to help define [the] tasks" needed to meet the crisis and
integrate them with social work.(4) Stanley P. Davies, an
executive of the New York Charity Organization Society and
president of the AASW, explained that individual social workers
and local groups had limited influence on national policy. The
national executive office of the AASW, although active in
lobbying and publicity, lacked the necessary strength and
representativeness. A national conference representing the
total membership would be a more effective vehicle for the
recommendations of professional social work to the federal
government.(5)

Contemporary observers described the resulting conference
in enthusiastic terms:

A room with long green covered tables, chairs down either
side, red folders full of material for discussion, about 200
representative social workers from 44 chapters of the AASW,
formed the setting for a professional experiment.(6)

Gertrude Springer, associate editor of The Survey, reported
that delegates were "sampling their own blood-stream, finding
it full of good red blood corpuscles. . . . Social workers
have discovered themselves as a coherent body with something to
say."(7)

What they said concerned a broad federal response to the
problems of the Depression. They recognized the importance of
existing programs: the FERA, National Recovery Administration,
Civilian Conservation Corps, and public works. But they urged
creation of a "permanent, comprehensive . . . adequate
system of welfare services to insure ourselves, as a people,
against the common hazards of our economic and social life."
They proposed continuation of federal employment projects and
development of state systems of unemployment insurance, a
federal employment service, low-cost housing, and an adequate
program for federally supported direct relief. Services
should be provided in an efficient and equitable way by properly
trained personnel.(8)

The conference recommendations referred to social
insurance and "possible changes in taxation methods," including
progressive increases in the higher brackets. Yet the overall

thrust was a moderate one. The delegates stressed creation of
a national program of public welfare rather than reconstruction
of the existing economic system.(9)
     The importance of the conference lay beyond its specific
recommendations for social welfare reform. Similar recommendations had already been made by an AASW Committee on Federal
Action, and the New York City social work community had been
lobbying for new social programs for several years. Yet the
AASW conference constituted the first national meeting of
professional social workers to discuss collective political
action and to accept responsibility for helping to shape public
policy.(10)
     Acceptance of that responsibility raised important
issues. What sorts of policies and programs should social work
endorse? How should the profession promote its proposals--
through expert testimony, lobbying, or more active forms of
political confrontation, including coalitions with other
organizations? Not only did the AASW and the Rank and File
organizations differ on these issues, but conflict also existed
within the professional association regarding the best
approaches to pursue. In addition, the profession had to deal
with political opposition to its involvement in policy making
and to compete with other interest groups in promoting its
recommendations. Internal debate and external forces shaped
social work responses to national economic problems in three
important periods: the pre-Roosevelt era, 1929-33, the First
New Deal, 1933-35, and the Second New Deal, 1935-37.
     Social workers had been among the first to call attention
to the growing problems of unemployment during the Hoover
administration. Well before the 1929 stock market crash,
settlement workers in the larger cities expressed concern over
increasing levels of joblessness. Family case work leaders
began to notice a troubling rise in relief expenditures.(11)
An editorial in The Family (March, 1930) urged practitioners to
broadcast the effects of growing unemployment. The editors
suggested use of the pamphlet "The Time to Plan is Now," put out
by the Family Welfare Association of America. The FWAA
publication described how social workers could make their
knowledge and experience available to others interested in the
problems of unemployment.(12) In a novel way of doing this,
social worker and poet Clinch Calkins used family histories
gathered by settlement workers for a book on the lives of the
unemployed.(13)
     By 1929, social workers questioned both the responsibility
and the capacity of private agencies to provide relief.
Earlier, the FWAA had suggested that member agencies shift from
relief work to family service. Now, the extent of public
agency involvement in relief work received increased notice.
Social work researcher Wayne McMillen told an NCSW audience
that the public sector accounted for an impressive 98 percent of
all relief disbursements in the city of Detroit.(14) Figures
from the Bureau of Social Statistics indicated that in 1928,
almost three-fourths of all relief in fifteen major cities had
come from public sources.(15) Clearly, as McMillen noted,
"government is already in the field of social work in a big
way."(16)

The increase in need following the 1929 crash soon proved too much, however, for many local governments to handle. In addition, the resources of private agencies, particularly in New York City, were fast running out. Yet demands that the federal government take action in meeting the crisis brought only a limited response. Miscalculating the most effective area for government intervention, President Hoover concentrated on reviving finance and expanding credit rather than dealing directly with unemployment and the decline in consumption.(17)

Hoover's faith in voluntary action and decentralized approaches to social problems kept him from choosing a strong role for the federal government in matters of relief. Both his 1930 Emergency Committee for Employment and the later Commission on Unemployment Relief were public relations committees designed to stimulate local initiative. Porter Lee, the sole social worker on the Emergency Committee, joined committee chairman Arthur Woods in an increasing impatience over the lack of stronger measures.(18)

As unemployment became more severe, other social workers joined in this impatience. New York social workers were among the earliest to organize in support of public funding of relief. Their action reflected the relative cohesiveness of the New York social work community, where major social service organizations shared close geographic proximity. In addition, New York social workers had already worked closely with three governors on welfare reform. Members of the group included Walter West, Linton Swift of the FWAA, Lillian Wald, Porter Lee, Harry Hopkins (director of the New York Tuberculosis and Public Health Association and about to be appointed head of Governor Roosevelt's Temporary Emergency Relief Administration, or TERA), and William Hodson. Hodson was a well-known social work administrator who headed the New York City Welfare Council, a coordinating body for 900 private agencies. His chief assistant was Jane Hoey. These people, who identified primarily with professional social work, were joined in political activity by members of a broader social welfare community: Paul Kellogg of The Survey, Frances Perkins, then state industrial commissioner, and Molly Dewson, president of the New York Consumers' League. For most of the group, political action meant individual and small group lobbying of political figures, based on social welfare expertise.(19)

Other social work groupings did exist. Jewish social service and foundation workers were located in another area of the city. Their leaders tended to work with socialist labor unions and political parties on the lower East side.(20) Harry Lurie was one of the most influential of this group. He directed the Bureau of Jewish Social Research. A highly intelligent man, whose background combined research and administration, Lurie "usually dominated committees of which he was a member" and was well regarded within the profession.(21)

Although differing political ideologies would later lead to differences in proposals for social change, for the moment New York social workers joined in a common push for expansion of local and state public relief programs. They were instrumental in the creation of the TERA. Yet even with city and state

involvement, it soon became apparent that more government help
was needed. Hodson made a significant move in this direction
in his "Open Letter to President Hoover" in the November, 1931
issue of The Survey. Hodson warned the president that
stimulating local effort was not enough. He urged serious
consideration of federal grants-in-aid to supplement
inadequate local relief funds. Hodson's letter received wide
publicity and support.(22)

     The Depression and its problems were important topics at
meetings of the NCSW. In 1930, social work leaders called
attention to the effects of the crisis upon relief
organizations and their clients.(23) The following year, they
recommended specific action. Jacob Billikopf, head of the
Philadelphia Federation of Jewish Charities, stressed the need
for unemployment insurance and federal provision of relief. A
representative of the Catholic Welfare Federation called for a
planned social economy. In 1932, Mary Van Kleeck proposed the
"integration of industries" and consideration of changes in
ownership of the means of production, based on the Soviet
Union's example. Van Kleeck, the director of industrial
studies at the Russell Sage Foundation, spoke for a radical wing
within social work.(24)

     These expressions of concern and suggestions for action
began receiving publicity outside of social work circles. The
New York Times covered C. M. Bookman's presidential address to
the 1932 NCSW. Bookman was a Community Chest executive. He
proclaimed the nation's failure to cope with the emergency and
called on Hoover to use federal resources to meet public relief
needs.(25) Noted social workers from New York and other cities
testified at congressional hearings on the need for increased
public relief. Settlement leader Helen Hall, Chicago Jewish
Charities executive Samuel Goldsmith, Grace Abbott, Billikopf,
Hodson, Swift, West, and others attended a series of Senate
hearings on unemployment from 1930 to 1933.(26)

     Social work leaders publicized the effects of social prob-
lems and consulted on their solutions. These roles were reason-
ably well accepted both within and outside the profession.
Exposure of social ills was part of the social work tradition.
Lobbying and testimony by well-known social work figures fit
with a growing stress on scientific expertise in business and
government. Yet as the Depression deepened, social workers
began to see the necessity of moving from individual actions to
a collective professional response.

     This idea raised troubling issues. Conscious of their
status as an emerging profession, social workers faced a
dilemma in responding to the national emergency. In their work
in both private and public agencies, they could not ignore the
results of the crisis. They saw at first hand what the Children's Bureau called

the accumulating misery . . . of [the] normally hard-working,
small spending families who through no fault of their own slip
farther and farther down until they become applicants for charity.(27)

They had begun to realize the inadequacy of individualized case work methods and the resources of existing agencies. Yet to go beyond these and suggest broader socio-economic solutions meant different methodologies and a more political and perhaps partisan stance on the part of the profession.

Was such a stance appropriate? Many social workers were unsure. Earlier, members of the profession had criticized William Hodson for heading a national committee of social workers in support of a presidential candidate.(28) A social work master's degree candidate encountered similar reactions when she interviewed Chicago members of the AASW in 1929 for a study on social work ethics. More than two-thirds of the respondents felt social agencies should not take an active part in any political activity.(29)

In part, such attitudes stemmed from the concept of impartiality as an important criterion for professionalism. Dependency upon philanthropists and the need to protect social welfare programs from political opposition further reinforced belief in a nonpartisan stance. Although social reformer Frances Perkins had become convinced that ongoing involvement in party politics would enable her to pursue particular goals, Grace Abbott's caution was perhaps more typical. As head of the Children's Bureau, Abbott believed an objective, nonpartisan stance was necessary to preserve the bureau's program.(30)

In addition, there was the assumption, particularly prevalent among case workers in the twenties, that reform activity was not "genuine social work." As Miriam Van Waters told the NCSW in her 1930 presidential address, concentration on legislative and constitutional reform led to neglect of "the concept of personality." Van Waters brought this emphasis on personality into her pioneering work in penology. She assured her audience that such a stress "sets the social workers apart from the reformer militantly urging a program of reform."(31)

Hesitations gave way under the stress of a prolonged depression. Major spokesmen within the field began to define collective social action as a professional responsibility. Gordon Hamilton was a prominent case work educator on the faculty of the New York School of Social Work. She argued the profession's responsibility "to support and promote mass measures for insurance, pensions, and the like . . . and to bear testimony in regard to the effects on people of tolerated political and economic systems." Eveline Burns, an economist by training, urged social workers to act as a group in clarifying public opinion regarding the issues at stake in social planning. Francis McLean, leader in family social work, proclaimed: "The family welfare movement accepts the fact that it can and must contribute to development of a more sensible economic . . . system."(32)

One of the first examples of collective action grew out of a 1931 New York City Conference on Federal Aid for Unemployment Relief. The meeting was called by Swift, Lurie, Kellogg, and several others. It included agency heads and directors of national social work organizations, such as the AASW, Catholic Charities, and the Associated Chests and Councils. The group established an ongoing steering committee, The Social Work Conference on Federal Action, whose purpose was to develop suggestions regarding relief programs and to gain a hearing with

legislators drafting relief proposals. The committee soon had
a national membership, including social work leaders from
Chicago.(33)
    The AASW national office was active in this committee and
also on its own. West testified in Senate committee hearings
on unemployment. Senator Robert La Follette and Representative Edward Costigan turned to the association for
information and advice in drafting relief legislation. An AASW
Commission on Unemployment was created by the Executive Committee in 1931. The commission was to "mobilize the results of
observation and experience of its members, [and] to make this
experience available" to legislators and others. The commission drafted a number of recommendations which were incorporated in the Costigan-La Follette relief bill of 1931. AASW
endorsement of this bill marked the first time the professional
association had supported pending legislation.(34)
    In 1932, the Conference on Federal Action group was
reconstituted as a committee within the AASW.(35) Swift, the
committee's chair, described its work as "the expression of the
professional social worker." In its early meetings, the group
concentrated on the matter of federal responsibility for
relief, rather than broader issues of social insurance and
national planning.(36)
    By 1932, a number of social work service and professional
organizations had coalesced in the call for federal relief. In
an open letter to Hoover, the AASW called for the matching of
state relief funds with federal funds whenever possible. The
FWAA, Catholic Charities, and other social welfare organizations took similar stands. Most of the delegates to the 1932
NCSW believed aid should be public and federally supported.(37)
    When Roosevelt took office in 1933, social workers were
ready with detailed proposals for action. They had access to
the president through Eleanor Roosevelt, Molly Dewson, now an
influential presidential advisor, and the new secretary of
labor, Frances Perkins. The creation of the FERA in May, 1933
was due in part to the efforts of Harry Hopkins and William
Hodson. Working through Perkins, they presented Roosevelt with
a plan for unemployment relief modeled after New York's TERA.
Perkins drew on their ideas in helping to draft subsequent FERA
legislation.(38)
    Roosevelt chose Hopkins, a hard-driving, innovative
social worker, to head the new relief administration. The FERA
was authorized to channel five million dollars to the states as
grants-in-aid. Hopkins soon ruled that federal emergency
relief funds were to be administered solely by public agencies.
Although private agency relief expenditures continued after
this date, supported in part by state and local monies, the primary responsibility for provision of material assistance now
passed from the private to the public sector.
    The shift necessitated a major overhaul in private agency
goals and functions, or what FWAA director Swift called "new
alignments between public and private agencies." If public
agencies were to handle the matter of relief, what now would be
the work of the private social work organization? Swift's book
on the topic, published by the FWAA in 1934, gave a comprehensive explanation of that new role.(39)

Swift applauded the entry of the federal government into the relief arena. His book spoke to a professional audience concerned with working out the resulting division of labor between public and private agencies. Swift defined the appropriate roles for these agencies by examining the characteristics of each. He saw the public agency as a government body responsible to the entire community. As such, it was subject to majority will and could not venture too far beyond the general level of community understanding. It had to relate to other governmental organizations, and its work could be affected by administrative changes in government. On the positive side, public agencies could draw upon the resources of the whole community. They carried a public mandate to help relieve social and economic inequalities. Despite a reputation for poor administration and inadequately trained staff, there was no inherent reason why public agencies could not become professional and efficient operations.(40)

Private agencies differed from public ones primarily in their constituency: a minority group of informed citizens interested in meeting certain needs not yet recognized as vital by the majority. A smaller constituency generally meant less resources. On the other hand, methods and goals were not subject to majority approval and control. This gave the private agency greater freedom to experiment.(41)

Swift believed that private and public agencies had unique but complementary roles to play in providing social services. As the official instrument of society in mitigating social and economic inequalities, the public agency could deal with dependency stemming from societal rather than individual causes. The private agency could work with those cases where dependency related to a family or individual's "own private incapacity to adjust."(42)

Swift noted "the common misconception" that use of the case work method distinguished the private from the public agency. He defined case work as a collection of methods, some of which were crucial to the administration of relief. He tried to avoid casting a narrow psychiatric function for private agencies. He stressed their capacity to experiment with a variety of services, which might later be taken over by public bodies. Yet his most concrete image of a private agency function was that of dealing "with personal maladjustments that will respond to case work treatment."(43) Swift thus strengthened a growing tendency to view the work of private agencies as centered on intrapsychic problems rather than environmental conditions.

Swift's conception of the private/public realignment was widely shared. Statements about the role of private agencies as innovators in new types of services appeared in contemporary descriptions of the private social services and in conference presentations and journal articles.(44) The notion of the private agency as best equipped "to care for clients requiring highly skilled and prolonged individual treatment" was also common. One writer argued that private family agencies should concentrate on situations where unemployment is caused by "deterioration in family morale or other internal problems."(45)

The proposed realignment met with certain counterargu-
ments. One was the traditional notion that only private relief
could effectively promote client self-reliance.(46) More
prevalent was the argument that private agency stress on individual maladjustment could erode the profession's developing
commitment to dealing with social and economic problems. Swift
countered that the distinction between public and private
agency work allowed social work to pursue a dual focus. The
profession could maintain responsibility for treatment of individual problems, and at the same time take on a broader responsibility for the stress caused by wholesale unemployment.(47)
How the profession should carry out that responsibility--
and what solutions for unemployment it should propose--were as
yet unclear. As the largest and broadest professional
organization, the AASW might be expected to represent social
work's collective "political voice." Some were skeptical
about whether it could do so. Joseph Levy, a leader in the Rank
and File Practitioners Group in the Chicago chapter, asked:

Can a professional organization, which bases its requirements
for membership on education and experience, rather than on
point of view, support a program of social change, many of
whose points may be controversial? Would it be wise for a
professional body to assume this function?(48)

While questions were raised about the AASW's political
function, national events demanded action. As Roosevelt began
establishing the programs of the first New Deal, Swift and his
Committee on Federal Action sensed the need for a wider scope.
While enlarging its policy concerns, the committee maintained a
judicious and scientific air. "Specially qualified persons"
were invited to a one-day hearing on national economic
objectives in May, 1933. The resulting proposals indicated the
committee's broader interest in social reform. They included
not only direct relief, but also social insurance, work relief,
and changes in taxation policy. In sum, the committee called
for national social and economic planning.(49)
This attention to comprehensive social and economic reform
aroused some concern within the AASW that the profession was
moving too far from its legitimate areas of expertise. Walter
West believed that social workers had been most effective in
their testimony regarding relief legislation. Here they
presented material based on firsthand experience. When they
moved beyond relief issues to minimum-wage laws and social
insurance, social workers had less adequate knowledge. West's
belief in expert testimony no doubt reflected his experiences
as part of the group of social work leaders in New York. He did
not deny social workers' rights to have opinions "beyond those
matters in which their professional experience gives them special competence." In fact, he hoped these opinions would "be
in support of such radical change" as the economic situation
required. But to allay "the fears of those who do not want
their professional organization to become a lobby organization," he predicted that the AASW was likely in the future not
"to involve itself deeply nor constantly in general federal
social legislation."(50) Yet despite the hesitations of West

and others, the work of the Committee on Federal Action had set the tone for such involvement. The call for action spread, at least for a time, to the larger AASW membership.

The move toward stronger political action meant that the association should "do more than just register opinions," according to President Davies.(51) It must shift from a committee phase of study and expert testimony to political activity based on the voice of the broader constituency. Initially the organization had relied on the efforts of leading figures in social work: executives, educators, researchers, and heads of professional organizations. The decision to call a Delegate Conference in 1934 reflected the belief of Davies and others in the AASW leadership that a broader base of power might strengthen the association's hand in Washington.(52)

The idea of broader representation in the Association's political activity appealed to many of the chapters. They responded quickly to a conference planning committee's call for preconference study of the issues to be discussed. Chapters were asked to think about proposals regarding work relief, taxation policies, and a comprehensive federal system of social services which included unemployment insurance and old age pensions. Discussion of a broad range of issues was thus carried out on a grassroots level throughout the Association.(53)

Two hundred delegates, representing three-fourths of the chapters, met in Washington.(54) Frances Perkins and Harry Hopkins addressed the conference, reporting on New Deal planning and federal social welfare programs. President Roosevelt sent his greetings. He assured conference participants that "social workers and I have the same objectives in common-- social justice for everyone."(55)

Recommendations resulting from the conference included establishment of unemployment insurance, continuation of both federal employment projects and direct federal relief, and creation of a permanent system of welfare services with participation of federal, state, and local governments. Delegates agreed that the AASW should play a role in planning and administering the new social welfare system.(56)

Conference delegates reached consensus quickly on many of the issues. Conflict did arise at several points. Edith Abbott made one of the major presentations regarding a comprehensive public welfare plan linking state and county programs with a permanent federal bureau of public welfare. Discussion following her presentation indicated that to some, such a system was not the final goal, but only a transitional step in a process of greater social and economic change.(57)

Ideological differences over program were in part related to a debate about tactics. This was seen most clearly in discussion about taxation proposals. Here participants differed over the appropriate role a profession should take in formulation of public policy. Harry Lurie, Katharine Lenroot of the Children's Bureau, and representatives of the Detroit and St. Louis chapters called for changes in the federal tax system to effect a redistribution of wealth. As Lurie put it, "The people who are holding onto the [purse] strings will simply have to let go."(58) Others objected. They felt social workers should be interested in the kinds of taxes used, and in increased tax

revenues, but not in the issue of redistribution. Many of the
objections were based on the argument that social workers, as a
professional group, lacked expertise in this area. People like
Lee, Swift, and Frank Bane, head of the American Public Welfare
Association, believed that social workers should reserve their
recommendations for areas in which they could speak with recognized authority.(59) The pursuit of changes in the economic
system through redistribution of wealth implied a shift in the
profession's focus and tactics. Grace Abbott protested:

I didn't think we wanted to assume we were a pressure group so
much as that we were a group that should lead in this field
that is our field and we should be organizing . . . and representing a program that we could stand by.(60)

      It is difficult to ascertain whether these objections
stemmed from ideological considerations, a commitment to a professional model of action based on expert opinion, or both.
Lurie chided the conference that the issue was not one "of
expertness but of politics." The majority of the delegates
appear to have agreed. After some debate, they voted approval
of a set of recommendations on taxation which acknowledged
America's "faulty distribution of wealth."(61)
      However, other proposals of the Delegate Conference
stopped short of a full program of reconstruction. Recommendations focused on improvement of the existing system. A more
radical set of changes was submitted to the meetings by Jacob
Fisher, an employee of the Bureau of Jewish Social Research in
New York and a leader in the Rank and File Movement. But
Fisher's recommendations were not discussed.(62)
      The Delegate Conference achieved a good deal of consensus
on social welfare policy and on the profession's basic responsibility for development and administration of such policy.
Yet it contained the seeds of division over ideology, the appropriate topics of professional concern, and the type of political activity the profession should pursue.
      Along with the rest of the American public, social workers
were confused about the causes of unemployment and its
remedies. Individual and organizational statements underwent
changes and reversals. Proposals of different groups overlapped. It is possible, however, to sketch in broad outlines
two trends of thought which were developing among social workers in the years of the Hoover administration and the first New
Deal policies. The first, a "radical program," stressed the
redistribution of wealth and power through reconstruction of
social and economic institutions. Basic changes in taxation
and the alliance of professional groups with the organized
labor movement were key elements in this program. Important
promoters of the radical view included younger, union-oriented
social workers such as Joseph Levy, a member of the Chicago
Practitioners' Group, and Jacob Fisher. Harry Lurie, an
administrator, joined other professional social workers and
researcher Mary Van Kleeck in urging major social change.
      While the radical viewpoint attracted a sizable audience,
particularly among the Rank and File, the majority of social
workers supported a more moderate program of reform. This

emphasized the responsibility of the government to guarantee a minimum level of economic security for all, through such measures as unemployment relief, public assistance, public works projects, and old age pensions.

Most of the heads of the established social work organizations--West, Swift, and Homer Folks, for example--supported reform rather than reconstruction. Educational and agency leaders such as Lee and Hodson followed suit. While the New York group had been in the forefront of promoting reform, they were quickly joined by well-known social workers in other parts of the country--the Abbotts, Kenneth Pray, director of the Pennsylvania School of Social Work, and Dorothy Kahn, executive director of the Philadelphia County Relief Board. The New York social work community's increased interest in public welfare muted the traditional rivalry between Chicago and New York. What differences remained related to more technical debate over how best to organize and run the new public social services.

The moderates' faith in the improvement of existing institutions soon drew fire from their more radical colleagues. Karl Borders, a Chicago settlement worker, expressed the radical perspective in vivid terms. He argued:

No intelligent social worker can fail to be concerned with the whole social and economic order in which his work is set. The logical pursuit of such a concern will bring him out a political and economic radical.(63)

Borders and others looked at the social distress around them and concluded that the American economic system had failed. They chastised social workers for not making "a resolute enough attack" on that system.(64) They saw social workers acting, consciously or unconsciously, as allies of the existing order. One critic noted:

Social work is really functioning as a stop gap in the present social crisis. . . . Unquestionably social workers are helping to postpone the inevitable reorganization of economic and political institutions.(65)

Division between the radical and moderate viewpoints, subdued at the AASW Delegate Conference, emerged in full strength at the 1934 National Conference of Social Work several months later. At the more broadly based NCSW, audiences were "swept off their feet" by the speeches of the charismatic Mary Van Kleeck.(66) To packed halls, Van Kleeck spoke of the inherent conflict between labor and capital. In this conflict, the government acted as protector of private property. Social work involvement in federal relief programs therefore meant upholding the status quo.(67)

Both admirers and detractors testified to the significance of Van Kleeck's speeches in mobilizing radical sentiment. Jacob Fisher proclaimed that her "stunning dissent" made social action a major issue in social work after a lapse of twenty years. Another admirer in the audience was Bertha Reynolds, a well-known psychiatric social worker and the associate dean at

the Smith College School of Social Work. She later recalled:
"The effect [of Van Kleeck's speech] was that of a strong wind
blowing through the Conference. The audience would not stop
applauding." Reynolds attributed her own turn toward Marxism
in part to Van Kleeck's arguments. Gertrude Springer, a writer
of more moderate leanings, described the "Van Kleeck sensation"
in The Survey: "The effect on her hearers was electric. The
younger and more volatile rose as to a trumpet-call. The
soberest were shaken."(68)

     Springer saw the 1934 NCSW as more radical than its prede-
cessors. In part this change could be attributed to the recent
rise of social work unionism. Public welfare protective
organizations, private agency discussion clubs, and practitioners groups in the AASW were gradually coalescing in the Rank
and File Movement. Although organization of a national
coordinating body was a year away, the movement had already
begun publishing its own journal, Social Work Today, edited by
Jacob Fisher.(69)

     The Rank and File Movement stressed broad social and
economic change as well as improvement of working conditions.
Many of its members were impatient with reformist approaches.
They scoffed at the AASW's "mystical faith in slow but sure
progress toward the good, the true, and the beautiful."(70)
The Rank and File groups held four meetings at the 1934 NCSW.
Participants stressed economic organization of workers as a
source of power for social change. They called on social workers to join with labor groups. They criticized New Deal
policies and joined Van Kleeck in challenging the social reform
response to Depression.(71)

     The ideas of the Rank and File were supported by older,
more established social workers. Harry Lurie was an active
proponent of unionism in social work. While he questioned the
use of tactics like strikes, Lurie agreed with the movement's
major goals. He belonged to several AASW social action committees, and chaired an important subcommittee on Outlining a
National Social Welfare Program. In this capacity, he had a
direct hand in the policy-making of the professional group. He
thus acted as a bridge between the militant younger social workers and moderates in the AASW.(72)

     Bertha Reynolds played a similar role. Well-established
in the field of psychiatric social work, she brought a measure
of credibility to the union group by supporting their ideas.
Reynolds sought to reconcile the tenets of Marx and Freud. She
wrote an important series in Social Work Today, in which she
stressed the complementarity of scientific study of the
economic behavior of society and that of the "psychological and
biological phenomenon in the lives of individuals." Case workers should use both kinds of knowledge in their work with clients.(73)

     Other well-known social workers shared parts, if not all,
of the radical perspective. They included group work
theoretician Grace Coyle, Marion Hathway of the Pittsburgh
School of Social Work, Eduard Lindemann, John Fitch, and Gordon
Hamilton of the New York School, and Wayne McMillen at the
University of Chicago. These individuals tended to sympathize
more with union complaints about poor working conditions than

with calls for radical social change. They concurred that the American system was flawed, but did not always join in a comprehensive program for social reconstruction.(74)

Part of their moderation seems to have stemmed from recognition of the difficulties of pursuing social change within the social agency context. It seemed risky to participate "in social program-building which donors and community leaders are likely to view as 'radical'."(75) Grace Coyle wrote perceptively about the sponsorship of social work agencies and programs by particular economic interests. As social work educator Mildred Mudgett observed, community chests and agency board members represented a class in American society which did not take kindly to challenges to the status quo.(76)

Even in the new federal agencies, social workers were hounded by politicians critical of "liberal" programs and determined to preserve a patronage system of political appointees in public jobs. One victim of the patronage system was Raymond C. Branion, a California state relief administrator and professional social worker, indicted on trumped-up charges of defrauding the U.S. government.(77)

Awareness of political pressures and agency constraints helped curb the growth of radicalism within social work. In addition, the commitment to moderate reform was an understandable response for middle-class professionals brought up with a belief in the adaptability of the American system. This belief encouraged social workers to feel that the New Deal's extension of existing social welfare measures would mitigate the problems of an industrial society.

Conflict between moderates and radicals colored the work of the AASW's Division on Government and Social Work. This division was established following the 1934 Delegate Conference, as an extension of the Committee on Federal Action. Swift continued as chairman. The goal of the division was to carry out the social welfare program of the AASW.(78)

The division soon developed internal problems. Much of the tension arose within a Sub-Committee to Outline a National Social Welfare Program, chaired by Lurie. Lurie, Van Kleeck, and other activists proposed an AASW political strategy which went beyond a "minimum program," or promotion of New Deal reforms, to a "maximum program": a protest movement using existing social welfare programs as points of attack. The maximum program suggested a planned economy and supported the "Lundeen Bill"--a radical social insurance measure--over the Wagner-Lewis Unemployment Insurance Bill.(79) Other members of the committee, including Grace Abbott and Paul Kellogg, supported the minimum approach. Swift backed the latter group. A majority of the subcommittee issued a policy statement endorsing the maximum program, but the Division Steering Committee refused to circulate the report at the 1935 AASW conference. Dorothy Kahn, president of the Association, and a strong supporter of New Deal measures, called Lurie "biased" and the maximum program "the impossible program." Lurie, in turn, accused the AASW leadership of censorship.(80)

In the face of such controversy, Swift argued that the association should limit its activities to those areas where members had achieved consensus: personnel and the adequacy of

relief standards. Not surprisingly, these were areas where
technical expertise seemed dominant over politics.(81)
     In June, 1935, Swift resigned as division chair. He
reported that the Steering Committee was full of differences of
opinion and "individualized approaches."(82) After Swift's
resignation, the political program of both the division and the
AASW seemed to founder. In part this was due to internal conflict over how best to proceed. More important, however, were
the 1935-37 changes in Roosevelt's programs to deal with
economic insecurity. In May, 1935, with Hopkins' concurrence,
the president terminated the FERA and created a broad program of
work relief. As federal direct relief was phased out, the
Works Progress Administration (WPA) was expected to take up the
slack. The Social Security Act, signed in August, established
social insurance for the elderly and several other categorical
groups. But general assistance--direct relief--was not
included in the program.
     The phase-out of federal direct relief was a blow to social
workers of varying political backgrounds. Both AASW members
and Rank and File practitioners believed in its necessity. The
Rank and File saw it as a needed stopgap, the AASW as a cornerstone of a permanent federal welfare program. Both groups
pointed to the inability of the WPA to handle all individuals
and families in need. For the Rank and File especially, there
was the added problem of staff cutbacks in the relief programs.(83)
     Social workers worried about their lack of influence over
these changes. In 1934, Roosevelt had assured AASW delegates
that they shared the same objectives. This seemed less true in
1935. Social workers had served on the President's Advisory
Council on Social Security. But neither they nor the AASW
could persuade the administration to include federal grants-in-
aid for all needy persons in the Social Security bill.(84)
     When the federal government terminated its direct relief
grants to states, social workers responded with a fervour remi-
niscent of that expressed during the Hoover administration.
The Board of Directors of the FWAA warned that a jobs program
could not absorb all the needy. The remaining relief needs
would be thrown back on states and localities ill-prepared to
meet them.(85) The AASW Exective Committee promised to use all
its influence to bring reinstatement of federal relief.
Despite its recent debate over political activity, the committee announced its intention to draw up relevant legislation.
West called on the chapters to supply supporting evidence.
Many chapters held mass meetings on relief.(86)
     The AASW thus renewed its efforts at national political
influence. This was due in part to the severity of the crisis.
In addition, the group was once again on "home ground." It was
expressing opinions not on national economic planning or on
changes in taxation, but on a traditional area of concern--
financial assistance. The gathering of chapter data and publication of results meant the resumption of a familiar fact-
finding role.
     Local chapters pushed the national office to pursue an
even more active role. They urged employment of a full-time
Washington representative to lobby the federal government.

Dorothy Kahn approved. As a public social service executive, she observed that social work was frequently misrepresented in Washington.(87)

West resisted the idea of a full-time lobbyist. He agreed the association could use such representation on a part-time basis. He himself was in frequent contact with Washington officials. Yet he argued that the major charge of the AASW was maintenance of professional standards and interpretation of social work to the public. The association lacked the resources for a full-scale political program. It had "no voting strength, no political power, and . . . no claim to the ear of Mr. Altmeyer or Mr. Hopkins except to state what we know on the basis of our experience." Despite Kahn's objections, West was able to convince the committee to hire a part-time publicity person rather than a full-time lobbyist.(88)

West envisioned an advisory rather than pressure group role for the association. He and other national officers continued efforts to reach the policy makers. West met with Aubrey Williams, Hopkins' assistant, in Washington. Yet when West stressed the need for federal public assistance, Williams emphasized the "degradity of relief." He told West "social workers were wrong in their thinking" about the shortcomings in the work program.(89)

Faced with such resistance, the AASW was in a quandary. Sensing the need to join with other groups in their protest, they began to plan a special national conference on relief, to develop cooperative action. Yet discussion of the conference revealed fears of domination by other groups and loss of autonomy. The Executive Committee rejected the suggestion of Grace Abbott as chair, fearing that "when the Conference was over, we might discover we didn't have much relation to it." They pondered cosponsorship with the Conference of Mayors, but worried that New York's Fiorello La Guardia might speak in opposition to their program.(90)

Finally, they were concerned that the conference might be dominated by the Rank and File Movement. The union movement had gained in strength with organization of a National Coordinating Committee and several national conventions. While West was sympathetic with Rank and File concerns, Grace Marcus argued: "I don't think that group should be given the floor or allowed to speak so much this year."(91)

Beneath this discussion lay several issues. One was the professional association's concern for autonomy and its sense that it had both a special stake and a unique expertise in the area of relief. The other was a question as to proper tactics. Though the AASW and the Rank and File raised similar objections to the relief cutbacks, they had different ideologies and pursued different forms of protest. Rank and File members engaged in mass meetings with labor groups and councils of the unemployed. They organized clients to obtain just and necessary relief. They sent large delegations "with appropriate demands" to visit the White House, the FERA, and the Department of Labor. Such approaches were at odds with the objective, advisory role envisioned by most of the AASW leadership.(92)

In the end, the AASW decided to hold a delegate conference on the relief issue, with invited outside speakers. The con-

ference would develop a platform on relief and other social welfare measures, to be promoted to social planners and the public.(93)

The Delegate Conference met in February, 1936. Kahn
charged the group to develop a program for governmental action.
She defined their role as "professional," not "political":

Our approach to this problem is through the single channel of
our professional knowledge and experience as social workers.
Whatever our alliances may be as citizens, here we have no
political or factional affiliations.(94)

The conference adopted a platform advocating a system of
federal grants-in-aid to states for public assistance. This
and other recommendations were published by the AASW in This
Business of Relief, a monograph intended to influence the
policy makers. In addition, the Division on Government and
Social Work submitted policy proposals to the Democratic and
Republican party platform committees.(95)

Yet the 1936 major party platforms showed no evidence of
influence by professional social work recommendations. Neither party endorsed general federal relief. After the
elections, the Democratic administration pursued its program of
work relief and implementation of the Social Security Act.
Dispirited, the AASW continued to lobby for a federal relief
bill. But in 1937, West asserted, "The era of considering our
job a sort of lobby job in Washington is over."(96)

Social welfare reform in general faced tough going after
1936. Gathering anti-New Deal forces were aided by the 1937
recession and the unpopularity of Roosevelt's attempts to pack
the Supreme Court. Although elected to an unprecedented third
term, the president was losing the power to start new programs.
The rumblings of approaching war distracted attention from
social policy.

Association activities in 1937 and 1938 indicate a gradual
retreat from attempts at active involvement in national policy
decisions on social welfare. Although the Delegate Conferences of those years repeated the policy recommendations of
previous meetings, they concentrated more on discussion of
internal structure and professional issues. Executive Committee members and others felt these issues, including membership
requirements and professional education, had been neglected in
recent years.(97) On the chapter level, members argued over
the propriety of social workers running for political office
and chapter support for political causes.(98) In general, the
organization began to debate whether its primary focus was professional practice or political activity.

At the same time, the association's involvement in social
welfare policy shifted to matters of professional staffing in
the developing Social Security programs and to the improvement
of public relief administration on the local level. In part,
this shift reflected changes in the national scene. The states
and localities had resumed responsibility for general relief.
The role of the federal government in a social security system
was widely accepted. Now the task was implementation of that
system on the state and local levels. But the association's

interest in administration and staffing also indicated a return
to a traditional concern with relief and with professional
standards.

Social workers had temporarily broadened their concerns
and moved toward collective political action during the 1930s.
As they did so, they debated program, tactics, and a professional commitment to political activity. Social change
proposals and methods tended to coalesce into two approaches.
The first stressed improvement of the existing system, with
social workers taking the role of experts in the design and
implementation of social welfare reform. The second cast
social workers as a protest group, often working toward more
fundamental socio-economic change.

The internal debate was affected by outside forces--agency
constraints, changing economic conditions and political cli-
mate, and shifts in social work's influence within administration circles. Agency and political pressures, and an image of
"true" professionals as nonpartisan and objective, encouraged
social workers to choose the expert role over that of political
activist. By the end of the decade, the AASW had returned to
the more comfortable position of a professional group concerned
with professional standards and practice. Outside forces and
internal questions about political involvement had combined to
limit social work's chances to influence broader social planning.

Notes

1. Jane Purcell Guild, "The Social Worker and the Depression," The Nation, CXXXVI: 667-68 (June 14, 1933).

2. Porter Lee, "Social Workers: Pioneers Again," Address before the Association of the New York School of Social Work, 1933, and published in The Survey Midmonthly, LXIX: 307-12 (September, 1933).

3. Harry Hopkins, "Current Relief Problems," Conference on Governmental Objectives for Social Work, 2/16/34, National Association of Social Workers Records, folder 66, Social Welfare History Archives, University of Minnesota, Minneapolis, Minn.

4. "The Conference on Governmental Objectives for Social Work," The Compass, XV: 1-2 (January, 1934).

5. "The AASW Calls a Conference," The Compass, XV: 4-5 (December, 1933); see also "The Conference on Governmental Objectives for Social Work," The Compass, XV: 1-6 (March, 1934).

6. "The Conference on Governmental Objectives for Social Work" (March, 1934), p. 1.

7. Gertrude Springer, "For Welfare and Security," The Survey Midmonthly, LXX: 67 (March, 1934).

8. "The Recommendations of the Conference," The Compass, XV: 7-9 (March, 1934).

9. Ibid.

10. "Report on Washington Meeting of AASW, February, 1934, on 'Governmental Objectives for Social Work'," Social Service Review, VIII: 145-46 (March, 1934); Stanley P. Davies, "President's Address," Conference on Governmental Objectives for Social Work, 2/16/34, NASW Records, folder 66.

11. Clark Chambers, Seedtime of Reform (Ann Arbor, Mich.: Ann Arbor Paper Backs, 1967), pp. 143-46; see also Linton Swift, "The Relief Problem in Family Social Work," The Family, X: 3-11 (March, 1929).

12. "The Time to Plan is Now," The Family, XI: 17 (March, 1930).

13. Clinch Calkins, Some Folks Won't Work (New York: Harcourt, Brace and Co., 1930), described in William Stott, Documentary Expression and Thirties America (New York: Oxford University Press, 1973), pp. 144-46.

14. McMillen, "Some Statistical Comparisons of Public and Private Family Social Work," National Conference of Social

Work, Proceedings (1929), pp. 514-27.

15. Josephine Brown, Public Relief, 1929-1939 (New York: Henry Holt, 1940), p. 55.

16. McMillen, "Some Statistical Comparisons," p. 522.

17. David Burner, Herbert Hoover: A Public Life (New York: Alfred A. Knopf, 1979), pp. 253-61.

18. Chambers, pp. 193-94.

19. For a comprehensive description of the affiliations and activities of New York social workers, see William W. Bremer, Depression Winters: New York Social Workers and the New Deal (Philadelphia: Temple University Press, 1984).

20. Ibid., p. 10.

21. Jacob Fisher, The Response of Social Work to the Depression (Cambridge, Mass.: Schenkman, 1980), pp. 68-69. Lurie had worked earlier in Chicago, where he earned the respect of Breckinridge and Edith Abbott. See, e.g., Minutes, Executive Committee, AASW, 9/28/33, NASW: Chicago Chapter Records, Box 20, Chicago Historial Society, Chicago, Ill.

22. William Hodson, "An Open Letter to the President on Federal Relief Appropriations," The Survey Graphic, LXVII: 144-45 (November 1, 1931); Chambers, p. 195.

23. NCSW, Proceedings (1930), pp. 233-49, 325-29, 341-57.

24. Jacob Billikopf, "What Have We Learned About Unemployment?" NCSW, Proceedings (1931), pp. 25-50; John Lapp, "Is Unemployment Permanent?" NCSW, Proceedings (1931), pp. 232-38; Mary Van Kleeck, "Social Planning and Social Work," NCSW, Proceedings (1932), pp. 294-300.

25. New York Times, LXXXI: 5 (May 16, 1932); see also LXXX: 29 (January 4, 1931) and LXXXI: 2 (September 26, 1931).

26. New York Times, LXXX: 1 (December 29, 1931); "Hearings Before a Sub-Committee on Manufactures, U. S. Senate, 72nd Congress, 1st Session, on S174 and S262," Social Service Review, VI: 174-78 (March, 1932); "Federal Relief Hearings," The Compass, XIV: 1 (January, 1933).

27. "Relief Statistics for 1930," Social Service Review, V: 109-10 (March, 1931).

28. Frank Bruno, Trends in Social Work (New York: Columbia University Press, 1948), pp. 319-20.

29. Lula Jean Elliot, Social Work Ethics (New York:

AASW, June, 1931), p. 36.

30. George Martin, Madame Secretary: Frances Perkins (Boston: Houghton Mifflin, 1976), pp. 165-67; Lela Costin, Two Sisters for Social Justice (Urbana: University of Illinois Press, 1983), pp. 108, 126-27.

31. Miriam Van Waters, "Philosophical Trends in Modern Social Work," NCSW, Proceedings (1930), pp. 3-19.

32. Gordon Hamilton, "Refocusing Family Case Work," NCSW, Proceedings (1931), pp. 170-88; Eveline Burns, "The Wider Implications of Social Planning," The Family, XIII: 72 (May, 1932); Francis H. McLean, "Present Day Problems in the Family Field," NCSW, Proceedings (1931), p. 161.

33. Minutes, Conference of Social Workers on Federal Aid for Unemployment Relief, 10/13/31, 11/29/31, 12/3/31, NASW Records, folder 195.

34. "A Statement by the Commission on Unemployment," The Compass, XIII: 1-2 (December, 1931); Minutes, Conference of Social Workers on Federal Aid, 1/32, NASW Records, folder 195.

35. Letter from West to Joanna Colcord, 11/23/32, NASW Records, folder 196.

36. Minutes, Committee on Federal Action on Unemployment, AASW, 5/4/33, 6/22/33, NASW Records, folder 196.

37. New York Times, LXXXI: 22 (May 30, 1932) and LXXXII: 2 (January 29, 1933); Paul Kellogg, "Relief Needs: Relief Resources," The Survey Graphic, LXVII: 463-67 (February 1, 1932); "Report of Chicago Conference on Relief Standards," Social Service Review, VI: 592-612 (December, 1932); Minutes, Conference of Social Workers on Federal Aid for Unemployment Relief, 10/13/31, NASW Records, folder 195; Editorial, The Family, XIV: 277 (December, 1933).

38. Martin, pp. 247-49.

39. Linton Swift, New Alignments Between Public and Private Agencies (New York: FWAA, 1934).

40. Ibid., pp. 11-12.

41. Ibid., p. 13.

42. Ibid., p. 39.

43. Ibid., p. 13.

44. See, e.g., Thomas Devine, "Essentials in A Community Program for Unemployment Relief," The Family, XIV: 166-68 (July 1, 1933); Recent Social Trends in the U.S.: Report of President's Research Committee on Social Trends, Vol 2 (New York:

McGraw-Hill, 1933), p. 1222; Robert Kelso, "The Community Chest and Relief Giving," NCSW, Proceedings (1930), pp. 233-38.

45. John P. Sanderson, "The Family Society of Tomorrow," The Family, XIV: 42 (April, 1933). See also Caroline Bedford, "Unemployment and Family Societies," NCSW, Proceedings (1931), p. 209; Lucia B. Clow, "What of the Future?" The Family, XV: 3 (March, 1934).

46. See, e. g., Mary Willcox Glenn, "On Consolidating Social Gains," The Family, XIV: 67 (May, 1933).

47. Esther Brown, Social Work as a Profession 2nd ed. (New York: Russell Sage, 1936), pp. 113-14; Linton Swift,"The Community Fund and Relief Giving," NCSW, Proceedings (1930), pp. 239-49. See also McLean, pp. 161-69.

48. Joseph Levy, "The Practitioners' Movement," (July, 1933), p. 4, NASW Records, folder 253.

49. "National Economic Objectives for Social Work," The Compass, XIV: 10-20 (December, 1933); Minutes of the Committee on Federal Action on Unemployment, AASW, 5/4/33; letter from Swift to Committee Members, 2/17/33, NASW Records, folder 196.

50. "The Association Program: Annual Report of the Executive Secretary," The Compass, XIV: 9-15 (June, 1933).

51. Davies, "President's Address," Conference on Governmental Objectives for Social Work, 2/16/34, NASW Records, folder 66.

52. Davies, "President's Address." It is difficult to ascertain just how the Delegate Conference idea developed, especially since the NASW Papers at the SWHA are missing the AASW Executive Committee Minutes for 1931-34. It is not clear how enthusiastic West was, for example. Grace Abbott gave the original suggestion for the conference format (a delegate conference in which participants were supplied with portfolios of written materials on the issues). She had attended a similar conference given by the AF of L. "Historical Development of the Delegate Conference," The Compass, reprint in Harry Lurie Papers, folder 2, Minneapolis, Minn.

53. "The AASW Calls a Conference," pp. 4-5; Instructions to Delegates, Chicago Chapter, AASW, 2/9/34, NASW: Chicago Chapter Records, Box 2.

54. Jane Hoey, "Credentials Report," Conference on Governmental Objectives for Social Work, 2/16/34, NASW Records, folder 66.

55. "The Conference on Governmental Objectives for Social Work," The Compass, XV: 1-6 (March, 1934).

56. "The Recommendations of the Conference," pp. 7-9.

57.   Proceedings, Conference on Governmental Objectives, 2/17/34, NASW Records, folder 67.

58.   Ibid., p. 275.

59.   Ibid., pp. 245-78. A similar debate took place at the 2/9/34 Membership Meeting of the Chicago Chapter. NASW: Chicago Chapter Records, Box 21.

60.   Proceedings, Conference on Governmental Objectives, 2/17/34, p. 265, NASW Records, folder 67.

61.   Ibid., pp. 275, 393-95.

62.   "Other Proposals and Recommendations," The Compass, XV: 9-10 (March, 1934); Proceedings, Conference on Governmental Objectives, 2/17/34, p. 314.

63.   Karl Borders, "Social Workers and a New Social Order," NCSW, Proceedings (1933), pp. 590-96. See also Borders, "Some Principles of Social Work in the Soviet Union," Social Service Review, V: 237-44 (June, 1931).

64.   Rev. Abba Hillel Silver, "The Crisis in Social Work," NCSW, Proceedings (1932), pp. 53-64.

65.   Guild, "The Social Worker and the Depression." See also Harry Lurie, "The Dilemma of the Case Worker," Social Work Today, III: 13-15 (October, 1935); Florence Davidson, "Case Workers and Society," letter to the editor, The Survey Midmonthly, LXVII: 555 (February 2, 1932).

66.   Jacob Fisher, The Rank and File Movement in Social Work, 1931-1936 (New York: New York School of Social Work, 1936), p. 22.

67.   Mary Van Kleeck, "Our Illusions Regarding Government," and "Common Goals of Labor and Social Work," NCSW, Proceedings (1934), pp. 473-85 and 284-303.

68.   Fisher, Rank and File Movement, p. 22; Bertha C. Reynolds, An Uncharted Journey (New York: Citadel Press, 1963), pp. 158-66; Gertrude Springer, "Rising to a New Challenge; The National Conference of Social Work Hears an Evangelist--And Likes It," The Survey Midmonthly, LXX: 179-80 (June, 1934).

69.   Fisher, Rank and File Movement, pp. 17-36.

70.   Irwin Rosen, "The Feasibility of a National Protective Association for Social Workers," Jewish Social Service Quarterly, X: 117-21 (September, 1933).

71.   Jacob Fisher, Response of Social Work, pp. 74-77.

72. Lurie, "Dilemma of the Case Worker," pp. 13-15; Lurie et al., "Should Social Work Employees Use Labor Tactics? A Symposium," Social Work Today, III: 5-7 (January, 1936).

73. Bertha Reynolds, "Re-thinking Social Case Work," Social Work Today, V: 8 (June, 1938).

74. Local 19 of the Social Service Employees Union had a chapter at the New York School of Social Work; members included Fitch, Lindemann, Hamilton, and Reynolds. Leslie Alexander, "Organizing the Professional Social Worker: Union Development in Voluntary Social Work, 1930-1950" (Diss. Bryn Mawr College 1977), p. 145. Hathway was a "Cooperator" of Social Work Today, and, along with Lindemann, a member of the American League against Fascism. Hathway Resumes, folder 1, Marion Hathway Papers, Social Welfare History Archives.

75. Letter from Mary Alma Cotter to Lurie, 7/10/33, Lurie Papers, folder 26.

76. Grace Coyle, "The Limitations of Social Work in Relation to Social Reorganization," Social Forces, XIV: 94-102 (October, 1935); Mildred Mudgett, "The Four Seasons" (Unpublished autobiography, Mildred Mudgett Papers, Social Welfare History Archives, p. 213).

77. Lillian Symes, "Politics vs. Relief," The Survey Graphic, XXIV: 8-10 (January, 1935); see also "The Ugly Head of Politics," The Survey Midmonthly, LXXI: 183-84 (June, 1935).

78. "Divisional Organization of the Association's Program," The Compass, XV: 4-5 (April, 1934); "Division on Government and Social Work," 7/26/34, Lurie Papers, folder 3.

79. Letter from Sub-Committee Secretary Helen Crosby to Lurie, 1/23/35, Lurie Papers, folder 4; "The Discussion Continues," The Compass, XVI: 6-7 (March, 1935); Memorandum, H. Lurie, 2/11/35, NASW Records, folder 210; "Report of the AASW Committee To Outline a National Social Welfare Program," n.d., Lurie Papers, folder 4.

80. Letter from Lurie to Grace Abbott, 10/30/34, Lurie Papers, folder 3; Kahn to Lurie, 1/1/35, and Lurie to Kahn, 1/15/35, Lurie Papers, folder 4.

81. Minutes, Steering Committee of Division on Social Work and Government, 1/7/35, Lurie Papers, folder 4; Minutes, Ad Interim Committee, AASW, 11/4/35, NASW Records, folder 21.

82. Minutes, Ad Interim Committee, AASW, 6/26/35, NASW Records, folder 21.

83. Fisher, Response of Social Work, pp. 127-31; Josephine Brown, p. 170; "The AASW Program for the Relief Emergency," The Compass, XVII: 2-5 (November, 1935); Statement to the President and the Federal Relief Administrator, The

Joint Committee on Public Assistance, Chicago, 12/6/35, NASW: Chicago Chapter Records, Box 20.

84.   Arthur Altmeyer, The Formative Years of Social Security (Madison: University of Wisconsin Press, 1966), p. 28; New York Times, LXXXIV: 18 (January 25, 1935); Chambers, p. 257.

85.   New York Times, LXXXIV: 2 (October 20, 1935).

86.   "The AASW Program for the Relief Emergency," pp. 2-5; Walter West, "The Relief Crisis," The Compass, XVII: 2 (October, 1935); "Social Workers Call a Mass Meeting," The Compass, XVII: 2-4 (October, 1935).

87.   Minutes, Ad Interim Committee, AASW, 10/10/35, NASW Records, folder 21.

88.   Ibid, 11/4/35.

89.   Minutes, Ad Interim Committee, AASW, 1/6/36, NASW Records, folder 21.

90.   Minutes, Ad Interim Committee, AASW, 12/2/25 and 1/6/36, NASW Records, folder 21.

91.   Minutes, Ad Interim Committee, AASW, 1/6/36, NASW Records, folder 21.

92.   Fisher, Response of Social Work, pp. 127-29; Minutes, Ad Interim Committee, AASW, 5/18/36, NASW Records, folder 21.

93.   Minutes, Ad Interim Committee, AASW, 2/7/36, NASW Records, folder 21.

94.   Dorothy Kahn, "The Occasion for the Conference," in AASW, This Business of Relief (New York: AASW, 1936), pp. 7-14.

95.   "Outline of a Federal Assistance Program," in This Business of Relief, pp. 162-69; Walter West, Foreword, in This Business of Relief, pp. 3-4; Fisher, Response of Social Work, p. 147.

96.   Fisher, Response of Social Work, pp. 150-51; Minutes, Ad Interim Committee, AASW, 6/19/37, NASW Records, folder 22.

97.   Fisher, Response of Social Work, pp. 176-78; Minutes, Ad Interim Committee, AASW, 2/10/37 and 8/11/37, NASW Records, folder 22; "Delegate Conference Program," The Compass, XVIII: 2-4 (February, 1937); Proceedings, AASW Delegate Conference, 1939, NASW Records, folder 75.

98.   Minutes, Executive Committee, 3/4/38 and 6/18/37, and Membership Committee, 3/10/38, Chicago Chapter, AASW, NASW: Chicago Chapter Records, Boxes 20 and 21.

5

Social Work and Public Service: Efforts Toward a Professional Public Welfare Program

In December, 1935, the Social Security Board appointed Jane Hoey head of its new Bureau of Public Assistance. Like her friend Harry Hopkins, Hoey was a professional social worker, with a diploma from the New York School of Social Work. Over the next few years, she and her staff developed a model for a professional public assistance program. Its implementation was only partly successful. The story of its creation and problems helps reveal the larger relation of professional social work to the development of a state/federal public welfare system between 1935 and 1940.

The relation between professional social work and public welfare was shaped by internal debates and external pressures. As in the controversies over involvement in national planning and reform and the responsibility of the profession to the new, untrained worker of the thirties, social workers differed in their views about public social services. Champions of public welfare had different conceptions about how it should be organized and staffed. Outside of the profession, politicians and established officials had their own ideas about structure and the use of social work.

Debates took shape around a variety of administrative principles. Yet the crux of the discussion was the nature of staffing of the new public services. Who would hold the public assistance jobs created by the Social Security Act? What kinds of training would prepare them for their functions? Jane Hoey and her team had definite ideas, which reflected an orientation toward professional social work. To adapt these ideas to the reality of the public welfare bureaucracy in a political milieu was to temper ideal standards by actual conditions. Outsiders as well as insiders defined the shape of social work.

In 1935 the profession had no clearly formulated ideal of the public welfare system and social work's relation to it. Certain basic principles were agreed upon: government should finance and administer general relief, it should provide social insurance, and a single federal agency should coordinate the two. Social work could promote and help plan for the incorporation of these principles into a broad program of social welfare. Here, professional leaders felt, lay their major expertise. Yet as the action changed from political debate and planning to actual administration, social workers became less clear and unified about their role. Should they maintain a responsibility to the developing public welfare enterprise? Or should they return to traditional concerns, including the advancement of case work theory and improvement of family agency practice?

Discussion about social work's role in administration and staffing of a public welfare system began within the American Association of Social Workers in 1926 with the creation of a Committee on Standards, Personnel, and Service in Public Agencies. Harry Lurie chaired the Chicago-based committee, whose members included Edith Abbott and Sophonisba Breckinridge. After several years' work, the committee recommended that (a) social work positions in public service should be professional, requiring social work training, and (b) they should be part of a civil service system and filled through competitive examinations, conducted by professional social workers.(1) The committee stressed professional expertise, incorporated into a civil service system, as the foundation of public welfare staffing.

After 1929 the AASW spent more time discussing federal responsibility for relief than the details of public welfare administration. But when association leaders turned to this topic, they supported the committee's stand. AASW President Stanley Davies declared that social workers should be in the forefront of organizing, developing standards, and directing public welfare. Public and private agencies should follow a single set of professional standards.(2) Members at the 1930 annual meeting accepted the committee's recommendation that the requirements for AASW membership be promoted as desirable personnel standards for public social work.(3) The 1934 Delegate Conference endorsed use of a merit system.

The Family Welfare Association of America developed similar positions. At the request of President Hoover's Organization on Unemployment Relief, the FWAA prepared a guide book on the organization and administration of public welfare agencies. This handbook stressed professional training for welfare personnel, including two years of professional social work training for case workers.(4)

The organization which devoted most time to personnel considerations in public welfare was the American Association of Public Welfare Officials. The AAPWO was not strictly a professional organization, as it focused on the broad field of public welfare rather than simply the profession of social work. Its membership, first brought together in 1931, consisted largely of public welfare officials. The group maintained ties with the AASW and other social work organizations, however, and professional social work leaders like Grace Abbott and Breckinridge were active members. The AAPWO was headquartered in Chicago and had a close relationship with the Chicago School of Social Service Administration throughout the thirties.

The AAPWO's goal was to promote a comprehensive, permanent public welfare program. High standards for personnel were essential. The AAPWO equated such standards with the qualifications for professional social workers. It established a committee on professional standards in public welfare, chaired by Grace Abbott. This committee endorsed professional training in a school of social work as a prerequisite for

employment.(5)
     As public welfare grew, state and local politicians found
relief a fertile field for patronage appointments. AAPWO
members saw the patronage system as a major obstacle to
professionalization. They pushed adoption of merit systems on
the state and local level.(6) "Insist upon qualified,
competent personnel in state and local administration"--this
was the message AAPWO field workers brought to state
governments which sought the group's help in welfare planning
during the Hoover administration.(7) Public welfare
officials, the AASW, and the FWAA all sought to incorporate
professional standards into a system of public relief free of
the spoils system, although the AAPWO was most active in pursuit
of this goal.
     The effort to improve public social services received its
greatest impetus from the pioneering work of Edith Abbott and
Sophonisba Breckinridge at the Chicago School. Breckinridge
came from a well-established Kentucky family and was the
daughter of a congressman. She attended Wellesley College.
After studying law, she was the first woman admitted to the
Kentucky bar. Clients did not seek her out, however. She went
on to the University of Chicago to complete a Ph.D. in political
science and a J.D. (the first earned there by a woman). Yet job
offers were few. In 1907, after three years with the Illinois
State Bureau of Labor, she joined the faculty at what was then
the Chicago School of Civics and Philanthropy. Later, she
helped reorganize the school into the university-affiliated
School of Social Service Administration. Bringing her
political and legal background to bear on social work training,
Breckinridge introduced the first course on public welfare
administration to be taught in a professional school of social
work.(8)
     Breckinridge's interest in public welfare was supported
and further advanced by her colleague, Edith Abbott. Born in a
Nebraska town near the old Overland Trail west, Abbott valued
her pioneer roots. Both her parents encouraged scholarship.
Abbott earned a Ph.D. in economics at Chicago and did
postgraduate work at the London School of Economics. She was
brought to the School of Civics and Philanthropy by
Breckinridge in 1908 and headed the SSSA from 1924 to 1942. She
helped found the Cook County Bureau of Public Welfare in 1925.
Like Breckinridge, she was a highly educated woman for whom
society offered few career possibilities. This situation
helped motivate their innovative work in new professional
areas.
     Abbott and Breckinridge pioneered in the development of
public welfare as a field of professional expertise. Both
women published widely and spoke frequently on public welfare
adinistration. Their scholarly Social Service Review increased circulation after 1930. At the Chicago School they
were impressive figures, Abbott a severe and imposing presence
dressed in black, Breckinridge a bright, sharp, bird-like
woman.(9) Devoted to a particular vision of public welfare and
the social work profession, they had little patience with those
who disagreed.
     Along with Abbott's more activist sister Grace, the two

took a broad view of the function of social work. They sought
to refocus its attention from narrow areas of case work
treatment to the broader field of social welfare. They felt
the profession should provide scientific knowledge about social
welfare problems and lead the way in improving institutional
responses. The program they developed at the Chicago School
was based in part on the British model of education for social
administration. It emphasized history, research, public
administration, and policy, especially law. Their students
joined them in social investigations of poverty, juvenile
justice, and the like, and wrote papers like "Legislative
Provisions for Children Born out of Wedlock in the State of
Michigan."(10) Theirs was an intellectual and scholarly
approach. Abbott argued that social service was not simply an
applied field, but an academic discipline in its own right.(11)
     They promoted reform in existing public welfare
organizations and systematic planning to meet social needs on
the national, state, and local levels. Abbott wanted states to
revise their poor or "pauper" laws. She wanted these to be
called "public assistance" laws. The new name would indicate a
more respectful, scientific approach to providing aid. She
objected to the traditional principles of residency and family
and local responsibility. Influenced by British example, she
promoted centralization of various forms of public assistance
under a single social welfare statute stressing combined
federal, state, and local responsibility. The new system
should be efficient and fair.(12)
     This system required a competent, professional staff.
"Partisan politics," Abbott exclaimed, "has long been the evil
genius of our public welfare program."(13) Politics
necessitated use of a merit system in the public social
services. This system should protect a particular kind of
competence needed in public welfare work. The Abbotts and
Breckinridge felt that clients were entitled to case work
services as well as monetary assistance. This was as true in
public agencies as in private ones. Graduate professional
social work training was necessary to prepare workers to render
such services.(14)
     On administrative levels, public welfare officials needed
expertise in public administration, personnel management, and
policy-making. The merit system should cover all the heads of
public welfare departments. All in all, as Edith Abbott told
the 1934 Delegate Conference, "We are never going to get a good
system until we have social workers in charge of it."(15)
     Although the AASW did not support all of the Abbotts' and
Breckinridge's proposals, the three women were widely
influential in social work circles. Their ideas informed the
philosophy and activities of the U.S. Children's Bureau, which
Grace Abbott directed from 1920 to 1934. This was the first
federal department to deal specifically with maternal and child
welfare issues. It stressed the importance of careful research
and expert planning in developing welfare programs.
     By the time the Federal Emergency Relief Administration
took form in 1933, various groups within social work had
formulated basic principles about public welfare. These
followed a high standards model of professionalism. Public

welfare should no longer be at the mercy of the politician.
Administrative and staff requirements--hopefully those of the
professionally trained social worker--should be protected by a
merit system. While the FERA was an emergency response to
unemployment, its staffing and service patterns could be
regarded as prototypes for a more extensive program.

The FERA drew its leadership from professional social
workers. Harry Hopkins had headed both private and public
agencies. Josephine Brown, his administrative assistant, came
from rural welfare and family services work. Together they set
up ambitious personnel requirements and educational plans for
the relief program's staff.

FERA regulations called for at least one trained and
experienced investigator in each local relief administration.
In addition, every relief agency should have one supervisor
"trained and experienced in . . . family case work and relief
administration" for every twenty investigating staff members.(16) Large city agencies could meet these requirements.
Private agencies often loaned their professional workers to
FERA agencies. Small communities and rural areas, unable to
draw on existing private agencies, employed people with no
specific training in social work. Of some 60,000 workers in
the State Emergency Relief Administrations, few were eligible
to join the AASW.(17)

Conditions were primitive in a number of relief offices,
particularly in rural areas. Alice Taylor Davis was a social
worker with private agency experience who worked as a district
case supervisor for the Missouri State Department of Public
Welfare in northeast Missouri. In Davis' judgement, many
offices in her district were well-run, but she recalls finding
case records filed among hardware items in a store which served
as one of the county relief offices. In another office, a
politically appointed relief board secretary read case records
out loud "to entertain the women in the WPA sewing room." On
Davis' recommendation, the secretary was immediately dismissed
and a qualified one appointed.(18)

Social workers fought to improve conditions in county
relief offices. Davis, for example, developed a case record
system and district staff training. She found relief staff
committed to their task, but overburdened with cases and hampered by their lack of social work preparation. Though it was
impossible to get experienced and trained workers into most
public welfare jobs, professionals in the public system continued to testify to its importance. Some, like Elizabeth
Dexter, had come into public relief from psychiatric case work.
Dexter was a field representative for the New York Emergency
Relief Administration. She argued that trained case workers
were best equipped to handle the bewilderment and embarrassment
of the applicant and to investigate the full range of client
problems.(19) The American Public Welfare Association also
stressed professional education and case work skills in its
consultation work with states.(20)

One way to meet the shortage of professionally trained
staff was to provide educational opportunities for workers
already on the job. Initially, Hopkins visualized the federal
government underwriting a special training program on a

national scale for public welfare employees. The plan would
have included grants to state universities to develop new
training programs in relief administration. Social work
educators, led by Abbott and Breckinridge, were aghast. How
could "poorly thought-out training plans" compete with the professional schools? Hopkins capitulated to Association of
Schools pressure. The FERA substituted a plan which awarded
scholarships to relief staff, to use for one semester's training in an established school of social work. Once again, the
standards issue interfered with innovative and broadly based
attempts to professionalize public welfare.(21)

Josephine Brown, the training program's director,
appeared to agree with her social work colleagues. Earlier, as
an expert in rural social work, she had stressed the importance
of using state agricultural colleges to train workers "in the
basics of social casework applicable to rural clients."(22) At
this point, however, she may have felt it politic to respect the
advice of AASSW leaders. She invited the Association of
Schools and the AASW to set up a joint committee to work with
her on training plans. She consulted with Abbott and
Breckinridge. Following the professional model of welfare
worker training, she decided in favor of AASSW-approved schools
for relief staff on educational leave. "Using fewer schools
means fewer students--but I'd rather do that and be sure of
higher educational standards."(23)

The AASW and the Association of Schools applauded this
approach. They felt that established professional schools
were the best recipients for federal training funds. They promoted the FERA plan even though they knew that training needs
outstripped the schools' capacity to educate people. Professional school enrollment for full- and part-time students in
the fall of 1934 was only about 5,000. Thousands more worked in
the State ERAs. The schools' proposal to handle the overflow was
on-the-job training. Even as they took FERA students, they
worried about loss of existing standards. They rejected a
number of FERA applicants whom they felt lacked the necessary
educational backgrounds or grade averages.(24)

Nevertheless, the scholarship program put over 1,100 workers in training in twenty-one schools of social work. A number
of workers from rural and small-town areas participated. As a
pragmatic supplement to professional training, the FERA also
helped establish short-term training institutes in some two-
thirds of the states.(25)

The training program was only funded for a year, yet it
established a particular model of staff development. This
included in-service training through short-term institutes.
However, the FERA stressed the professional curriculum in
schools of social work as the preferred vehicle for public welfare training.

Staffing and training for the FERA were first steps in
building a professionalized public welfare system. Next came
Jane Hoey's Bureau of Public Assistance (BPA). It was one of
three divisions of the new Social Security Board established in
1935. Roosevelt's Committee on Economic Security had rejected
the idea of federal responsibility for an ongoing general
relief program. In agreement, Roosevelt abolished the FERA and

proposed instead a national system which combined work relief, social insurance, and federal-state categorical assistance to dependent children and the aged.

When the FERA was abolished, social workers were concerned about adequacy of funding and staffing in public relief. They knew that most state and local departments picking up the general relief function would be unable or unwilling to maintain the relief levels and standards of administration developed under the federal program. These older poor relief agencies, which had continued to function alongside the state ERAs were often inadequately staffed and poorly administered. The battle for professional standards now shifted to the states and localities. The hope of help from the federal administration lay in the influence Hoey's bureau might exert upon states developing their categorical aid programs.

Hoey, like Hopkins and Brown, came to the federal welfare program from professional social work. Educated at a Catholic college in Washington, D.C., she received her diploma from the New York School of Social Work in 1916. She first worked as an assistant to Harry Hopkins, then secretary of the New York City Board of Child Welfare. After a stint with the Red Cross Home Service, she moved to the New York Welfare Council. Her brother, James Hoey, was a member of the New York State Assembly. Through him, Jane met prominent political figures: Al Smith, Robert Wagner, and Franklin Roosevelt. For six years, she served as a Smith appointee and the only woman on the New York State Crime Commission. She took credit for helping Roosevelt set up the TERA in N.Y. and for recommending Hopkins as its director.(26)

Although Hoey had prominent political connections, including a friendship with the Roosevelts, she regarded her appointment to the Bureau of Public Assistance as based on her professional experience and training. Confident in her abilities and ideas, Hoey valued her classification as an expert. She eagerly pursued her notions about how to build a professional public welfare service. Her feistiness in this campaign received both praise and criticism.(27)

Hoey "started from scratch" when she assumed the directorship in January, 1936. Around her flowed the excitement of federal officials inaugurating new social programs. Though excitement was high, manpower was low. Hoey began with a mandate from the federal government and three staff members. One of her first decisions was to gather together "the most competent staff I could get." She requested "professionally trained and experienced workers in public welfare." The Civil Service Commission balked, arguing that a college degree was ample background. But when Hoey made a personal appeal to the commission and threatened to resign, her staffing requirements were accepted.(28)

Having made her point that professional competence was the key to successful operation of the bureau's program, Hoey set out to define that program. She decided on a centralized administration of all three categorical components: assistance to the aged, the blind, and dependent children. In doing so, she departed from the tradition established by the Children's Bureau and its friends at the Chicago School. The bureau was now led by Katharine Lenroot, who had been Grace Abbott's assistant from 1922 to 1934. Following the direction set by Abbott and Julia Lathrop before her, Lenroot stressed a specialized, intensive approach to the problems of a particular population--dependent children and their mothers. The Children's Bureau focused professional expertise from several fields--economics, public health, nursing, and social work--on planning services to meet the needs of the "whole" child.

The clash between the approaches of the Children's Bureau and the Bureau of Public Assistance indicates differences of opinion within professional social work as to the proper shape of a federal public welfare program. On the broadest level, this was a debate over whether to promote (a) a comprehensive public welfare system under a single unit of the federal government, or (b) a plan which selected certain groups for specialized care, and allowed for some division of labor among federal departments in responding to their needs. Some proponents of the first view suggested provision of federal assistance on a general basis, rather than through the categories established by the Social Security Act. Others simply spoke of a single administration for all public welfare activities. Hoey, AASW leaders Dorothy Kahn and William Hodson, the AAPW, and Josephine Brown promoted the comprehensive plan. Lenroot, Breckinridge, the Abbotts, and the child welfare field supported the second approach, particularly in reference to the Children's Bureau.(29)

As Director of the BPA, Hoey sought a comprehensive program of federal aid. On the state and local levels, she recommended inclusion of general assistance along with categorical aid in a single administrative department. As Lenroot later described it, Hoey "believed in a generic approach to . . . public assistance, which would knot everything together in one program, so that you could be flexible."(30)

The Children's Bureau, on the other hand, sought a more selective approach. This stemmed in part from the rather elitist stress on public welfare expertise characteristic of the Chicago School, in part from the fear that the taint of public welfare would contaminate child welfare in the eyes of politicians and the public. In addition, the bureau believed that the problems of families with fatherless children were not temporary ones like those of the unemployed. These children and their families required long-term aid, not subject to the vagaries of relief.(31)

The push for a separate child welfare program came also from the ambition and drive of the bureau's new leader, Katharine Lenroot. Like Breckinridge and Hoey, Lenroot came from a well-connected political family. Her father, a Republican, had worked closely with the progressive La Follettes as a legislator in Wisconsin. He later served in the U.S. Senate. Lenroot "was brought up on the idea of public service." Acquaintanceship with men like the La Follettes and Louis Brandeis reinforced her interest in social reform. After earning a B.A. in sociology at the University of Wisconsin, she worked as a researcher for the Wisconsin Industrial Commission. She left the Commission in 1914 to join the staff of the Social Service Division at the Children's Bureau.(32)

     As she rose in the bureau's ranks, Lenroot played a growing
role in attempts to expand the organization's areas of responsibility. During the Hoover administration, she conceived the
idea of a federal aid program for child welfare, but was unable
to get appropriations for demonstration projects in the states.
When Roosevelt's economic security program was being planned,
she fought to have the Aid to Dependent Children category placed
within the bureau's bailiwick. In this, she had the strong
backing of the child welfare field. Yet supporters of a unified welfare system, with FERA officials in the lead, won out.
Following the recommendation of the President's Committee on
Economic Security, Congress assigned the ADC program to the
Social Security Board and a smaller child welfare program to the
bureau.(33) This move may have had as much to do with Congress'
growing disenchantment with "standards" (seen as an emphasis at
the Children's Bureau) as with the committee's report.(34)

     Contemporary observers have commented on Lenroot's
aggressiveness in promoting the Children's Bureau point of
view. This drive could be attributed to dedication to service-
-"she equated the Children's Bureau with all the children of the
U.S."--or to empire-building.(35) Jane Hoey, for her part,
pursued her own ideas with fervour. While their personal relationship was amiable, and the two agencies often worked
together, Hoey and Lenroot were strong leaders who represented
broader constituencies within social work.

     In setting up the federal assistance programs, Hoey
stressed the importance of adequacy and efficiency in meeting
clients' needs. She saw competent, professional personnel as
crucial to both goals. On the federal level, experts were
needed to develop guidelines, transmit these to the states, and
help write legislation to set up state programs which would
qualify for federal grants-in-aid. Hoey affirmed the
importance of states' autonomy in developing programs adapted
to local conditions. But she wanted an experienced field staff
which could advocate fairness and adequacy.(36)

     Hoey pushed for the same competence on state and local lev-
els. Her message to the states was "get trained people as
quickly as possible, put them in your key positions." She recommended professional social workers as directors of public
assistance and child welfare and urged states to require at
least a bachelor's degree for case workers, so they would be
eligible for enrollment in a school of social work. A competent case work staff was vital to efficient determination of
eligibility and promotion of clients' independence.(37)

     It was politically and often legally impossible for the
BPA to establish and enforce minimum personnel requirements for
state and local agencies. State merit systems had not been
mandated by the Social Security Act. In many states, officials
failed to recognize public assistance as a social work program
requiring technically trained personnel. States often had res-
idence restrictions, prohibitions against requiring special
education and experience for public jobs, and limitations on
the amount of salary possible. State departments did not have
full control over local governments. Political appointments
flourished on both state and local levels. Hoey and her staff
had to rely on powers of persuasion and whatever weight their

own expertise would carry in promoting the importance of
trained and experienced personnel.(38)
    The BPA was able to require that state proposals include
formal plans for objective selection and promotion of personnel.   The bureau recommended "consultation with individuals
technically familiar with the character of the work." It also
promoted use of open competitive examinations and development
of a merit system.(39)
    For political but also practical reasons, personnel in the
state and county categorical aid programs were often inexperienced and inadequately trained. In Wisconsin, for example, one-
fourth of the county directors had not graduated from high
school, and less than 8 percent had completed college.   In West
Virginia, the chief of the State Bureau of Social Service was a
professional brought in from the outside.   Yet only one supervisor in the state office had an M.A.   In most states, case work
positions were held by people with B.A.'s or less, often with no
experience.(40)
    In an effort to cope with this situation, the BPA actively
promoted educational leaves and in-service training for public
assistance personnel.   At first, Hoey wanted states to release
some of their better people for education at AASSW-approved
schools.   But such leaves were difficult to arrange, as the
Social Security Board had no provision for financing them and
many states could not spare personnel to attend a year's worth
of training.(41)
    Although the schools of social work and the professional
organizations were aware of the needs for public welfare training, they offered no comprehensive plan.   Both the AASW and the
Association of Schools participated in a committee to advise
the BPA and the Children's Bureau on training and personnel.
The committee included Walter West, Breckinridge, Kenneth Pray,
and Gordon Hamilton.   These representatives of the social work
establishment were reluctant to accept modifications of the
graduate professional school approach.   The group was unable to
develop a workable response to training needs.
    Many graduate schools enrolled public assistance workers
among their part-time students, but they were not able to accommodate all those who desired training.   Scholarships were limited. For those who could attend, either on a part-time basis or
on full-time educational leave, the curriculum was often irrel-
evant.   Before 1930 few schools provided course work in public
welfare. The University of Chicago was a notable exception.
Most social work education prepared students for case work in a
private agency.
    Moreover, many schools, particularly in the Northeast,
emphasized psychiatric case work.   The thirties witnessed a
decided increase in courses in psychiatry and its application
to social work. Psychiatric social workers moving into the public agencies saw a new arena for pioneering, a chance "to
transfuse another section of society with mental hygiene concepts."(42)   At this time, a division developed between followers of the "functional" and the "diagnostic" theories of case
work.   The functional school drew on the teachings of Otto Rank
and stressed the importance of agency objectives, short-term
treatment, and client responsibility in the case work process.

The diagnostic group had a Freudian base and used a psycho-analytically oriented model of treatment.

Although the functional approach was later seen to have important implications for public case work, the immediate effect of the division was a draining away of energies which might have been focused on development of training for public welfare work. Educator Mildred Mudgett recalls a lunch with functionalist leaders Jessie Taft and Virginia Robinson:

[They] were still so much under the spell of . . . Otto Rank, that the courses [at the University of Pennsylvania school] contained little other information. The relevance of Supreme Court decisions for students of social work was not in their field of interest.(43)

At its height, according to case work theorist Helen Perlman, the controversy "tore the field apart." Perlman describes a social work conference in 1938, where a waiter in the host hotel restaurant asked "what side of the room do you want to sit on, the diagnostic or the functional?"(44)

While eastern schools argued about Freud and Rank, social work educators in other parts of the country paid more attention to building curriculum in public welfare administration and practice. The Chicago School played a major role. Well before the Depression began, Breckinridge and Abbott had established their public welfare and policy-oriented curriculum. Chicago-trained educators Marion Hathway, Arlien Johnson, Elizabeth Wisner, and others carried this approach to their respective institutions in Pennsylvania, California, Louisiana, and else-where. Gradually, material on public welfare began to be seen as a legitimate part of social work education. About half the schools had faculty with expertise in public welfare content by 1937, and by the end of the decade almost all schools offered at least one course in the area.(45)

Yet training for public social welfare, while it received greater attention during the thirties, never really challenged the dominance of the private case work tradition in social work education. The AASSW included public welfare and social legis-lation content in a minimum curriculum adopted in 1932. In 1933, the Association set up committees on course content in Public Welfare Administration and Social Legislation, chaired by Breckinridge and Abbott respectively.(46) Yet schools tended to pay lip service to public welfare course require-ments, while continuing to stress the case work core. Speaking as chair of the AASW Division on Personnel Standards four years later, Grace Marcus observed: "It is unquestionable that the dominance of casework in professional education is dispropor-tionate to its place in the future scheme of things."(47)

While Hoey did not abandon her faith in professional social work education for public assistance workers, the private case work focus of many schools figured in her growing reliance on in-service training programs. Even more important in this decision were the limited resources of the professional schools and the concentration of these schools in urban areas. Hoey was also becoming increasingly aware of the need for a spe-cial kind of training to equip people to function in a bureaucratic organization and to carry out specific welfare functions as determined "by statute, charter, rule, and regulation."(48)

Hoey had established a training division within her own bureau in 1936. By the end of 1938, the BPA recommended that each state establish a staff development program "to increase the capacity of every state and local staff member administering public assistance." While this program should encourage formal education through leaves, its major responsibility was in-service training. Appropriate topics for such training arose from the daily problems of the agency. They included the agency's organization, its relationship to the federal government, legal provisions, and policies for establishing eligibility. In addition, staff development should cover knowledge of community resources and case work skills.(49) Hoey thus experimented with an immediate and practical alternative to graduate professional training.

The BPA's Division of Technical Training, headed by social work educator Agnes Van Driel, helped states develop their programs. The division worked through the bureau's regional representatives, who consulted with state departments of public assistance. The consultants suggested use of supervision and staff meetings for training purposes. They encouraged development of agency libraries and passed along a "Selective Book List" developed by the BPA. This list covered the classics on public welfare--including works by Breckinridge and Robert Kelso's Science of Public Welfare--as well as material on personnel management, public administration, social work as a profession, and case work technique.(50) The division also produced its own publications, including Common Human Needs by Charlotte Towle. A well-known case work theorist, Towle had been engaged by Van Driel to write a basic training document on human needs in relation to public assistance. Towle's book emphasized case work treatment. It was balanced by another training manual by Grace Marcus, which stressed issues of eligibility and benefit amounts and cautioned against over-interference in clients' lives.(51)

The BPA thus envisioned a broad program. It would utilize traditional social work material related to case work and private agency practice, but would draw also from public administration, law, the social sciences, and the burgeoning public welfare literature. This vision of agency-based training tailored to the needs of a new public welfare worker was far more flexible than the standard social work stress on graduate education. Yet even so, the BPA faced great difficulties: workers with limited formal education, supervisors with no professional training, lack of clarity about staff functions, and little state support. By late 1938, the BPA had consulted with twenty-nine states on staff development, and most training programs were still in a beginning phase.(52)

The Bureau made slow headway in efforts to encourage modern methods of relief administration and staffing. By 1938, only fifteen state agencies had worked out specifications for all personnel positions in public assistance. Thirty had developed requirements for some positions; four had none at all.(53)

The minimum personnel requirements set out in state

specifications fell short of Hoey's goals. As of August, 1936, only three states required education for the director or other staff people in the state office. Most required social agency experience for supervisory positions, but not for the director. Local directors were generally expected to have the B.A., but senior case workers rarely needed more than a high school degree. Beginning workers were often required to have experience, but only two states called for a college degree.(54)

In its attempt to raise personnel standards, the BPA was supported by the AASW. The 1937 Delegates Conference marked a shift in interest from national policy-making to involvement in state and local problems of government and social work. Chapters were urged to study and communicate the role which social work could play in the public social services. They were encouraged to work with state and local authorities to define administrative principles and personnel standards.(55)

The AASW's turn toward issues of public welfare standards in the states occurred for a variety of reasons. First, the association found it increasingly difficult to make an impact on federal policies. Second, with the dissolution of the FERA and creation of the Social Security Administration, much of the "action" in public welfare had shifted to the states. Finally, the profession could attempt to diffuse its internal debate over political involvement by taking action in an area where social work influence and expertise seemed more legitimate--the professionalization of public welfare.

Many chapters formulated specifications for public welfare positions and submitted these to their state welfare departments. The suggested requirements were often higher than the more realistic recommendations of the BPA--for example, one or two years of graduate training for case work positions. Few states responded fully to such recommendations. One exception was Louisiana, where active involvement by professional social workers, such as Elizabeth Wisner at the Tulane School of Social Work, combined with a favorable political atmosphere to create a modern, professionalized public welfare system.(56)

The AASW joined the BPA and the APWA in calling for a merit system. In a related effort to secure public recognition of social work expertise, the AASW began promoting the idea of state certification or licensing plans. The association acknowledged the difficulty of achieving this goal, since social workers had not yet clearly defined the content of their profession. For this reason, the 1935 Delegate Conference advocated voluntary rather than legal certification. California and Missouri were the only states to develop such certification during the thirties.(57)

Professional social workers' attempts to get involved in the business of personnel standards and civil service met with only limited success. Part of this stemmed from their inability to define social work functions, part from their high standards approach. In addition, the AASW was bidding for attention among other organizations with more recognized expertise in public welfare. The Civil Service Assembly and the APWA were actively involved in job analysis and standard setting. Gordon Hamilton worried that unless social workers "take a rather vig-

orous position, I think we may be left out of the planning."
Walter West responded:

It is difficult for us to find our place. . . . The APWA feels
enough self-conscious about its position that it is anxious not
to have any of the regular social work organizations too closely
identified with its programs.(58)

    This stand on the part of the APWA--a cautious organiza-
tion of public welfare administrators who had to work closely
with political figures--suggests the bad press of social workers in political circles. Here lay a major source of difficulty for the AASW, Hoey, and all social workers involved in
professionalizing public welfare. These individuals pushed
the notion of expertise in public service, a notion which struck
at the very heart of political power on the state and local levels. In addition, the idea of a public welfare program based on
professional, scientific knowledge and skill ran counter to
strains of localism, racism, and populism in many American communities.
    Surveying the public welfare scene, delegates at the 1937
AASW conference declared, "In no other field of governmental
operation is the elimination of politics so vital."(59) Some
political officeholders used public welfare benefits to garner
votes. In the early thirties, the governor of California
enclosed a congratulatory letter with each of the first checks
sent to recipients of old age assistance. The letter implied
that the governor was responsible for such aid. In Ohio,
according to Hoey, public assistance workers brought ballots
along with the checks.(60)
    Despite BPA requirements that states submit formal plans
for selection of personnel, use of the spoils system continued.
Governors picked political favorites to head state welfare
departments. Local authorities fought to keep relief agencies
within their control. As Edith Abbott noted, there was a con-
certed effort "on the part of local political leaders to make
the new program recognize the claims of the local chieftains."
Abbott warned that since FERA "the poor law services are drifting back to the old system of petty incompetence and are becoming more political and more unskilled day by day."(61) It is
significant that the merit systems proposed in legislation creating the FERA and the Social Security Administration were
eliminated from both these bills in Congress.
    Political control made life difficult for professional
social workers. The Arizona AASW chapter was described by a
visitor from the national office as

a most pathetic group, chiefly employees from the Department of
Public Welfare, each of whom is very insecure due to the dismissal of [a co-worker] and re-organization of the department
on a political basis. They are literally afraid to lift their
voices on any professional topic--trained social workers are
anathema, and if they advocated civil service, they would all
lose their jobs. . . . The new state board would love to fire
them all and make jobs for party workers.(62)

So much for professional ideals.   In the words of a Chicago
School graduate, working in Peoria, Illinois:

I guess our basic disillusion here has been the extreme political toying with public welfare. . . . The Chicago school's public welfare program, and the personalities directing that
school symbolized for us some near idols in public welfare.
Coming to the back yard of the Chicago school, and getting
acquainted with the terribly backward welfare programs here
hasn't been conducive for maintenance of idols or illusions.(63)

     The policies and activities of the politicians reflected
the localism, racial discrimination, and fears of the expert
found in many communities.   Such fears and prejudices were soon
to contribute to the rise of McCarthyism and purges of government and other institutions. During the FERA and the early years
of social security, they led to disapproval of "outside social
workers" interfering in the lives of local residents and of "so-
called trained social workers" administering public funds.   In
Denver, Colorado, a hotbed of antiprofessional feeling, a local
newspaper proclaimed, "No outside worker can go into a county
and tell the conditions or needs."(64)
     Reactions against social workers were part of a larger
campaign against New Dealers emerging on the Far Right.   As
early as 1934, Elizabeth Dilling's Red Network identified
Eleanor Roosevelt, Frances Perkins, and prominent social work
figures as Communists.(65)
     Racism was also a potent force in the welfare systems of
some states and localities.   Texas excluded noncitizens (that
is, Mexicans) from its programs; New Mexico and Arizona discouraged Indians from applying.   Nevada had no ADC program for
twenty years, to avoid giving money to Indian children.   In
Mississippi, counties were informally instructed to put a 10
percent quota on the number of black citizens receiving
assistance.(66)
     These inequities and patterns of political corruption,
along with poor administration, were the kinds of things that
many professional social workers sought to counteract.   Hoey
stressed the importance of state autonomy and the adapting of
programs to local conditions.   Yet she could be aggressive in
her attempts to get states to run more equitable programs.   She
tells of one governor calling the executive director of the
Social Security Board to complain: "That red-haired devil of
yours is in my office.   She's telling me certain things that I
need to do." Where states used discriminatory policies in their
relief programs, Hoey used threats of public hearings to get
them to stop.(67)
     Such "meddling" on the part of social workers brought
strong reaction from the politicians.   They fought merit systems and argued against the professionals' claim to public welfare jobs.   U.S.   Representative Fred Vinson of Kentucky said
of the merit system, "No damned social workers are going to come
into my state to tell our people whom they shall hire."(68)   The
Nebraska legislature's hostility toward social work, and especially toward Ernest Witte, a former regional representative of

the Social Security Board, almost brought the closure of the
state university school of social work which Witte headed.(69)
In Colorado, the governor "thoroughly detested social workers"
and refused to support their attempt to pass public welfare legislation. Commenting on the defeat of these bills, the
Colorado House and Senate whips confided to BPA field worker
Valeska Bary:

At the regular session the social workers presented a string
of goals; but they made themselves so objectionable that we
decided to turn down every one of them, although there were some
that we wanted to vote for. We had to teach them a lesson.(70)

The lesson sometimes extended to politically motivated
investigations of "fraud" and "mismanagement" in public welfare
departments, during the era of the FERA and later. An early
example was the 1935 investigation of the New York City department in which a special committee of aldermen looked into
charges of "waste and extravagance." A worried Los Angeles
chapter of the AASW warned social workers to be prepared for
local political investigations and "the advent of politicians
and so-called business men and women in the social work
divisions of the public relief departments."(71) The chapter's warning was prophetic. Similar investigations occurred
in places like Detroit, Atlanta, and the state of Pennsylvania.
Particularly shocking to social workers was the 1938 firing of
Dorothy Kahn, head of the Philadelphia public welfare department, apparently for her lack of loyalty to local politicians.(72)
The most flagrant practices of political manipulation were
brought to a halt by the 1939 amendments to the Social Security
Act. These gave the Social Security Board authority to require
states to establish a merit system in order to receive federal
grants in public assistance and unemployment compensation.
The merit provision, long advocated by social workers, represented a milestone in welfare legislation. Yet the merit system did not guarantee the acceptance of professional social
work qualifications for public welfare jobs. In 1943, many
state systems still prescribed low levels for beginning visitor
positions. "An encouraging number" required a year of professional education for supervisors, but few prescribed the
full two years of such training.(73)
The public welfare staffing situation in the early forties
failed to meet either the demanding ideals of the AASW and the
Children's Bureau, or the more realistic goals of Jane Hoey and
her staff. The AASW visualized its membership requirements as
effective qualifications for public welfare work. The Children's Bureau and the Chicago School pressed for graduate
social workers. Because of its small size, the Children's
Bureau was more successful in achieving this goal in its own
operations. Working on a much larger scale, Hoey wanted at
least B.A. workers, but many states did not comply.
Responses to the continued staffing problem reflect the
differences between the various schools of thought in social
work. Following a high standards model of professionalism, the
Chicago School, the Children's Bureau, the AASW, and the Asso-

ciation of Schools maintained their emphasis on graduate education. They were skeptical about other kinds of public welfare
training. Hoey, on the other hand, became more willing to
experiment with new training methods, such as in-service training and undergraduate education for social work.
     Hoey's approach reflected in part a definition of the
functions of the public assistance worker that differed from
the conception of the Children's Bureau and the Chicago School.
Although the distinction has been exaggerated, there existed a
definite division over the place of "services" in the public
welfare worker's role. Lenroot prided herself on the specialized services provided by the Children's Bureau: case work,
education for mothers on child care, health services, referral
work, and the like. She felt that "this type of effort was
practically ignored in the early problems of dealing with a
large aid to dependent children program, with questions of
eligibility uppermost in people's minds."(74)
     The ability to offer specialized services was an important
point in Edith Abbott's argument for a federation of separate
categorical aid programs rather than the inclusion of as many
welfare functions as possible under a single umbrella. Abbott's
idea was fought by both Hoey and the AASW. In spirited
reaction, Abbott told an NCSW audience:

With regard to the method of providing special care for special groups, we have been challenged recently by some of our
eastern friends, who in the rather grand, N.Y. manner labeled
this policy 'categorical relief' and told us [it] was not
approved.(75)

     Other social workers, from the private case work tradi-
tion, made their bid for the inclusion of services in public
welfare. They stressed the need for relationship building,
careful listening, and "an individualized approach to human
problems."(76) This stress on case work services provided a
way for social workers to legitimize involvement in public
assistance.
     The criticisms of the BPA's lack of attention to services
were not entirely fair. At the 1937 NCSW meeting, Hoey assured
participants that the BPA had "deemed inadequate any state program which has not included service. . . . Stress has been laid
on the need for preventive work and rehabilitation." Yet when
asked about the services issue years later, Hoey retorted, "I
think public assistance [i.e. money] is one of the most
important services to people, when you're starving."
Intensive case work or rehabilitative work did not make sense in
a situation of large case loads and inadequately trained staff.
Yet Hoey's emphasis on eligibility determination and attention
to government regulations suggests a bureaucratic model of service adapted to a new type of large-scale welfare program.(77)
     The demands of this new program caused Hoey to be more
receptive than the social work establishment to new types of
social work education. Concerned with "maintaining standards," the AASW and the Association of Schools criticized
attempts of schools like Wayne State to focus on education for
the staffs of public agencies. Such schools might be "forced

to make compromises which seriously affect the development of integrated professional education."(78)   Social work educators were willing to explore the idea of one-year graduate programs in areas of the country which lacked established schools, but they felt these should be first steps toward two-year schools.

The one idea which both the AASW and the school people adamantly opposed was the notion of undergraduate training for social work.   State universities, and particularly land grant colleges, had begun to suggest such training as a way to meet public welfare personnel demands in their states.   The AASW and the Association of Schools saw this move as a serious threat to professional education.   Hoey, however, was willing to talk to the undergraduate people and suggest courses which would prepare individuals for public welfare practice.(79)

In building a permanent public welfare service, Hoey gradually moved away from the highly professionalized models suggested by other social workers.   In her development of in-service training objectives and new conceptions of service, she looked to a new sort of bureaucratic public assistance work. She differed from other social workers in her stress on rules and efficiency, but echoed their ideals in her concern for adequacy and equity.

The broader field of social work, caught in a debate between standards and public service, lost the chance for meaningful involvement in the development of the new public programs. Although representatives of the AASW and the Chicago School were concerned about staffing the public social services, they recommended a selective, high standards approach which was impossible to implement.   Kahn and Abbott encouraged the use of professional social workers as administrators and policy makers.   But they were joined by others in discouraging new kinds of social work education for the bulk of the staff.

Hoey tried a broader route to the professionalization of public services.   Yet this approach had only limited success. Large numbers of untrained workers continued to staff the public agencies.   These agencies did not take a leadership role in social welfare in the forties.(80)   Hoey's goal foundered for lack of support within social work, opposition by politicians, and the sheer size of the task.

A number of social work practitioners had viewed their work with public agencies as purely temporary.   While there, they stressed clinical over economic services.   With a New Deal safety net firmly in place, they returned to private agency work in the forties. Many schools of social work continued their case work thrust.   Public welfare gradually resumed its role as a peripheral concern of professional social work.

Notes

1. Minutes, Executive Committee, AASW, 10/2/26 and 6/17/27, National Association of Social Workers Records, folder 2, Social Welfare History Archives, University of Minnesota, Minneapolis, Minn.; Annual Meeting, AASW, 5/16/27, folder 2; "Personnel Standards in Public Agencies," The Compass, IX: 1-2 (June, 1928). The idea of professionalism in the public services had been stressed earlier by proponents of mothers' aid laws like Homer Folks. William W. Bremer, Depression Winters: New York Social Workers and the New Deal (Philadelphia: Temple University Press, 1984), p. 77.

2. Stanley Davies, "Working Toward One Professional Standard--Public and Private," Social Service Review, VI: 436-49 (September, 1932). See also Frances Taussig, "Social Work--Past, Present, and Future," The Compass, XIII: 1-4 (June, 1932).

3. "Standards for Public Agencies," The Compass, XI: 3 (June, 1930).

4. Rose Porter, Organization and Administration of Public Relief Agencies (New York: FWAA, 1931). See also Leah Feder, "The Relationship of Private Case Working Agencies to Programs of Public Welfare," Social Forces, IX: 515-25 (June, 1931).

5. Grace Abbott, "Developing and Protecting Professional Standards in Public Welfare Work," Social Service Review,, V: 389-94 (September, 1931); "Official Proceedings of AAPWO," Social Service Review, VI: 489-90 (September, 1932).

6. Lorena Hickok, One Third of a Nation, ed. Richard Lowitt and Maurine Beasley (Urbana: University of Illinois Press, 1981), pp. 8-9, 15-16, 124-25; L. A. Halbert, "A Review and Forecast of the Work of the American Association of Public Welfare Officials," Social Service Review, V: 353-66 (September, 1931). For a detailed history of the AAPWO, see Narayan Viswanathan, "The Role of the American Public Welfare Association in the Formulation and Development of Public Welfare Policies in the U.S.: 1930-1960" (Diss., Columbia University, 1961).

7. Viswanathan, p. 4.

8. Anthony Travis, "Sophonisba Breckinridge, Militant Feminist," Mid-America, LVIII: 111-18 (April, 1976); "Sophonisba Breckinridge," Encyclopedia of Social Work (New York: NASW, 1971), pp. 84-85.

9. Steven J. Diner, "Scholarship in the Quest for Social Welfare: A Fifty-Year History of the Social Service Review," Social Service Review, LI: 24 (March, 1977); impressions from interviews with SSSA students of the Thirties; Lela Costin, Two Sisters for Social Justice (Urbana: University of Illinois

Press, 1983), pp. 3-25, 160-61.

10. Costin, pp. 59-61; "Legislative Provisions for Children Born out of Wedlock in the State of Michigan," (Paper written by SSA student Paulette Kahn for Child Welfare 313, 1937).

11. Edith Abbott, "Some Basic Principles in Professional Education for Social Work" (1928), in Abbott, Social Welfare and Professional Education (Chicago: University of Chicago Press, 1942), pp. 66-67.

12. Edith Abbott, "Revision of State Poor Laws," The Compass, XV: 18-21 (March, 1934).

13. "Public Welfare and Politics," National Conference of Social Work, Proceedings (1936), p. 27.

14. "How Secure Administrative Skill with Professional Competence for State and Local Public Welfare Service?" NCSW, Proceedings (1936), p. 497.

15. Abbott, "Public Welfare and Politics," p. 36; Minutes, Executive Committee, Chicago Chapter, AASW, 11/9/33, NASW: Chicago Chapter Records, Box 20, Chicago Historical Society, Chicago, Ill.; Proceedings, Conference on Governmental Objectives in Social Work, 2/17/34, p. 287, NASW Records, folder 67.

16. FERA, Rules and Regulations #3, July 11, 1933, cited in R. Clyde White and M. K. White, Research Memorandum on Social Aspects of Relief in the Depression (New York: Social Science Research Council, 1937), pp. 150-52.

17. Josephine Brown, Public Relief, 1929-1939, (New York: Henry Holt, 1940), p. 277; Marjorie Anne Merrill, "Lessons Learned in Personnel Selection and Management in the Emergency Relief Administration," NCSW, Proceedings (1936), pp. 538-47.

18. Alice Taylor Davis, unpublished manuscript; letter from Davis to author, 5/15/86.

19. Davis, letter to author; Elizabeth Dexter, "Has Case Work a Place in the Administration of Public Relief?" NCSW, Proceedings (1935), pp. 155-65. See also Ruth Taylor, "Problems the Public Welfare Field Presents to the Professional Social Worker," Bulletin of the New York School of Social Work, XXVII: 4-11 (July, 1934).

20. Virginia R. Dosher, "Fifty Years of Looking Ahead," Public Welfare, XXXVIII: 30-31 (Winter, 1980); the AAPWO changed its name in 1932.

21. Edith Abbott, "Education for Social Work," Social Work Year Book (1935), pp. 113-21; Minutes, Subcommittee on

Training Courses, National Membership Committee, AASW, 6/18/34, NASW Records, folder 53; Costin, pp. 227-28.

22. Emelia E. Martinez-Brawley, "Josephine Chapin Brown," in Walter I. Trattner, ed., Biographical Dictionary of Social Welfare in America (Westport, Conn.: Greenwood Press, 1986); Martinez-Brawley, unpublished manuscript. Brown had developed her expertise as executive secretary of the Dakota County (Minn.) Welfare Association and as associate director in charge of eighty southeastern states at the Family Welfare Association of America.

23. Martinez-Brawley, unpublished manuscript; Minutes, Executive Committee, AASSW, 7/7/34; letter from Brown to Mildred Mudgett, 5/15/34; Brown to Breckinridge, 5/27/34, Council on Social Work Education Records, Record Group I, Box 4, Social Welfare History Archives; Josephine Brown, p. 282.

24. Memorandum, Advisory Committee to FERA, n.d. (ca 5/34), CSWE Records, I-4; Brown asked the schools to be more flexible in their entrance standards, but they refused. Letter from Frank Bruno to Brown, 10/12/34; Memo from Breckinridge to Executive Committee, AASSW, 11/2/34, CSWE Records, I-4.

25. Edith Abbott, "Education for Social Work," pp. 113-21.

26. "Jane Hoey," Encyclopedia of Social Work, 1971, pp. 582-83; The Reminiscences of Jane Hoey, Social Security Project, 1965, pp. 1-10, Oral History Collection of Columbia University (hereafter Hoey, COHC); Blanche D. Coll, "Jane Marguretta Hoey," in Barbara Sicherman and Carol Hurd Green, eds., Notable American Women, The Modern Period (Cambridge, Mass.: Harvard University Press, 1980), pp. 341-43. Permission to use the Hoey interview was given by The Trustees of Columbia in the City of New York.

27. Hoey, COHC, pp. 1-10.

28. Ibid., pp. 10-13; Charles McKinley and Robert W. Frase, Launching Social Security (Madison: University of Wisconsin Press, 1970), pp. 147, 164-65.

29. Hoey, COHC, p. 51; "Summary of the 1937 Delegate Conference Sessions," The Compass, XVIII: 2-6 (March, 1937); "An Outline of the Position of the AASW in Respect to Governmental Employment, Social Insurance, and Assistance Programs," 1938, NASW Records, folder 211; AASW Delegate Conference, 1940, NASW Records, folder 77, pp. 84-143; "Resolutions Adopted at the Annual Meeting of the American Public Welfare Association, May 23, 1934," Social Service Review, VIII: 528-29 (September, 1934); Josephine Brown, pp. 308-12; The Reminiscences of Katharine Lenroot, Social Security Project, 1965, pp. 103-105, Oral History Collection of Columbia University. Permission to use the Lenroot interview was given by The Trustees of Columbia in the City of New York.

30. Lenroot, COHC, pp. 52-54; see also Hoey, "Next Steps in Public Assistance," NCSW, Proceedings (1945), pp. 148-60.

31. Lenroot, COHC, pp. 52-54.

32. Ibid., pp. 1-20; "Katharine Lenroot," Social Service Review, VIII: 368-69 (June, 1934).

33. Dorothy Kahn chaired an advisory committee on public assistance, which consulted with the Committee on Economic Security; Lenroot, COHC, pp. 34-40, 103-5; Costin, pp. 223-24.

34. Gertrude Springer, "In Predominantly Rural Areas," Survey Midmonthly, LXXVII: 38-39 (February, 1941); Costin, p. 224.

35. The Reminiscences of Charles Schottland, Social Security Project, 1965, pp. 1-16, Oral History Collection of Columbia University. See also Helen Valeska Bary, "Labor Administration and Social Security, A Woman's Life," interview conducted by Jacqueline K. Parker, 1974, p. 138, Suffragists Oral History Project, Regional Oral History Project, University of California, Berkeley, Calif., Permission the Bancroft Library. Permission to use the Schottland interview was given by The Trustees of Columbia in the City of New York.

36. Hoey, COHC, pp. 13-15.

37. Ibid., pp. 61-76; Hoey, "The Federal Government and Desirable Standards of State and Local Administration," NCSW, Proceedings (1937), pp. 440-45.

38. "Standards for Personnel Administration of State Public Assistance Agencies," BPA, 12/1/38, p. 3, Social Security Records, Box 94, folder 631, National Archives, Washington, D.C.; McKinley and Frase, p. 26; Martha Derthick, Uncontrollable Spending for Social Services Grants (Washington, D.C.: Brookings, 1975), p. 21.

39. Memo, Hoey to Oscar Powell, Executive Director Social Security Board, 12/22/38, Social Security Records, Box 94, folder 631.3; "Plan of Bureau of Public Assistance for Developing an Adequate Personnel Program in State Public Assistance Agencies," 12/1/38, Social Security Records, Box 94, folder 631:3; BPA, "Standards for Personnel Administration."

40. "Report of the BPA on Assistance to States in Personnel Training Programs," 11/30/38, Social Security Records, Box 94, folder 631.3, p. 11.

41. Hoey, COHC, pp. 61, 76; BPA, "Memorandum to Executive Director, Social Security Board," 12/21/37, Social Security Records, Box 94, folder 631.34; BPA, "Report of the BPA on Assistance to States in Personnel Training Programs."

42.   Alice J. Webber, "The Psychiatric Social Worker in
Public Welfare," Newsletter, American Association of Psychia-
tric Social Workers, IV: 13-15 (January, 1935), AAPSW Ephemera,
NASW Records.

43.   Mildred Mudgett, Secretary, AASSW, "Report to the
Executive Committee," 10/35, p. 8, Grace Browning/Mary Houk
Papers, Social Welfare History Archives; Mildred Mudgett, "The
Four Seasons" (unpublished autobiography, Mildred Mudgett
Papers, Social Welfare History Archives), p. 229.

44.   Mary L. Gottesfield and Mary E. Pharis, Profiles in
Social Work, (New York: Human Sciences Press, 1977), pp. 108-
10.

45.   Mudgett, "Four Seasons," p. 234; AASSW Directory of
Faculties of Member Schools, 7/1/37, Browning/Houk Papers;
Esther Brown, Social Work as a Profession, 4th ed. (New York:
Russell Sage, 1942), pp. 67-69.

46.   Minutes, Executive Committee, AASSW, 2/11/33, CSWE
Records, I-4.

47.   Chairman's   Report   on   the   Discussions   and
Recommendations of the Division on Personnel Standards, AASW,
11/2/37, NASW records, folder 63.

48.   BPA, "Relationship Between Welfare Agencies and
Schools of Social Work," attached to Memo, Hoey to Arthur
Altmeyer, Chairman, Social Security Board, 3/7/38, Social
Security Records, Box 94, folder 641.34.

49.   Hoey, COHC, p. 76; Memo from Hoey to Oscar Powell,
Executive Director, Social Security Board, 12/12/38, Social
Security Records, Box 94, folder 631.3; "Report of the BPA on
Assistance to States in Personnel Training Programs," pp. 1-2.

50.   "Report of the BPA on Assistance to States in
Personnel Training Programs," pp. 3, 66-69, and Appendix,
"Outline of Orientation for Public Assistance Workers."

51.   Charlotte Towle, Common Human Needs (Washington,
D.C.: Social Security Board, 1945); Grace Marcus, The Nature of
Service in Public Assistance Administration (Washington, D.C.:
U.S. GPO, 1946).

52.   Memo from Hoey to Chairman, Social Security Board,
11/29/38, Social Security Records, Box 94, folder 631.3.

53.   Ibid. The number of agencies described (49)
includes one in Hawaii.

54.   Memo, Frank Bane to Altmeyer, 8/21/36, Social
Security Records, Box 94, folder 631.3.

55.   Memo, Walter West to Chapter Chairmen, 11/4/38, NASW

Records, folder 233.

56. "Facts About Personnel Standards," prepared for 4th Annual Conference, AASW, 1937, NASW Records, folder 99; Florence Sytz, "Relations of a Standard of Education and Training to Professional Practice," NCSW, Proceedings (1936), pp. 100-7.

57. Leonard D. White and Wayne McMillen, "Civil Service and Social Work," The Compass, XVII: 15-21 (April, 1936); Government and Social Work Division, AASW, "Outline on Position of AASW in Respect to Governmental Employment Social Insurance, and Assistance Programs," 1938, NASW Records, folder 211; Ellen C. Potter, "Certification of Social Workers," The Compass, XVII: 10-14 (December, 1935); Walter West, "Social Work as a Profession," Social Work Year Book (1935), pp. 935-36. California passed the first certification law in 1945.

58. Minutes, Ad Interim Committee, AASW, 6/19/37, pp. 2-5, NASW Records, folder 22.

59. "Federal Employment and Assistance Programs," Statement Adopted by Delegate Conference, 2/21/37, The Compass, XVIII: 7-9 (March, 1937).

60. Bary, pp. 150-76; Hoey, COHC, p. 82; but see also Gilbert Steiner, Social Insecurity: The Politics of Welfare (Chicago: Rand McNally, 1966), pp. 87-88.

61. Abbott, "Public Welfare and Politics," pp. 32-33; see also Bary, p. 2; McKinley and Frase, pp. 156-60, 182-92.

62. Letter from Joanna Colcord to West, 7/12/37, NASW Records, folder 232.

63. Letter from A. Mitzer to Hathway, 11/1/42, Marion Hathway Papers, folder 11, Social Welfare History Archives.

64. Records of Mary Phares Grievance Case, NASW Records, folder 38; Rocky Mountain News, 7/2/33, clipping in Records of Grievance Procedure Committee, Denver, Colo., 1933-34, NASW Records, folder 34.

65. Joseph P. Lash, Eleanor and Franklin (New York: Signet Books, 1971), pp. 760-63.

66. Hoey, COHC, pp. 42-49; Hickok, pp. 240-41.

67. Hoey, COHC, pp. 64, 42-49.

68. Quoted in George Martin, Madame Secretary: Frances Perkins (Boston: Houghton Mifflin, 1976), pp. 354-55.

69. Letter from Agnes S. Donaldson (faculty member at University of Nebraska School of Social Work) to Hathway, 5/24/39, Hathway Papers, folder 8.

70. Bary, p. 243. Bary prided herself on being diplomatic and not "coming on" like a social worker. She helped get categorical aid legislation through the Colorado legislature. She criticized Hoey for being too abrupt in her dealings with governors.

71. Open letter from NYC Chapter, AASW, to Mayor La Guardia, 4/35, AASW Records, folder 212; "Road to Chapter Strength," Annual Report of the President, L.A. County Chapter, 1934-35, The Compass, XVII: 12 (September, 1935).

72. Chapter Activities, Michigan, 1937-42, NASW Records, folder 221; "Another Political Investigation," The Compass, XVI: 5 (April, 1935); Karl and Elizabeth de Schweinitz Papers, Box 4, folders 30 and 31, Social Welfare History Archives.

73. Marion Hathway, "Education for Social Work," Social Work Year Book (1943), p. 195.

74. Lenroot, COHC, pp. 104-7.

75. Edith Abbott, "Public Assistance--Whither Bound?" Presidential Address, NCSW, Proceedings (1937), p. 7.

76. Marjorie Smith, "Social Case Work in Public Assistance," NCSW, Proceedings (1944), pp. 319-25; Helen E. Hayden, "Case Work Possibilities in a Public Assistance Program," NCSW, Proceedings (1944), pp. 326-34.

77. Hoey, "The Federal Government and Desirable Standards of State and Local Administration," pp. 440-45; Hoey, COHC, p. 55; Martha Derthick, The Influence of Federal Grants: Public Assistance in Massachusetts (Cambridge, Mass.: Harvard University Press, 1970), pp. 129-31.

78. Minutes, Subcommittee on Technical Requirements, AASW, 12/30/37, NASW Records, folder 54.

79. Memo, Hoey to Powell, 2/27/39, Social Security Records, folder 631.34.

80. Nathan Cohen, Social Work in the American Tradition (New York: Dryden Press, 1958), p. 255.

6

Confusion and Consolidation: Professional Identification During World War II

At the end of the 1930s, the American Association of Social Workers moved toward greater cohesion as it pursued the goal of professionalization in social work. Disputes over membership policies subsided. Calls for political activism diminished. Over 10,000 strong, the organization could be expected to interpret social work's services and goals to a country facing continued economic difficulty and the threat of world war. Yet in 1941, the AASW was caught up in intense internal conflict. The election of Chicago's Wayne McMillen as president in 1940 brought a renewed challenge to the association's model of an exclusive profession which would play, at best, an objective, consultative role in social planning. McMillen's election led to a crisis in association leadership which lasted until 1943. Its sources included political, regional, ideological, and interpersonal differences. The confusions it revealed paralleled other confusions within social work as a whole. In addition, social work continued to face problems with its external environment. As a result, the profession lost an important opportunity for involvement in planning and service during the war and postwar years.

This was a crucial time for the profession. World War I, viewed at first by social workers as a threat to social progress, had brought new ideas about reform and an expansion of welfare programs. The Second World War offered a similar chance for involvement in planning and services on community and national levels. Yet social workers experienced several dilemmas. Should they support American neutrality or collective security? If involved in the defense effort, how should they promote and define their role? What suggestions did they have for postwar planning and how forcefully should these be presented? Did national problems, as well as AASW difficulties, call for new and broader forms of professional organization? Should they build coalitions with other social work groups?

An underlying issue was the familiar problem of the relation of professionalism and political action. Though not debated as vigorously as in the 1930s, it continued to provoke discussion and argument and figured in the AASW's internal conflict. This organizational conflict, set within a larger debate over involvement in the war effort, illustrates both the strengths and weaknesses of social work from 1940 to 1946.

The AASW's preoccupation with internal concerns could not

have come at a worse time. The situation in Europe had been
steadily deteriorating since Hitler came to power in 1933.
From 1938 on, German and Italian militarism made American participation in war more and more likely. Although isolationism
had strong proponents in American society, many people were
coming around to President Roosevelt's view that the U.S. must
take action in support of the Allies. Social workers, like the
rest of the American public, were confused and alarmed. They
debated neutrality versus involvement in the Allies' cause.
Although mainstream social work settled this dilemma fairly
quickly, the Rank and File Movement suffered damaging internal
division.

Up through 1940, most social work leaders urged American
neutrality. Social workers were not unaware of the effects of
the rise of fascism. In 1933, they set up a Hospites program to
support refugee colleagues in Europe.(1) Aid to loyalist Spain
was a popular cause in social work circles. Relief to Spanish
Civil War victims was promoted at AASW chapter meetings and in
Survey editorials.(2) Yet most social workers believed that
domestic reform was America's best defense against communism
and fascism. The theme that defense must come from within
dominated the 1940 National Conference of Social Work, where
President Grace Coyle urged participants to support noninter-
vention.(3)

Belief in neutrality was in part a heritage of the World
War I pacifist tradition of Jane Addams, Lillian Wald, and others. It stemmed also from commitment to recently developed
social services and the fear that military preparedness would
undercut extension of New Deal reforms. A rise in tensions
abroad and political conservatism at home had already caused
FDR to reorder his priorities away from social reform. Similarly, Harry Hopkins had shifted his attention from New Deal
programs to war preparedness.

At the 1940 AASW conference, President Harry Greenstein
warned delegates of those "who will say that since national
defense is so important . . . people who want . . . broad social
programs ought to 'sit down and quit rocking the boat.'" He
promised that social workers would persist in pushing for a comprehensive social welfare system.(4) At the National Conference of Social Work meetings in 1940, over a thousand social
workers signed a peace and neutrality petition. The statement
argued that war abroad did not justify cutting into badly needed
social services at home.(5)

The following months witnessed the Battle of Britain and
the fall of most of Europe to the Axis forces. Neutrality
became less and less attractive to social workers. Participants at the 1941 NCSW backed the war effort. The conference
"was packed with willing and ready servants waiting to do
Washington's bidding."(6) Social workers now argued the
importance of social services in defense programs. They proclaimed that the need for social workers was more urgent than
ever and began planning how best to meet the summons they hoped
would come.(7)

Decisions about wartime involvement were more complicated
for one group within social work. Many members of the Rank and
File Movement regarded the Russian government as a leader in the

international progressive cause. They maintained this commitment long after many liberals turned away in disillusionment.

Not all social work unionists were strict followers of the
Soviet line. By the late thirties, many Rank and File groups
had moved from discussions of social reform to preoccupation
with bread-and-butter issues and the process of formal affiliation with organized labor. Yet the foreign policy positions of
Social Work Today seemed to follow the Communist line. These
positions led to serious conflict within the movement.(8)

After 1935, Social Work Today promoted a Popular Front
philosophy. Editorials supported Roosevelt's second New Deal.
They stressed the need for collective security in the face of
the rising threat of fascism.(9) This position was radically
reversed when Hitler and Stalin signed a nonaggression pact in
August of 1939. The Popular Front philosophy was dead. Social
Work Today now urged American abstention from a war between cap-
italist and imperialist nations.(10)

Social Work Today was joined by radicals like Mary Van
Kleeck in denouncing Roosevelt's moves toward mobilization in
1940. Van Kleeck warned that war subordinated the needs of the
people to the needs of the military. Others in the movement
were severely troubled by the shift in policy.(11) One social
worker active in the thirties recalls listening to union leader
Joe Levy agonizing over whether to switch allegiances.(12) The
dilemma for Jewish social workers was particularly acute.
Three months after the Stalin-Hitler pact, Harry Lurie aban-
doned his earlier sympathies with Russian socialism. Lurie now
joined Max Lerner in an attempt to build a "strictly American"
radicalism.(13)

Radicals disagreeing with the neutralist position opened
fire on Social Work Today. They formed a Committee of Social
Work Unionists for Britain and Democracy which denounced the
journal for following a Communist line. Noninterventionists
set up an opposition group. Both groups aired their views at
the 1941 NCSW. Within a month, the conflict was ended. Hitler
invaded Russia, and Social Work Today became an all-out supporter of military aid to the Allies.(14)

Debates over American involvement in the war took their
toll on the radical movement in social work. Leaders like
Lurie accused other radicals of following a pro-Russian line.
The rapid reversal of Social Work Today's editorial policy following the German invasion of Russia discredited the journal in
the eyes of many unionists. The resulting loss of support,
along with ongoing financial difficulties, led to the journal's
demise in 1942.

The Rank and File Movement was no longer a strong force in
social work affairs, though it lived on in the form of social
work unions. Part of this was due to internal struggle over
allegiance to Soviet policies. Diffusion of the movement was
also the result of a shift of attention to building union membership and seeking formal affiliation with the AF of L and the
CIO. These activities had at last gained a measure of
respectability within the larger profession, so that the split
within the Rank and File was accompanied by greater
rapprochement between unionists and the social work establishment.(15)

     Rank and File debates over ideological commitment to the
Soviet Union were one factor inhibiting social work's involvement in national wartime planning. Another was organizational
and political dissension within the AASW. Hints of this conflict appeared in the middle and late thirties. Open dissent
emerged in 1940.
     In 1938, the AASW had begun a period of self-examination.
Active involvement in politics and public welfare planning gave
way to discussion of organizational composition and goals. At
the request of the 1938 Delegate Conference, the 1939 meeting
concentrated on issues of participation, purpose, and structure. Delegates reached consensus on a number of points. They
agreed that the AASW should continue its selective membership
policy. They described the major areas of organizational focus
as practice, personnel standards, professional education,
administrative structures affecting practice, and, finally,
social programs.(16) They sought a stronger role for chapters
and individual members in the association's program. In line
with this goal, they supported substitution of a large National
Board, elected entirely by the membership, for the existing
Executive Committee, over half of whose members were appointed.
     The Delegate Conference of 1940 went further toward formu-
lating common goals. Participants unanimously passed an "AASW
Position on the Public Social Services." This recognized the
federal government's responsibility for "a broad national program of work, insurance, assistance [and] employment services,"
staffed by trained, competent personnel. In another unanimous
action, the conference reaffirmed a commitment to graduate
social work education as the basic qualification for professional practice.(17) They thus continued their support of a
high standards model of professionalism.
     Despite such unanimity, the conferences indicated con-
tinuing disagreement on a number of issues. This disagreement
was low-key. It arose largely when discussion turned to trans-
lation of principles into action. The Chicago chapter was
active in this dissent. Wayne McMillen's leadership in
presenting the chapter's point of view hinted at the larger battles yet to come.
     McMillen did social research for the Chicago School, then
joined the faculty in 1931. Breckinridge viewed him as "a
great acquisition."(18) By 1938, he was a professor of social
economy. He was a strong supporter of Edith Abbott's ideas on
public welfare and promoted these at AASW national meetings.
He was active in the Chicago chapter and chaired the group from
1936 to 1938. Interest in broad social issues underlay his
decision to run for Illinois state senator in 1938. Yet the
real focus of his activism was organizational structure and
strategy, both on the community level and within the professional association.
     McMillen was a complex blend of organizational "in-
fighter" and sound, likable academician. A bachelor who lived
with his mother, he was one of the few men tolerated by the for-
midable Abbott-Breckinridge team. He was a member of Phi Beta
Kappa and had a bachelor's degree from the University of Iowa
and a diploma from the University of Montpellier in France. He
received his Ph.D. from the Chicago School in 1931. Before

joining the Chicago faculty, he directed community surveys and wrote <u>Measurement</u> <u>in</u> <u>Social</u> <u>Work</u>. At Chicago, he taught courses in community organization, research, and statistics. Students and peers remember him as a solid, principled individual.(19)

Yet McMillen was forceful in conducting debate and promoting his ideas. Moreover, he represented one of the association's strongest chapters. The Chicago chapter, with 968 members in 1939, was second in size only to New York. It represented 9 percent of the association's total membership.(20) From 1932 to 1938, it carried on a strong social action program. Better organized than many chapters, it had an active Practitioners Group and Committee on Social Legislation.(21)

During the New Deal years, the Chapter, like the national office, used lobbying, publicity, and expert testimony. It transferred these to the state and local levels, particularly after 1935. Under McMillen's activist leadership, the chapter pursued a new tactic to deal with a state relief crisis in 1936.

In the summer of 1936, the Illinois Legislature refused to use a state surplus to offset shortages in WPA appropriations. In conjunction with social work union groups, the chapter responded with an ambitious plan.(22) Chapter members set up a series of public meetings throughout the city. Using community organization techniques, the AASW canvassed neighborhoods and worked closely with churches, civic groups, and other local organizations. Together they succeeded in holding thirty-four community meetings and loosing a barrage of letters and telegrams to legislators, city officials, and the media. Overall attendance at the meetings was estimated at 9,000 people. One participant reported that echoes of the meetings were reverberating through City Hall.(23)

The chapter had for some time sought greater support from the national office for its political activities. In 1937, the group asked for financial help in hiring a full-time executive secretary, but was turned down by Walter West, who stressed the association's limited resources.(24) At delegate conferences, chapter representatives promoted the ideas of the Chicago School regarding public welfare. These ideas, such as Abbott's commitment to services and categorical aid programs, were often rejected by the association's leadership and its "Eastern wing."(25)

The chapter played an active role in the evaluation of association purposes and structure. Although it accepted the general format of the AASW Statement of Purpose presented to delegates for ratification at the 1939 conference, the chapter pushed a more definite commitment to the improvement of social conditions. McMillen, who had consistently argued the legitimacy of professional involvement in social action, presented the chapter's view that the AASW should give top priority to social problems. The Chicago position called for political action "through interpretation of social needs to the public at large, to legislators, and to organized groups."(26)

In debating the Chicago chapter's proposals, some chapters objected to a nationally determined commitment to any specific priorities. New York and Cleveland argued that organizational programs should respond to the demands of immediate situa-

tions.Other chapters were more direct in rejecting social
action as a primary focus of the association. They described
professional practice as the association's major concern.(27)
Still others accepted social work's commitment to social action
but adhered to the position developed in the thirties: such
activity should be limited to areas in which social work had
specific expertise. Dorothy Kahn and Linton Swift, proponents
of that view, chaired the AASW committee which prepared the
Statement on Purpose. New Jersey was the only chapter which
conspicuously supported the Chicago position.
    Delegates voted four to one to accept the Statement on Pur-
pose as originally proposed. They did, however, agree to some
stronger wording on improving social conditions, as proposed by
the Chicago group.(28)
    On issues of organizational structure, the Chicago chap-
ter's views were more widely shared. Until then, the association had tended toward centralized control by the national
office, supported by executive boards made up mostly of New
Yorkers and other Easterners. West had been criticized by some
association members for assuming too much autonomy, particularly when he fired his assistant executive secretary, Florence
Taylor, in 1938.(29) Taylor had been assigned as staff person
to a subcommittee of the National Membership Committee. West,
concerned as usual about maintaining high membership standards,
attempted to oversee the subcommittee's work. Conflict
between West and Taylor over what she termed his "attempt to
control the opinions of a national committee" led to her firing.(30) Gordon Hamilton then resigned as chair of the
National Membership Committee. She criticized West for his
rigid interpretation of membership requirements and for his
refusal to follow democratic processes within the organization.(31)
    At the 1939 Delegate Conference, the Chicago chapter and
other groups called for more control of the association by the
membership. They felt the Delegate Conference should set major
policy emphases for the Association's programs. These emphases should then be translated into action by chapters, with the
assistance of the national office. The Chicago group thus promoted a more cohesive and active professional association,
based on stronger chapters, with major direction coming from
the membership.(32)
    This would be a more politicized organization. Chapter
delegations would come to the conference with specific
instructions as to how to vote on various proposals. Candidates for national office would run on platforms. In an
attempt to move control away from the eastern seaboard, Chicago
argued that the newly created National Board should have
regional representation.(33)
    These suggestions for a stronger, more broadly repre-
sentative association reflected regional conflicts in social
work. The Chicago program was supported by chapters outside of
the metropolitan Northeast. Californians reported feeling
"far away from New York." They liked the idea of a national
program based on delegates' interests. Easterners responded
with worries about sectionalism. New York's Elizabeth Dexter
professed not to understand why regional representation mat-

tered to people "[whose] common identification is professional social work." The New York chapter was particularly opposed to the practice of instructing delegates.(34)

Yet these rifts had not polarized the organization. Several Chicago suggestions on structure were passed. Discussion of issues was often good-natured, and New York and Chicago sometimes saw eye-to-eye on an issue. On one such occasion, the association president quipped to a delighted audience: "Ladies and gentlemen, when Chicago moves the adoption of a New York recommendation, that is history."(35)

The relaxed attitude toward disputes did not last. Shortly after McMillen became president in the fall of 1940, he began to fault the national office and particularly its chief executive officer, Walter West. These criticisms culminated in a series of formal charges by McMillen. While a number of the charges appear inconsequential--Executive Office inefficiency, failure to get mail out on time--others were more substantial. McMillen accused West of taking too strong a hand in association affairs. He claimed that West had subverted the president's right to appoint committees. He criticized West's delay in carrying out National Board policies promoting closer relations between the national committees and the chapter.(36)

The motives for McMillen's actions are not entirely clear. One observer accused him of "gestapo tactics."(37) Others suggested that he and his chapter had been used by a "rump group" of dissidents within the organization "to disrupt the national [office]."(38) However, a number of his charges reflected issues raised earlier by the Chicago chapter. Moreover, other chapters had complained about West to McMillen and the National Board. Many of the complaints were based on a feeling "that the National Staff and Board [were] dominated by the East coast and New York."(39)

Although there was undoubtedly a personal element in the West-McMillen fight, there were also important philosophical differences between the two men. These concerned both the structure and function of the professional organization.

McMillen attributed many of the difficulties between himself and West to the executive secretary's resistance to increased delegate participation and a stronger role for the president in interpreting membership thinking to the national office. McMillen believed the most successful structure for the association would be a decentralized one in which chapters carried out most of the organization's program. He argued that the association would be more effective politically if chapters dealt with welfare legislation and administrative issues on the state and local levels.(40)

However, McMillen realized that many in the organization, and particularly its leadership, supported a strong national program. He therefore argued that members be given as much participation in that program as possible. He proposed that program objectives be democratically selected at delegate conferences and that national committees work closely with chapters in carrying out these goals. Nominees for president of the association should run on platforms. Once elected, the president should relay ideas of the membership to the national staff.(41)

These proposals would create a more democratic organization and, McMillen hoped, a more politically active one.
McMillen disagreed with West's stress on development and maintenance of membership standards as the single most important
goal of a professional association. He supported high standards and criticized moves to lower them in order to broaden
membership, but he believed that the stress on standards should
be subordinated to a broad program of service to the community.
"Professional function," he stated, "is thus touched with a
true public interest."(42)

In McMillen's eyes, the "public interest" called for
social work's involvement in social reform. Based on experience and "well-documented evidence," social workers should
propose remedies to social problems.(43) Like West, McMillen
realized that professional social workers were not numerically
powerful. West's solution to this was to rely on fact-finding
by the chapters and expert testimony by a small group of leaders. McMillen's approach was a more politically active one.
He proposed alliances with other organizations, in which social
work could share its specialist knowledge. Social work would
thus influence other groups in the electorate to promote particular social reforms.(44)

McMillen's views were those of an "insider" in the profession, rather than a radical member of the Rank and File. He
did not see the AASW as a protective association open to anyone
in social work. He believed in professional standards, but he
felt strongly that professionalism entailed responsibility to
broader social needs. "How . . . in good conscience," he
argued, "can social workers ignore politics?"(45)

West disagreed with many of McMillen's ideas and responded
to McMillen's charges with restrained anger. He denied accusa-
tions that he was responsible for the organization's problems.
West had headed the association's staff for thirteen years. He
identified strongly with its policies and program. He believed
in the importance of national leadership and was uncomfortable
about the notion of giving the Delegate Conference power to
determine organizational priorities.(46)

West was not a professionally trained social worker, but a
journalist who had entered the field through an interest in public relations and agency administration. Yet he was deeply
committed to the importance of professional standards based on
graduate education. He was convinced that pursuit of standards
was the association's most important function. His view of the
AASW as a body of experts studying and reporting on social
issues was incompatible with McMillen's stress on broader
political alliances.(47)

The AASW National Board, investigating McMillen's charges
against West, invited both men to make formal statements
regarding the association's problems. West gave a perceptive
description of conflicts caused by limited resources, regional
differences, and Rank and File groups' concerns about agency
executive influence in the association's program. He might
have added that he himself had earlier urged the Executive Committee to broaden the geographic base of national committee
memberships. He had also been more receptive than most to Rank
and File ideas, arranging at one point for expression of these

in The Compass.(48)
      Yet West believed that professional purpose should rise
above such tendencies toward divisiveness. He described the
source of the current crisis as "the insistence on political
formulas and political means of operation." Such methods
"exposed the organization's original professional purposes and
procedures to increasingly serious jeopardy."(49)
      McMillen's views on association difficulties were more
directly tied to issues of participation and control. He
pointed to the general membership's discontent and lack of
involvement in organizational activities. He urged development of strength at the chapter level. His interest lay not in
limiting debate, but in opening up avenues for the expression of
differences.(50)
      Two models of a professional association were thus
presented. One stressed centralized organization, the all-
importance of standards, and utilization of an expert role in
political activity. The other emphasized democratic participation in decision-making and a major commitment to broad-based
social action.
      The National Board essentially supported West's model.
It ruled that McMillen had overstepped his role as president.
The board found his conduct unprofessional and damaging to the
organization's integrity. With a bow to the legitimacy of two
of the charges against West, the board supported the executive
secretary's overall performance. Yet in a surprise move, the
board asked for West's resignation. They explained that the
seriousness of the crisis made it difficult for him to remain in
the national office. They then voted to request McMillen's
resignation as well.(51)
      West resigned early in the spring of 1942. The organiza-
tion had been caught up in crisis for two years. The
West/McMillen affair was so complex that at one point the entire
Executive Committee of the National Board resigned on a vote of
"no-confidence" by the Delegate Conference. A sharp drop in
dues payments added to an existing budget deficit.(52) Other
staff members resigned. One stated she had spent her time
largely on administrative problems and "overcoming the obstacles which recurrently interfered with program activities."(53)
      Slowly, the association began to pick up the pieces.
Grace Coyle replaced acting president Frank Bruno in October,
1942. Coyle was a highly regarded group work specialist who
taught at the School of Applied Social Sciences of Western
Reserve University. Under her guidance, the Executive Committee selected Joe Anderson, also from Western Reserve, as the new
executive secretary. A year after West's resignation,
Anderson took over as head of the national office.(54)
      Lack of strong AASW leadership in 1940-43 and continuing
indecisiveness over political action hampered social workers'
attempts to define the profession's role in the U.S. mobilization movement. Social workers hoping for professional influence in government circles deplored the internal crisis which
prevented association leaders and staff from fulfilling that
role. An editorial in Social Work Today observed that organizational paralysis had left AASW members without a group

voice.(55)   A Los Angeles member noted, "The Association,
because of its own war, has not played the proper role in the
war which really matters, that against fascism."(56)   Public
welfare administrator Louis Towley expressed a similar theme to
Gertrude Springer of The Survey. Towley wrote of the need for
social work to have spokesmen among the planners.   Ideally the
AASW might fill this role, "but of course that organization is
in no shape now nor will it be for a year . . . to turn its energies outside itself."(57)

Social work could make an important contribution to the
war effort. As Towley proclaimed, the field was "well-fitted
to be the servant of democracy." Because of its humanism and
respect for the dignity of the individual, the profession could
help adjust the urgent needs of society to the particular needs
of each citizen.(58)   But social work required legitimization
as a profession essential to the defense effort.

Officials were often slow to grant this legitimacy.
Social workers argued their usefulness on draft boards and
their potential for helping the army with medical discharges
and AWOL personnel.(59)   The American Association of Psychiatric Social Workers announced its willingness to cooperate
with government and armed forces personnel in mental health
activities.(60)   The profession stood ready to help develop and
staff housing, health, and other essential welfare programs.
Yet social workers were not initially assigned to draft boards.
They had difficulty getting army commissions. The psychiatric
branch of the armed services turned first to psychologists and
nurses before using social workers.   The Veterans Administration did not have a classification for professional social work
jobs until late in the war.(61)   In Washington, the newly
established Office of Defense, Health, and Welfare Services was
not initially sympathetic "to the essential nature of welfare
services" or to utilization of social work professionals.(62)

The inability of the AASW to act as a strong agent for the
profession contributed to the delay in recognition of social
work's potential.   The familiar lack of agreement within the
field over who constituted a qualified social worker further
impeded official declaration of social work as an essential
occupation.   The profession also suffered from its failure in
the previous decade to establish itself firmly within the public social services.

Where it did involve itself in public services, social
work continued to face political opposition to its standards.
Moreover, conservative Congresses had begun to dismantle New
Deal programs.   Both the Civilian Conservation Corps and the
WPA were terminated in 1943.   In a country jittery about sabo-
tage and fifth-column activity, persecution of supposed left-
ists increased.   Representative Martin Dies used his House Committee on Un-American Activities to track down subversives in
government.   The Far Right linked New Dealers and social workers with communism.(63)   One victim of such suspicions was
Bertha Reynolds, who, because of blacklisting, was unable to
get a job with the American Red Cross.(64)

Despite these problems, social workers did become involved
in government defense and welfare programs. By the spring of
1942, Joanna Colcord could report to Louis Towley:

The Office of Defense, Health, and Welfare Services is honey-
combed with social workers; the office of Civilian Defense has
recently acquired Hugh Jackson and Ralph Blanchard. . . . Fred
Hoehler is giving part time to the Army's morale division.
There are social workers in the U.S. Civil Service Commission .
. . and in the Bureau of Old Age and Survivors Insurance, not to
mention the Bureau of Public Assistance and the Children's
Bureau, which they own and operate entirely.(65)

Colcord's report was overoptimistic. The numbers of
social workers in wartime government welfare programs was
relatively small. Individually, social workers were active in
promoting these programs and the role of the profession within
them. Yet they lacked a collective voice to state policy positions and carry out joint planning. In 1942, the AASW had set
up a Committee on Organization and Planning of Social Services
in the War. The group was to explore the impact of war on
social work, the unmet needs that social work could fulfill, and
the profession's relationship to the government. Yet partly
because of the association's internal difficulties, the committee was barely off the ground a year later. At best, it focused
on study of wartime problems and formulation of statements for
discussion at delegate conferences. The lack of a more active
program was blamed on the shortage of staff in the national
office.(66)
The competition which existed between those social work
organizations actively involved in defense and welfare programs
made the need for a common meeting ground even more imperative.
Concern about conflicts between the Children's Bureau and the
Bureau of Public Assistance caused the AASW to avoid appointing
representatives of either organization to its wartime planning
committee. Shortages in social work personnel led groups like
the Red Cross to actively recruit social workers already
employed by public and private agencies. Social work administrators and AASW officials spoke resentfully of these raids on
agency staff.(67)
In an effort to deal with rivalries and the lack of common
planning, social workers created two inter-organizational
bodies. The War Time Committee on Personnel in the Social Services was a joint venture of the AASW, the Association of
Schools, the psychiatric and medical social work groups, and
the newly organized American Association for the Study of Group
Work. The committee sought to organize and coordinate attempts
to increase the supply of social workers for war and postwar
programs.(68)
A second group, the Interim Committee for Joint Planning
in Social Work, had a more far-reaching mission. This committee was set up by representatives of several social work professional bodies "to develop some form of organization through
which American social work opinion could be mobilized on matters of broad social concern and policy."(69) The committee's
founders felt the AASW was not representative enough to speak
for social work as a whole.(70)
The Interim Committee included both organizational representatives and leading lay and professional figures. Gordon

Hamilton and Harriett Bartlett figured prominently in the work
of this and the personnel committee. Bartlett, who chaired
each committee for two years, had had a distinguished career in
the Social Service Department of Massachusetts General Hospital
and was president of the American Association of Medical School
Workers. Interested in the cohesion of the profession, she
hoped the Interim Committee would provide a structure which
would enable social workers "to keep the broader social issues
and responsibilities of the whole field more clearly before
us."(71)
     Neither committee was entirely successful in its goals.
The personnel committee worked on improving the status of
social workers in the armed forces and the V.A. It became a
committee of the AASW, where it consulted with the Office of
Community War Services on occupational definitions and federal
aid for social work students. The group was disbanded in
1946.(72)
     The Interim Committee on Planning had difficulty building
a group capable of representing the varied and conflicting
philosophies within social work. A major problem was defining
the field in order to decide who should be included in a social
work planning group. The committee spent two years attempting
to establish organizational structure and goals and methods of
operation. These efforts did not proceed beyond the planning
stage. The committee was absorbed by the National Social Welfare Assembly, which was formed in 1946. The assembly was a
collection of representatives of national social welfare
organizations and stressed an agency rather than a professional
association point of view.(73)
     Nevertheless, both committees constituted important
attempts to build broader coalitions within professional social
work. While the internal difficulties of the AASW hastened the
turn to such structures, the creation of these particular
groups indicated a desire for a new type of organization which
could unite the various segments within the field.
     The war years continued to challenge social work. Man-
power demands expanded at a rapid rate. The number of social
work positions had already almost doubled between 1939 and
1940. Despite cutbacks in New Deal programs, wartime brought
expansion and experimentation in social welfare. Yet the profession did not play a leading role.
     The creation of the Federal Office of Defense, Health, and
Welfare Services marked a step forward in the direct provision
of government health and welfare services to local communities,
especially defense industry boom towns. Veterans' benefits
provided another type of social welfare, which by 1950 embraced
almost one-third of the total population. Yet social workers
did not figure prominently in either program.
     On the private level, the Red Cross expanded its Home Ser-
vice activities, providing information, counseling, and
financial assistance to armed services personnel and their
families. In 1941, six national agencies, including the YMCA,
the Jewish Welfare Board, and National Catholic Community Services, founded the United Service Organization for National
Defense. The organization was an important experiment in
cooperation between private agencies and the federal govern-

ment. Although both the USO and the Red Cross employed professional social workers, they were essentially volunteer operations with a small number of trained staff.(74)

Even though the employment of professional social workers
was not huge, expansion in war-connected agencies created a
drain on others, especially in the public social services.
Louis Towley reported from a public welfare department in
Minnesota: "Our staff has pretty well been knocked to pieces,
especially in the counties . . . Red Cross is taking most of the
good workers and we are not getting recruits."(75) A Children's Bureau official noted the "shocking number of vacancies"
in child welfare divisions in the states. School of social
work enrollments fell as young men joined the armed forces. In
an attempt to deal with shortages of trained personnel, two-
thirds of the professional schools of social work in the AASSW
accelerated their programs to year-round operations. As a
stopgap measure, public and private agencies brought in large
numbers of volunteers.(76)

The AASW's continued stress on high personnel standards
hindered creation of a social work professional work force
large enough to staff new and established agencies. The association's internal problems and the ongoing debate about the
profession's commitment to social planning undercut involvement in government welfare and defense programs.

Social workers did make strides on the practice front during the forties. The war years brought demands for different
kinds of practice. A new clientele appeared, requesting services, not relief. Clients sought help in locating housing,
day care, and rehabilitation programs. Social workers became
aware of the need for information, referral, and short-contact
services. Psychiatric skills received renewed emphasis as
social workers were called upon to help deal with service-con-
nected mental disorders and the adjustment problems of families
in wartime. Social workers found jobs in counseling programs
in unions, industry, and business. Group work and community
organization rose in importance.

As the country moved from defense concerns to anticipation
of postwar society, the federal government turned to issues of
postwar planning. Here again, social work's lack of cohesion
and its debates over political involvement undercut its
potential contribution to the planning exercise.

Both AASW and Interim Committee leadership verbalized the
need for expansion of social welfare programs after the war.
Yet neither organization played a major role in planning this
expansion. An Association of Schools report noted that "postwar planning for social welfare services does not seem to have
proceeded beyond prophecies that there will be an unprecedented
need for them."(77)

In the case of the Interim Committee, lack of action
stemmed from the inability to weld a variety of social work
groups into an organization with a common program. The AASW's
involvement in postwar planning was hindered by internal crisis, lack of funds, and continuing debate over the amount and
type of social action appropriate to a professional group.

A number of AASW leaders accepted the legitimacy of the
association's involvement in promoting social legislation and

social reform in the postwar years. Yet they differed among
themselves as to the actual strategies which the association
should employ. Some promoted direct sponsorship of social legislation. Others argued for a public relations approach in
which the AASW made its views known to the community at large.
Kenneth Pray assured a 1945 NCSW audience that social reform was
an integral part of social work practice. Yet he was hesitant
about direct political activity, finding it "utterly inappro-
priate . . . for the [professional] association to use its
influence on behalf of one or another party or candidate in a
political contest in which other than strictly social issues
are at stake."(78)   The AASW continued to reject suggestions to
move the national office from New York to Washington, D.C.(79)
     By and large, the association limited itself to study of
issues and development of position papers to send to public
officials, with occasional forays in support of specific legislation. The Committee on Organization and Planning of the
Social Services, established in 1942, soon turned to discussion
of postwar planning. The committee formulated statements on
medical care and foreign relief and set up subcommittees to
develop material for the chapters on social security, full
employment, and services to youth.(80)
     One subcommittee reviewed the Report on Security, Work,
and Relief Measures prepared by Eveline Burns for Roosevelt's
National Resources Planning Board. Based on this review, AASW
President Grace Coyle cabled Roosevelt the association's
"hearty support of the [report's] proposals" for extension of
the nation's social reform programs. The planning committee
also submitted suggestions on social welfare to the Republican
and Democratic national committees in 1944. Yet despite these
activities, the committee felt the association should be careful about attempting to cover too much ground. It suggested
choosing a limited number of areas in which to try to exert
influence.(81)
     One such area was national health insurance. The associa-
tion favored the Wagner-Murray-Dingell bill, which provided for
a comprehensive national health system. Yet when the bill was
attacked by the American Medical Association and other critics,
the AASW proceeded to tread cautiously. The office decided
simply to send chapters a summary of the positions of various
groups regarding a national health program. The bill was
killed in 1944. It was not until 1948 that an AASW Delegate
Conference came out strongly in favor of universal, compulsory
health insurance.(82)
     The association had a mixed record in other areas of public
policy. It was one of the most active of social work organizations in supporting war relief programs, such as the United
Nations Relief and Rehabilitation Adminstration.(83)   It was
less decisive on matters of civil rights, an important national
issue in the forties. Despite the protests of the Chicago
chapter and several others, the association participated in the
1941 NCSW meetings in segregated New Orleans.(84)
     The lack of a dominant commitment to social action was
evident in the organizational priorities established by the
National Board in 1945. In a discussion of the association's
future program, the board placed "influencing public social

policy" fourth in a list of five priorities.(85)

Frustration over the lack of a strong social action program led a group of politically inclined social workers to form the Social Work Action Committee in 1944. Spearheaded by Harry Lurie, the committee planned to engage in lobbying and publicity to promote social action on health and welfare issues. In an attempt to avoid "the restrictions of professional associations," the committee opted for an open membership policy. Anyone connected with a social agency could belong.(86)

The committee developed a Call for Action, urging full employment after the war and an equitable distribution of national resources. It conducted a survey on the effects of demobilization and defense cutbacks, and submitted this to President Truman in 1945. However, like the Interim Committee, the group failed to achieve its projected national organization. Attempts to coordinate activities with the AASW fell through. Two years after its founding, the group folded.(87)

Social work's inability to make a strong mark in war and postwar social planning stemmed from a variety of causes. Debate over professionalism versus social action, the stress on higher standards, inter- and intra-organizational conflicts, and the conservative move against the New Deal all played a part.

Yet while it lost opportunities through indecision on social action issues in the mid-1940s, social work showed signs of strength in other areas. Under the guidance of Grace Coyle and Joe Anderson, the AASW began to rebuild. Anderson was a personable man with broad administrative experience. He helped the AASW develop a set of priorities which stressed important professional goals--establishment of social work licensing, improvement of professional education, and study of new developments in social work practice. Though lower in priority, an interest in public welfare was maintained. The association reversed a several years' budget deficit in 1943. Membership, which had dropped during the war, rose back to 10,000 in 1944.(88)

Anderson encouraged cooperation of the AASW with other organizations. He had worked actively with Bartlett to develop the Interim Committee on Joint Planning. Though the various efforts at building broader social work organizations were not immediately successful, they helped people think about the possibilities of a more coordinated field. The crisis of war brought not only confusion and divisions but also the resolution of certain conflicts.(89) The Rank and File Movement was divided by the neutrality issue, but lived on in the less radical, more widely accepted social work employee unions.

The 1940 census found 70,000 individuals employed in social work. This constituted a 75 percent increase over 1930. Practice was still centered in large cities, and regional differences maintained their salience. Yet leadership was no longer so concentrated in Chicago and New York and the competition between these two centers had given way to a more diffuse picture. While Abbott and Breckinridge, Hoey, Lenroot, and Hamilton were still prominent, other names had appeared--Grace Coyle at Western Reserve, Marion Hathway at the Pittsburgh School, Joe Anderson, Harriett Bartlett in Massachusetts,

Kenneth Pray in Philadelphia, and Arlien Johnson out on the west
coast. (90)
     Spurred by internal and external forces, social work was
turning to an interest in case work and professional concerns.
The tension between these interests and social action would not
disappear. But the field was moving toward broader organizational structures within which these tensions could be played
out.

Notes

1. Confidential Memorandum on Hospites, AASW, 1933, National Association of Social Workers: Chicago Chapter Records, Box 2, Chicago Historical Society, Chicago, Ill.

2. See, e.g., Minutes, Executive Committee, Chicago Chapter, AASW, 6/18/37, NASW: Chicago Chapter Records, Box 20.

3. Grace Coyle, "Social Work at the Turn of the Decade," National Conference of Social Work, Proceedings (1940) pp. 3-26; Thomas Lyle Olson, "Unfinished Business: American Social Work in Pursuit of Reform, Community, and World Peace, 1939-1950" (Diss., University of Minnesota, 1972), pp. 45-51.

4. Proceedings, Delegate Conference 1940, p. 40, NASW Records, folder 77, Social Welfare History Archives, University of Minnesota, Minneapolis, Minn.

5. Walter West, "Editorial," The Compass, XXI: 2 (July, 1940); Olson, p. 48.

6. Olson, pp. 65-66.

7. "Social Work and the National Defense," The Compass, XXI: 3-5 (August, 1940).

8. Jacob Fisher, The Response of Social Work to the Depression (Cambridge, Mass.: Schenkman, 1980), p. 186.

9. Ibid., p. 204.

10. Olson, pp. 42-43. See, e.g., Mary Van Kleeck, "Social Work in the World Crisis," Social Work Today, VII: 8 (March, 1940); Frank C. Bancroft, "Social Work and Defense," Social Work Today, VIII: 7-10 (October, 1940).

11. Van Kleeck, p. 8; Olson, pp. 42-43.

12. Interview with D. E. Mackelmann, March 15, 1979.

13. Olson, p. 43.

14. Olson, pp. 61-65; Fisher, pp. 217-20; Albert Deutsch, "Let's Face Facts This Time," Social Work Today, IX: 3-6 (November, 1941).

15. See, for example, Virginia P. Robinson, "Is Unionization Compatible with Social Work?" The Compass, XVIII: 5-9 (April, 1939).

16. AASW, Handbook for Delegate Conference, 1940, pp. 15-18, AASW Records, Box 9, folder 76; "Executive Committee Report to 1939 Delegate Conference on 1938 Conference Proposals," The Compass, XX: 3-19 (April, 1939).

17. Proceedings of 1940 AASW Conference, p. 50, NASW Records, folder 77; "AASW Statement on Standards for Social Work Personnel," Passed at Delegate Conference, 5/25/40, NASW Records, folder 148.

18. Letter from Breckinridge to Marion Hathway, 12/10/27, Marion Hathway Papers, folder 6, Social Welfare History Archives.

19. Interviews with Paulette Hartrich, July 23, 1979, Rita Novak, May 8, 1979, and D. E. Mackelmann, March 15, 1979; Who's Who in Chicago (Chicago: A. N. Marquis, 1941); Directory of Members of the American Association of Social Workers (New York: AASW, 1936).

20. "Chapter Membership Count," The Compass, XX: 18 (December, 1939). The New York City chapter had 1,232 members and total AASW membership was 11,179.

21. Minutes, Membership Meeting, 2/1/32, 10/6/33; Minutes, Executive Committee, Chicago Chapter, AASW, 9/8/33, 11/9/33, 8/2/34, NASW: Chicago Chapter Records, Boxes 20 and 21.

22. Minutes, Membership Meeting, Chicago Chapter, AASW, 6/18/36, NASW: Chicago Chapter Records, Box 21.

23. Ibid.

24. Minutes, Executive Committee, Chicago Chapter, AASW, 12/7/37, NASW: Chicago Chapter Records, Box 20.

25. Ibid.

26. Wayne McMillen, "The Professional Base for Social Action," in American Association of Social Workers, Four Papers on Professional Function (New York: AASW, 1937), pp. 7-21; Proceedings, AASW Delegate Conference, 1939, pp. 70-97, NASW Records, folder 75.

27. Proceedings, AASW Delegate Conference, 1939, pp. 84-86.

28. Ibid., pp. 70-97; "Report on Informal Conference Discussion of Purpose and Structure Proposals," The Compass, XX: 8-11 (July, 1939).

29. "Report of the Executive Committee," The Compass, XX: 7-9, 14 (December, 1938); Minutes, Executive Committee, Chicago Chapter, AASW, 6/7/39, NASW Records: Chicago Chapter, Box 20.

30. Florence Taylor, Statement to Special Committee in Confidential Report, Special Committee to President Greenstein on Facts and Issues Involved in Dismissal of Mrs. Florence Taylor, AASW, New York Chapter, n.d., NASW: New York Chapter Records, Chapter Office, New York, N.Y.

31. Letter from Hamilton to West, 10/4/37, NASW: New York Chapter Records.

32. Proceedings, AASW Delegate Conference, 1939, p. 17; Proceedings, AASW Delegate Conference, 1940, NASW Records, folders 75 and 77.

33. Proceedings, AASW Delegate Conference, 1939, NASW Records, folder 75.

34. Ibid., pp. 196-98.

35. Ibid., p. 198.

36. "Draft of Progress Report of Executive Committee to Delegate Conference," 5/41, NASW Records, folder 15; Minutes, Executive Committee, AASW 5/16-17/41, and 4/12-13/41, NASW Records, folder 22; Report of the Special Study of Program, Policies and Operations of the AASW by the Executive Committee to the National Board, 2/42, NASW Records, folder 9.

37. As reported by J. Siebole in letter to Louis H. Towley, 3/16/42, Louis Towley Papers, folder 12, Social Welfare History Archives.

38. Memo to Chapter Chairmen, Elizabeth Mills, Asst. Exec. Secy., AASW, 8/6/42, NASW Records, folder 24.

39. Report of the Special Study of the AASW, 2/42.

40. Wayne McMillen, "The American Association of Social Workers and the Future," Social Service Review, XVI: 452-61 (September, 1942).

41. Ibid.; Minutes, Executive Committee, AASW, 5/16-17/41, NASW Records, folder 22.

42. McMillen, "The American Association of Social Workers and the Future," p. 446.

43. Wayne McMillen, "Social Workers and the Democratic Process: Social Work and Politics," Social Work Today, VII: 20, 30 (January, 1940).

44. Ibid.; McMillen, "The Professional Base for Social Action."

45. McMillen, "Social Workers and the Democratic Process," p. 30.

46. Walter West, "Statement about Association Program," 2/11/42, NASW Records, folder 5.

47. Ibid.; West, "The Association Program," The Compass, XIV: 9-15 (June, 1933).

48. West, "Statement about Association Program;" Fisher, pp. 98-99.

49. West, "Statement about Association Program."

50. Wayne McMillen, "Statement about Association Program," 9/25/41, NASW Records, folder 5.

51. "Special Study of Program, Policies, and Operations of the AASW;" Minutes, National Board Meeting, AASW, 5/42, NASW Records, folder 11; Minutes, Executive Committee, AASW, 5/16-17/41 and 7/19-20/41, NASW Records, folder 22; "National Board Decisions on Future Plans for the Association," The Compass, XXIII: 3-6 (March, 1942).

52. Minutes, Executive Committee, AASW, 5/30/41 and 11/1/41, NASW Records, folder 22.

53. Letter from Elizabeth Mills to Grace Coyle, 12/10/42, NASW records, folder 232.

54. Letter from Frank Bruno to Walter West, 3/18/42, NASW records, folder 15.

55. "The AASW Crisis," Social Work Today, IX: 8 (April, 1942).

56. "Report to Membership on Results of Mail Vote," 8/6/42, NASW Records, folder 23; Memo to Chapter Chairmen from Elizabeth Mills, 8/6/42, NASW Records, folder 24.

57. Letter from Louis Towley to Gertrude Springer, 4/18/42, Louis Towley Papers, folder 12.

58. Ibid.

59. "Social Work and the National Defense," pp. 3-5.

60. Leona M. Hambrecht and Mildred H. Hurley, "Participation in the National Defense Program," Newsletter, American Association of Psychiatric Social Workers, X: 15-17 (Winter, 1940-41).

61. Minutes, Executive Committee, AASW, 7/18-19/45, NASW Records, folder 25; "Comments of Elizabeth Ross on the Development of Social Work in the Armed Services and Veterans' Administration," n.d., in Karl and Elizabeth De Schweinitz Papers, folder 93, Social Welfare History Archives.

62. Arlien Johnson, "Professional Education for Social Welfare Services in War Time, A Preliminary Report," 12/31/42, Grace Browning/Mary Houk Papers, Social Welfare History Archives.

63. John Morton Blum, V Was for Victory: Politics and American Culture during World War II (New York: Harcourt Brace

Jovanovich, 1976), pp. 234-41.

64. Bertha C. Reynolds, An Uncharted Journey (New York:
Citadel Press, 1963), p. 240.

65. Letter from Joanna Colcord to Towley, 5/5/42, Towley
Papers, folder 12.

66. Minutes, Executive Committee, AASW, 11/14-15/42,
NASW Records, folder 24; Eileen K. McCracken, "Progress Report
of the Committee on Organization and Planning of Social
Services in the War and Post War Periods," The Compass, XXIV:
12-13 (April, 1943); Minutes, Committee on Organization and
Planning of Social Services, AASW, 6/11-12/43, NASW Records,
folder 61.

67. Minutes, Executive Committee, AASW, 11/14-15/42,
NASW Records, folder 24; letter from Elizabeth Mills to Joanna
Colcord, 5/7/43, NASW Records, folder 232; Mary Irene Atkinson,
Child Welfare Division, Children's Bureau, to Marion Hathway,
3/30/42, Marion Hathway papers, folder 12; Towley to Springer,
3/28/43, Towley Papers, folder 13.

68. Minutes, Executive Committee, AASW, 2/5-7/43, NASW
Records, folder 25.

69. Comments by Harriett Bartlett, 5/72, attached to
records of Interim Committee for Joint Planning in Social Work,
1944-46; Memo, Bartlett to Joe Anderson, 9/18/44, in Harriett
Bartlett Papers, folder 9, Social Welfare History Archives.

70. Interview with Harriett Bartlett, August 20, 1979.

71. Memo, Bartlett to Anderson, 9/18/44, p. 3, Bartlett
Papers, folder 9.

72. Minutes, Executive Committee, AASW, 7/18-19/45, NASW
Records, folder 25; Joseph P. Anderson, "Social Work as a
Profession," Social Work Year Book (1945), pp. 449-54.

73. Memo from Harriett Bartlett to Interim Committee
members, 10/22/45, Bartlett Papers, folder 9; Ray Johns,
"National Association in Social Work," Social Work Year Book
(1947), p. 333.

74. Geoffrey Perrett, Days of Sadness, Years of Triumph
(New York: Coward, McCann, and Geoghegan, 1973), pp. 325-56:
Red Cross Service Records, Accomplishments of Seven Years:
1939-1946 (Washington, D.C.: American National Red Cross,
1946); Operation USO, Report of the President (USO, 1/9/48).

75. Letter from Towley to Springer, 4/28/43, Towley
Papers, folder 13.

76. Johnson, "Professional Education for Social Welfare
Services in War Time"; Almena Dawley, Presidential Address,

Association of Psychiatric Social Workers, 5/13/42, Browning/Houk Papers.

77. Johnson, "Professional Education for Social Welfare Services in War Time," p. 6.

78. Kenneth Pray, "Social Work and Social Action," NCSW, Proceedings (1945), p. 358.

79. Minutes, Membership Meeting, Chicago Chapter, AASW, 3/12/42, NASW: Chicago Chapter Records, Box 21.

80. Minutes, Executive Committee, AASW, 1/7-8/44 and 7/28-29/44, NASW Records, folder 25; Reports of Committee on Organization and Planning of Social Services, 12/30/43 and 2/16-17/45, NASW Records, folder 61.

81. Press Release, "Social Workers Back Resources Board Report on Security, Work, and Relief Measures," 3/12/43, NASW Records, folder 237.

82. Olson, pp. 297-301.

83. Ibid., pp. 209-16; "Statement on Principles on Foreign Relief and Rehabilitation," The Compass, XXV: 9-11 (April, 1944).

84. Minutes, Executive Committee, Chicaago Chapter, AASW, 9/8/41, NASW: Chicago Chapter Records, Box 20.

85. Minutes, National Board Meeting, AASW, 3/45, NASW Records, folder 12.

86. "To Social Workers: A Call to Action," The Compass, XXV: 25-28 (April, 1944); Olson, pp. 135-39.

87. Olson, p. 311.

88. Arlien Johnson, "Social Work as a Profession," Social Work Year Book (1943), pp. 511-19. Nurses had increased by 21 percent; teachers had decreased 1 percent.

89. Interview with Harriett Bartlett, August 20, 1979.

90. Johnson, "Social Work as a Profession," pp. 512-13.

7

Public Service Versus Professional Standards:
Conflict in Social Work Education in the 1940s

Social work was becoming a more unified profession by the mid-1940s. The American Association of Social Workers regained much of its prewar strength, the Rank and File challenge subsided, and preliminary attempts were made to coordinate the work of various professional organizations. Yet social work education entered the most divisive period in its history. The conflict related largely to the now-familiar tensions in social work: selectivity versus breadth in professional membership and training, high standards versus "practicality" in personnel matters, and profession-building versus public service in practice. The intensity of the battle indicates the persistent nature of such tensions, even in periods of rapprochement. How social work educators resolved the crisis gives insight into the comparative importance of profession-building in social work in the 1940s and the 1950s.

Conflict in social work education in the 1940s centered on the question: should professional education take place at the graduate or the undergraduate level? Underlying this question was a more fundamental issue, only partially recognized within the field. This concerned the nature and degree of social work's responsibility to the public social services, and in particular to the staffing of those services.

The conflict crystallized with the formation of a new educational organization, the National Association of Schools of Social Administration. The group coalesced at a 1942 meeting of the Southwestern Social Science Association. Here, faculty involved with undergraduate social work curricula at several southern and western colleges and universities formed an organization to improve the quality and prestige of undergraduate social work education.

The group included both sociologists and social workers. Much of their teaching took place in sociology departments. Their courses had evolved largely in response to the expansion of the public welfare system in the thirties and the lack of formal training of most welfare workers. Their schools were located in regions not served by graduate social work programs. In organizing to promote undergraduate social work education, these faculty challenged the move toward specialized graduate education so successfully championed by Edith Abbott, Sophonisba Breckinridge, and the American Association of Schools of Social Work. The strength of the challenge suggests the limitations of that graduate education in the thirties and forties.

These limitations mirrored ongoing difficulties in social work. A small group of graduate schools faced a massive demand for social work training. Similarly, a selective AASW had been called upon to give recognition to large numbers of new social workers, many of whom lacked formal professional qualifications. Geography figured in both situations. An elite group of professionals in urban areas was asked to respond to the needs of the rest of the country. Schools of social work were challenged to go beyond private agency training and provide education in public welfare case work and administration for rural as well as urban areas.

Both in educational and professional organizations, demands to adjust to new situations clashed with desires to improve professional standards. The conflict between narrow professionalism and a broader concept of the field had been an important element in the dispute between Walter West and Wayne McMillen in the AASW. Now that conflict moved to the arena of social work education.

Three interest groups challenged the authority of the twenty-year-old Association of Schools to make policy for all of social work education. The first was composed of state university and land grant college administrators, who were concerned with the training of personnel for all types of state service and who resented the interference of specialized accrediting agencies. The second consisted of heads of departments of sociology, who criticized the AASSW's "unnecessarily high professional standards in a too limited definition of the scope of social welfare."(1) The third group was made up of social workers, particularly in rural areas, who were disturbed about the large number of untrained workers in the public social services.

The three groups coalesced in the movement toward a new social work accrediting organization. This movement began in the late thirties, when state universities and land grant colleges started developing social work courses for an expanding public welfare personnel. Many did so because of the failure of the AASSW to meet public welfare training needs on a broad scale. This failure was due in part to lack of resources among the graduate schools of social work. It stemmed also from AASSW adherence to a particular model of social work education: graduate education, stressing case work, generally housed in a private institution, and located in an urban area.

Most of the AASSW member schools were severely underfinanced in the thirties. In 1934-35, the total budget of twenty-two out of twenty-nine schools was about $1,100,100. Forty-seven percent of this amount went to the three largest schools.(2) The majority of schools were located in urban areas in the East and Midwest, in part because these offered agencies with the professionally trained staff seen as necessary for field work supervision. The cities were also a source of jobs for graduates. The association viewed development of schools in rural areas as a risky business, particularly because of the lack of field work opportunities in those areas.

Attachment to a model of professional education oriented toward case work hindered expansion of schools and development of public welfare training. Most of the established schools maintained a case work base and added public administration and welfare courses in a piecemeal fashion. These schools generally felt they should train for higher levels in public welfare administration, rather than for the frontline job of welfare case worker. When new schools did try to prepare personnel for all levels of public welfare, as in the case of Wayne State, Michigan State, and other public institutions, the Association of Schools called them "one-sided" and "non-professional" and denied them admission to the organization without major changes. Some educators criticized these programs for failing to see the case work core as the heart of social work education.(3)

Above all, the AASSW, like the AASW, was determined to raise and solidify professional standards. The schools' association had reached a certain critical mass--by 1936, thirty-two schools belonged. Yet the education provided by these schools was uneven. Most still offered training on the under-graduate as well as graduate levels. Courses varied from school to school. There was no standard professional curriculum. Several different types of field work education were employed.

Under the leadership of Breckinridge and others associated with the Chicago School, the AASSW now sought to standardize the course of training and to establish graduate education as the only proper level of professional education for social work. In 1932, the association approved a minimum curriculum to be required of all new schools. One year of courses would have to be on the graduate level. In 1937, the association ruled that schools applying for membership after 1939 would have to have a two-year graduate program.(4) The association made this change largely because of the belief in graduate education as the symbol of professional status in the U.S. Graduate school educators often equated social work education with preparation for medicine or law. They were insulted when their programs were compared to those for nursing or public school teaching.(5)

By the end of the thirties, then, the AASSW had committed itself to the idea of a single graduate professional degree in social work, based on a relatively standardized curriculum. At the same time, the organization was becoming more autonomous. It no longer held its annual meetings in conjunction with the meetings of the AASW, NCSW, and social science organizations. In 1937, the AASSW met independently of these organizations for the first time. In a series of skirmishes between the AASW and the schools' association in the thirties, the professional group argued its responsibility to test the validity of social work training in practice. Yet gradually the AASSW established its primacy in the area of educational standard setting. In 1936, the association began to explore the possibility of becoming an official accrediting body.(6)

A strengthened AASSW's pursuit of the graduate school model for social work education did not mesh well with existing training needs, especially in public welfare. As more and more untrained and inexperienced people went to work in the public social services, undergraduate institutions across the country began to see the possibilities for a more immediate and elementary training than the social work graduate schools were prepared to offer. Courses in social welfare, history, public welfare administration, and even social work methods began appearing in these institutions, particularly in schools located in rural areas of the Midwest, Far West, and South. These areas were those least well served by graduate schools of social work. The need for local training of public welfare workers fit well with the regional service mission of many state universities and land grant colleges. A number of these institutions began to develop undergraduate programs to furnish personnel to state social welfare agencies.

Most often, undergraduate social work training began in departments of sociology. Both sociologists and social workers taught the courses. The location of undergraduate training in sociology departments added to tensions between the graduate school establishment and undergraduate programs. Social work educators had long been ambivalent in their dealings with sociologists, recognizing some mutual goals and theoretical backgrounds, but fearing domination by the academic discipline. Many graduate schools resented continued control by the sociology departments from which they had developed. Several schools of social work still had sociologists as deans, and some sociology departments still fought to keep their social work programs from advancing to the graduate level.(7)

Despite these tensions, undergraduate programs were willing to seek direction from the AASSW. Yet at first the association responded minimally to the needs of colleges and state universities and their requests for help. When a state school whose program was unable to meet AASSW requirements publicized its complaints, the association did establish a committee to study the problems of state universities attempting to achieve AASSW approval.(8) The committee was composed of people from state university-affiliated schools which already belonged to the AASSW. While the group reported some concerns on the part of such schools, it noted that they believed "it would be suicidal to [withdraw from the association]." The fact that this was an in-house committee suggests the limits of the AASSW's concern about the needs of developing programs not yet eligible for membership. In fact, in the period 1936-41, discouragement of developing programs received more attention from the Executive Committee than the encouragement of new endeavors.(9)

State universities at least had the potential to build graduate programs and seek AASSW membership. Land grant and other colleges were generally restricted to undergraduate training. If they characterized such training as "professional," they ran into difficulty with the AASSW. More and more, the association was coming to define undergraduate social work education as preprofessional preparation for the graduate curriculum. In 1936, the association's Curriculum Committee studied the matter of appropriate prerequisites for admission to schools of social work. The committee supported the existing AASSW philosophy that such prerequisites should be broadly defined, such as "20 hours in the social sciences."(10) This committee and others stressed that technical professional training should not be given to undergraduates. Instead,

undergraduate institutions should offer background courses in
the social and behavioral sciences, the history of social welfare, and the field of social work. Under no circumstances
should schools offer field training or courses in case work
skills.(11)

The goals and problems of undergraduate institutions, and
the position of the AASSW, are graphically expressed in an
exchange of letters between Breckinridge and W. Kumlien, a professor of rural sociology at South Dakota State College of Agri-
culture and Mechanical Arts. In 1935, Kumlien wrote
Breckinridge, then President of the AASSW, requesting her
advice regarding an undergraduate social work program being
developed by his department. The program would concentrate on
training rural social workers. Kumlien explained:

Our interest . . . in undertaking such a project has arisen
largely from the fact that the Midwestern rural states have
great difficulty in attracting and keeping professionally
trained social workers who understand rural problems . . . we
see no way of remedying the situation except to tackle the problem from the grassroots and try to build up at least one school
in each state that can train farm-reared people.

The proposed program had been carefully thought out. It
included courses offered by rural sociology and other social
science departments. For its professional component it would
employ a trained social worker from the state welfare commission. The social worker would teach case work courses and
supervise trainees placed in public welfare departments.
Kumlien reported that a number of rural sociology departments
at land grant colleges were considering similar programs. He
suggested a joint conference with the AASSW to work out the
terms of a plan for rural states.(12)

Breckinridge's reply (four months later) was regretful but
firm. "Writing you isn't very easy," she explained. She
argued that rural social work was "no more to be taught in rural
communities than rural medicine or rural law." Practice in
rural areas demanded a wide range of skills and knowledge, best
taught in an urban setting, with some additional information on
rural culture. Voicing the long-term distrust of sociologists
felt by the SSSA and other social work faculty, she added:

The sociologist has much to give in the general effort at social
reform, but the disastrous effects of having schools of social
work developed during the World War as subdivisions of departments of sociology has never been overcome, and the [AASSW] is
only now emerging into a state of professional competence. . . .
In order to be admitted to the Association now a school must be
an independent, separate entity.

Regretting that what she had to say was "so ungracious,"
Breckinridge rejected South Dakota State's entire plan.(13)
Essentially, Breckinridge was arguing that professionalism
depended on educational autonomy and on the dominance of urban
graduate schools with a particular set of standards. Her position was reflected in AASSW philosophy. As Breckinridge

explained, the attitude of the association "might be described as believing thoroughly in birth control," keeping institutions out in order to be assured of graduate quality in social work education.(14)   To adhere to this philosophy, schools like the George Warren Brown School of Social Work in St. Louis dropped their undergraduate programs outright and concentrated on graduate training.(15)

Nongraduate, less autonomous programs, especially in rural areas, posed a threat to the high standards model of professionalism in social work.   Pursuance of this model often meant refusal on the part of the graduate school people to tackle the issue of how best to educate rural and public welfare social workers.

In the undergraduate-graduate debate, the AASW generally reinforced the AASSW's position. Professional education was a major part of the professional organization's definition of a bona fide social worker. In accepting courses taken by applicants in nonmember schools, the AASW did recognize the limited availability of training in AASSW-approved schools. The AASW Committee on Technical Requirements, chaired by Gordon Hamilton, felt it should offer support to developing programs. Yet the committee was reluctant to approve of programs "whose primary objective is to meet public social work demands." Such programs, Hamilton felt, could be "forced to make compromises which seriously affect the development of integrated professional education."(16)

In addition, the U.S. Children's Bureau strongly supported graduate-level professional training. The Bureau of Public Assistance took a more flexible stand. Its needs for personnel were much greater than those of the more selective Children's Bureau.   Jane Hoey saw a role for colleges and universities in the education of public social service workers. Undergraduate curricula could include courses on current economic and social problems, and some special programs might even offer field work in social agencies. Hoey urged that the Social Security Board confer with college and university presidents, deans of schools of economics, political science, and sociology, and representatives of the AASSW, in order to plan future training for professional and technical positions in the social insurances and public welfare.(17)   In the late thirties, representatives of the BPA consulted with the Association of Land Grant Colleges, the National Association of State Universities, and individual institutions regarding training plans.(18)   Yet the BPA, and Hoey herself, did not give unqualified support to professional education on the undergraduate level. Hoey's ideal for social work education remained the graduate school model developed by the AASSW. Nevertheless, she and her organization were willing to discuss the possibilities of a variety of kinds of training: in-service programs, institutes, undergraduate courses, and graduate education.

Many groups--the federal departments, state social service agencies, the AASSW, the AASW, college and university administrators, and academic sociologists--felt they had a stake in social work education in the late thirties. No one organization was in charge of educational planning. New programs, particularly on the undergraduate level, wondered where

to turn for advice or formal approval. Two attempts at leadership in social work and public welfare education emerged from
this vacuum. The first was short-lived, but was a warning of
the more successful challenge to the AASSW to follow.

In 1938, the president of the University of Oklahoma, W. B.
Bizzell, sent a memo to forty state universities which did not
belong to the AASSW. The memo criticized the philosophy of the
association and suggested the organization of a new accrediting
group. Bizzell was then president of the National Association
of State Universities. He was joined in his protest by J. J.
Rhyne, head of the university's Department of Sociology.
Rhyne's department administered a one-year graduate program in
social work that had had repeated difficulty in getting
accepted to AASSW membership.(19) Rhyne and Bizzell suggested
seven reasons for establishing an independent organization.

1. The AASSW program was not adaptable to many educational
institutions outside of the very large ones.
2. The association reflected the goals and structure of
privately endowed schools of social work.
3. The association did not sufficiently recognize rural needs.
4. Social workers in the public welfare services were paid
with public funds, so universities with state support should be
allowed to train them for these positions.
5. The AASSW was "an autocratic organization dominated by the
thinking of two or three schools" and concerned with "maintaining its own positions at the expense of the needs of the field."
6. Members of teaching faculties in AASSW schools lacked cred-
itable academic ratings in terms of higher degrees.
7. A too-rigid curriculum was imposed on member schools.(20)

This catalogue of AASSW sins was not unique to Bizzell and
Rhyne. Other universities and land grant colleges had begun
openly to criticize the Association of Schools.(21) As one
sociologist in a social work program noted, "The fat is in the
fire . . . the recent protest of W. B. Bizzell . . . has kindled
a long smoldering issue. . . . AASSW standards were set up
largely without the active collaboration of the responsible
administrative heads of the colleges and universities affected
by them."(22)

The activities of the state universities and land grant
colleges led to alarm in AASSW circles. Rumors flew that a
rival accrediting organization was in the making. Association
officers were concerned that "public officials are critical of
the Association."(23) In addition, the BPA and the American
Public Welfare Association had become more vocal in their concerns over training needs. The president of the AASSW, Wilbur
Newstetter, warned that the organization was "in the most critical position in its history."(24)

The AASSW responded to the crisis in three ways. First,
the organization set up an Advisory Committee on State
Universities and Membership Requirements, consisting largely
of representatives from member schools in state universities.
Newstetter suggested to the land grant college and state
university group leaders that their organizations appoint a
committee to meet with the association committee. A Joint Com-

mittee on Accrediting, chaired by John Tigert, was subsequently
established. This group represented the majority of colleges
and universities in the country. Its creation was a response
in part to the desire of institutions of higher education to
keep accreditation in general from leading to "excessive external control."(25)

The two committees held several joint meetings, consisting
largely of conciliatory efforts by the association to respond
to the state university grievances. While refusing to consider
the notion of professional training on the undergraduate level,
the association indicated willingness to explore a special membership for schools with a one-year graduate program.(26)

A second approach to the Bizzell challenge was that time-
honored mechanism: a study. In February, 1938, the AASSW
received funding from the Rockefeller Foundation for research
in the area of professional education for the public social services. Newstetter publicized the grant as confirmation of "our
own recognition of the responsibilities of the association for
the public social services."(27) Care was taken to establish a
study advisory committee with representatives from the state
universities, federal and state agencies, and public welfare
organizations, although no land grant colleges appear to have
been represented.(28)

Finally, the AASSW launched a field consultation service
for developing schools. This service was to become a major
weapon in the association's fight against the undergraduate
training movement. Marion Hathway, a protégée of Abbott and
Breckinridge, had just become full-time executive secretary of
the AASSW.(29) In 1938, she toured a number of western
universities and discovered "a revolt against all accrediting
groups."(30) Nevertheless, the state universities seemed anxious to achieve and maintain AASSW membership status. Hathway
noted their fear "of what the land grant colleges are about to
do in undergraduate education." Recognizing this common
ground--a commitment to graduate-level professional training--
Hathway offered suggestions to the state universities regarding
development of their social work programs.(31)

Reporting back to her Executive Committee, Hathway suggested that the AASSW establish a membership category for
schools offering a one-year graduate curriculum. On her recommendation, Bizzell's University of Oklahoma was accepted on a
provisional basis. Hathway reiterated that the undergraduate
colleges should be guided toward building a preprofessional
rather than a technical social work curriculum.(32)

Faced with the state universities' challenge, the AASSW
responded in a conciliatory manner, but with an eye toward co-
opting its critics. Its special membership category for one-
year graduate schools had the blessings of the APWA, the federal
welfare agencies, and the Joint Committee on Accrediting of the
State Universities and Land Grant Colleges. Eventually, seven
state universities, including Oklahoma, took advantage of the
new membership opportunity.(33)

The one-year graduate school compromise quieted the state
university protest but left many land grant colleges and other
undergraduate institutions out in the cold. It was much more
difficult, philosophically, for the AASSW to respond to their

demands than to those of the universities. Shortening the graduate preparation of some social workers was one thing; accepting the legitimacy of professional preparation on the undergraduate level was another. In its final report on the Rockefeller-sponsored study, published in 1942, the association clung to a belief in advanced education as the cornerstone of professional status.

The study used interviews with federal, state, and local officials and a survey of course offerings by schools of social work "to analyze the training needs of the social services established or expanded under the Social Security Act and to evaluate the role of the schools of social work in the preparation of personnel for these services."(34) The final report, Education for the Public Social Services, bore the imprint of Abbott and Breckinridge in its approach to the public social services. The report characterized these services as a matter of human need as well as right. These were professional services, as distinguished from the "over-the-counter administration of doles." They demanded special insight and understanding of individuals in their environments, an understanding best attained through graduate professional preparation for the field of social work. Thus a major recommendation of the study was that jobs in the public services be filled by graduate-trained social workers. When such social workers could not be found, college graduates with social science preparation should be utilized. Rejecting other suggestions for the training of public service workers, the report insisted that no consideration be given to establishment of professional training on the undergraduate level.(35)

The AASSW was unwilling to sacrifice the graduate school standard in an attempt to meet public service training needs. Yet the one-year graduate school compromise did not generate enough new programs to meet those needs. Undergraduate institutions continued to develop professional training courses. With no hope of acceptance by the AASSW, a number of these programs joined forces at the 1942 Southwestern Social Science Meetings in Dallas. Here the "seven deadly sins" of the AASSW were again enumerated. Within six months, the National Association of Schools of Social Administration had emerged. Its charter members included social work programs in land grant colleges, private colleges, and state universities. Southern and southwestern institutions formed the nucleus, but the group included schools from all over the U.S.(36)

The new organization was in part the brainchild of Austin Porterfield. Porterfield was a sociologist at Texas Christian University in Fort Worth. He had been in contact with J. J. Rhyne and faculty of other institutions regarding the problems of non-AASSW member programs. Porterfield criticized the AASSW for its attempt to pattern social work education after medical schools and for its lack of attention to regional needs. He noted that thirty of the forty-eight states had no member schools in the association.(37)

When the NASSA was officially formed in September, 1942, Porterfield was chosen its first president. J. J. Rhyne became the group's secretary. Founders of the NASSA deliberately chose a loose, informal structure. They sought to keep the

association as democratic as possible. They charged no membership fee, and deferred "until a later time" any stipulation of
curriculum content or faculty qualifications for member
schools.(38) All this was in marked contrast to the formal
structure and standard-setting mission of the AASSW.

The philosophy of the NASSA closely mirrored the earlier
arguments of Bizzell and Rhyne. The new organization noted the
severe lack of trained personnel for the public social services. It argued that "the graduate schools of social work
have never met more than a fraction of the demand for fully
qualified workers."(39) These schools trained 4,000 to 5,000
students a year; public services employed 40,000 to 50,000
workers. While several years of advanced training might be
desirable, it was at the moment impractical.

The NASSA argued that social work training must be brought
within the reach of workers in all parts of the country. In
addition, training programs should be sensitive to regional
social service needs. The present situation called for practical, basic, and localized training. Standards could be
raised once the emergency was past. A sensible solution was
development of undergraduate social work training in
educational institutions across the country.

The NASSA struck a responsive chord with its promotion of
undergraduate social work education. The state universities
and land grant colleges' Joint Committee on Accrediting
strongly supported the new organization.(40) By December,
1942, twenty colleges and universities had joined. Word of the
new association began to reach AASSW and graduate school circles. AASSW members soon realized that the issues raised by
the state university challenge had not really been dealt with--
or smoothed over--as previously thought. The director of the
social work program at the University of Denver warned a colleague of the threat to social work education represented by
formation of the NASSA. "I think we have made a mistake in not
prescribing more of an undergraduate curriculum. Theirs
sounds very good."(41)

Others agreed that the AASSW had not dealt realistically
or effectively with the state university protest and social
service training needs. Stuart Chapin was a sociologist who
had headed the AASSW's Advisory Committee on State Universities
and Membership Requirements. He wrote Gordon Hamilton, now
president of the association, of his disturbance over the creation of the NASSA. "Some years ago," Chapin noted, "we were
able to deflect this trend" toward a new organization. But
now, due to AASSW neglect and the rising interest of powerful
state institutions, social work's control over professional
training was being challenged.

Chapin saw the danger of a rival accrediting organization,
backed by impressive educational forces. He warned:

The support for the new association stems from the most powerful
. . . combine of institutions of higher education in the country. This combine is 'big politics' educationally speaking,
and quite apart from its threat to established . . . standards
of professional education for social work, it is likely that
many member schools of the AASSW may be forced to join the new

Association _also_ as a measure of self-preservation.(42)

At first, however, the AASSW avoided confrontation, or even direct contact, with the new group. Watchful of the undergraduate movement, the association continued its program of consultation regarding preprofessional education, encouraging undergraduate curricula which would prepare students for graduate schools. The association did soften its stand to recognize the role of a "planned four year [undergraduate] curriculum" in providing personnel "which would be more immediately useful to an agency." But the group refused to accept skills training on the undergraduate level.(43)

Various forces conspired to bring the NASSA and the AASSW into more open conflict. The University of Oklahoma and other schools began to announce their intention to withdraw from the AASSW.(44) The Joint Committee on Accrediting, frustrated with the AASSW's lack of movement, formally recognized the NASSA as an accrediting body in December, 1943. This meant there were now two accrediting groups in social work. The chairman of the Joint Committee, John Tigert, persuaded Katharine Lenroot to call a conference of interested parties in Washington to discuss NASSA/AASSW relationships and education for the public social services. Alarmed, the AASSW began a series of attempts to deal more directly with the NASSA and the threat it posed.(45)

AASSW and NASSA relationships over the next several years were marked by mutual suspicion, co-optation, and occasional open hostility, interspersed with periods of negotiation and compromise. No less than three committees grappled with the question of who would control education in social work. Powerful and interested "outsiders"--the federal agencies, the Joint Committee on Accrediting, college and university administrators, and public welfare groups--added their weight as partisan supporters or mediators. The period ended with formation of a new social work accrediting organization, the Council on Social Work Education, in 1952. Yet its creation did not mean final resolution of the conflict over levels of training. Underlying this conflict were crucial questions about the nature of professionalism and the respective roles of higher education and professions in meeting national manpower needs.

The first official contact between NASSA and AASSW representatives was the 1944 conference called by Tigert and Lenroot. This was attended by representatives of the two school associations, universities and colleges, and several federal departments. A major outcome was the formation of a Continuation Committee to study problems related to undergraduate social work and training for public welfare. The Continuation Committee included delegates from the Joint Committee on Accrediting and the Children's Bureau. It was cochaired by Anne Fenlason of the AASSW and Ernest Harper of the NASSA.(46)

Ernest Harper headed the NASSA from 1945 to 1947. A sociologist, he chaired the social work program at Michigan State. One contemporary has described him as an articulate and "peppery" man who made good use of his background in community organization. He was an active proponent of undergraduate training for the public social services and a moving spirit in the undergraduate group throughout the forties.(47)

The Continuation Committee's one and only meeting served to clarify positions and "claims to turf." The NASSA and the state universities sought formal recognition of undergraduate training and the granting of an M.A. at the end of the first graduate year of social work. The AASSW was willing to compromise on a fifth-year M.A., if the actual professional degree could be retained for completion of the two-year graduate program, over which the association had accrediting powers. The task of certification of fifth-year M.A. degrees could perhaps be shared with the NASSA.(48) In the area of undergraduate education, the AASSW sought ongoing control over course content.

With positions clarified, but not reconciled, the committee set up another, more permanent group, the Joint Committee on Education for Social Work. This group was restricted to the two school associations and was authorized by both organizations at joint annual meetings in 1945. At the same meetings, both organizations recognized a B.A. in social work.(49)

The decision to hold joint meetings was one sign of the serious attention being paid to working out a solution to the split within the field. Pressures from federal departments and educational interests added to the sense of urgency. A relatively neutral outside organization, the Russell Sage Foundation, supplied the new committee's chairwoman, Esther Brown. Brown could be a mediator between two opposing groups.

The Joint Committee on Education took its mission of negotiation and cooperation seriously. The group produced a set of mutually agreed-upon recommendations which established a system of accommodation between the two organizations. Yet as often happens in peacemaking efforts, the parent organizations themselves took a harder line than their negotiators. In this case, the hard line came primarily from the AASSW, which refused to accept the advice of its own representatives on the Joint Committee.(50)

The Joint Committee presented eight recommendations to the AASSW and the NASSA. These included proposals for a comprehensive study of social work education and for development of a broadly constituted commission or council on social work education. The two existing educational associations could merge into this new organization, which would assume responsibility for all accrediting in the field of social work. In the meantime, the committee recommended that the two associations divide accrediting between them, with the NASSA accrediting B.A. and one-year M.A. schools, and the AASSW reviewing six-year M.S.W. schools. In addition, the committee recommended an Interim Committee on Social Work Education, with a broader membership than the present group. This committee would pave the way for a national council.(51)

The NASSA approved all eight of the Joint Committee's recommendations. The AASSW Board of Directors, after much debate, passed only three--the suggestions for a study of social work education, a national council, and an interim committee to plan for these developments. The proposition which aroused the greatest argument was that suggesting a temporary division of the accrediting field. This the AASSW Board of Directors refused to approve. Board members balked at accepting the NASSA as an equal in educational standard-setting. Even in agreeing to the idea of a new commission on social work education, AASSW leaders saw the Association of Schools as the dominant member of that commission.(52)

NASSA officers were dismayed by the AASSW board's actions. The undergraduate organization had increasingly come to favor a cooperative arrangement with the Association of Schools. In part, this stemmed from the realization that the NASSA was not strong enough, financially or organizationally, to maintain an autonomous accrediting role. In 1946, the group had thirty-two members out of a possible ninety schools.(53) Graduate education was better established and the AASSW commanded greater resources. Now, the AASSW decision threatened joint efforts. Harper wrote a colleague, "This action means that all the work of the Joint Committee has been lost and we are right back where we were in the fall of '44." Referring to the proposed Interim Committee, Harper quipped, "One committee follows another like the numbers on . . . a wheel of fortune."(54)

The Joint Committee on Accrediting was equally perturbed. The committee attributed the setback to AASSW stalling. Tigert wrote Harper that the AASSW action would probably mean the land grant colleges and state universities would cast their lot with the NASSA and in the future "recommend that our members work with that organization and have no relations with the AASSW.(55)

A variety of groups--the AASSW, the Joint Committee on Accrediting, the federal agencies--had hoped for cooperation among the various interests in social work education. Yet achieving such cooperation was proving a difficult task. Important barriers kept the NASSA and AASSW apart. The two associations differed in educational philosophy, attitudes toward professionalism, and degree of commitment to public welfare. The problem was in a sense one of different constituencies with different goals. The AASSW responded largely to a set of demands internal to a profession: the need to develop autonomy, raise standards, and strengthen the profession's educational base. The NASSA responded primarily to external forces: the demands of the institutions of higher education and social welfare, and those of the public at large.

The AASSW reflected the profession's desire for recognition and autonomy in its attempts to control the entire system of social work education. Like the AASW, the AASSW saw standard-building as serving a dual purpose. Higher standards would help win public respect for the profession and would weed out elements threatening the association's control. AASSW members heeded the message of profession-builders like Abbott, Breckinridge, and Hamilton. They believed the main function of the association to be "development of standards of professional education." This education was the symbol of professional competence, intended to convey to the public that social work demanded distinctive knowledge and skills acquired only through specialized training.(56)

To justify extending influence over the developing undergraduate programs, the AASSW spoke of education for social work as a continuous and connected process. Undergraduate social work training should not be seen as a separate and independent entity. Rather, it was one part of a system planned and guided by the social work education establishment. Graduate school educators were particularly concerned to keep undergraduate sociology departments from usurping the guidance role. This led, unfortunately, to some disparagement of the importance of sociological content in social work education.

In trying to influence undergraduate developments, AASSW members were in a peculiar position. Their belief that graduate education was a prerequisite for professional status meant they could not sanction "professional" education at the undergraduate level. Yet undergraduate programs existed. The AASSW thus had the difficult task of acknowledging and bringing undergraduate programs within its sphere of influence, while preventing them from expanding in size or function. Their solution was to devise a limited role for undergraduate social work, a role which greatly reduced the possibility of the profession's involvement in training for the public social services.

The NASSA faced a different set of constituencies and priorities. The presence of sociologists in undergraduate social work programs helped create an emphasis on the social sciences, particularly sociology, in undergraduate training. The NASSA emphasized the careful integration of social science and social work courses in the undergraduate curriculum. This was in contrast to the AASSW, which did not specify any particular pattern to the social science courses taken in preprofessional education.(57)

State welfare departments also influenced the NASSA. They put pressure on public educational institutions to provide brief, accessible social service training. Harper, for example, recalls the influence of the state welfare department on the Michigan State program.(58) Direct alliances between NASSA member programs and state welfare agencies were not common. Yet in states like Arkansas, Michigan, and Kentucky, the welfare system began to recognize undergraduate social work training in job requirements.

Social work practitioners and educators in southern and western rural regions joined in the push for localized public welfare training on the undergraduate level. Such workers saw the AASSW and its goals as an obstacle in meeting training needs.

In response to those needs, the NASSA proposed "establishment of a hierarchy of training levels to match the requirements of various job levels, from beginning public assistance positions, to the most highly specialized forms of social work." The group did not wish to train mere technicians, and sought instead to provide students with an introduction to major social work skills, applicable to local public welfare jobs.(59)

The demand for regional training created something of a dilemma for the NASSA. Programs which were "regionally appropriate" might be quite different from one another. How could the NASSA build itself as a nationally recognized accrediting body if there were no common standards among members? Although the NASSA adopted a minimum set of educational standards in

1945, and tightened these somewhat in 1948, this was not enough
to dispel AASSW criticism of the group's lack of educational
leadership.(60) Had the NASSA been a stronger group, with more
direct public welfare department backing, it might have developed a broad-scale, more uniform training system for the public
social services. Such a system would have promoted a generic
training drawing on the social sciences as well as social work
knowledge and skills.

The differences in the two organizations' approaches led
to the late forties impasse and to an outburst of mutual suspicion and hostility. One AASSW member spoke of "the mediocre
quality of thinking within the [NASSA] group."(61) Harper in
turn characterized an AASSW official as "unsympathetic,
domineering, and inclined to railroad things through [joint
committees]."(62) Mattie Cal Maxted, a social worker at the
University of Arkansas and one of the founders of the NASSA,
complained that AASSW leaders had "never had an original idea in
their lives."(63)

Maxted, Harper, and other NASSA officers saw the Association of Schools as unsympathetic to public welfare training
needs and eager to control social work education. They felt
the group was not to be trusted. Their suspicions were not
unfounded. The AASSW made covert but deliberate attempts to
woo NASSA member schools, particularly state universities, into
the association's ranks. The president of the AASSW, Ben
Youngdahl, suggested to the executive secretary that she make
"an oblique suggestion [to Harper] to make application in our
association." Dissidents like J. J. Rhyne were carefully
courted. Sue Spencer, the executive secretary, assured
Youngdahl that if they could get the membership of Harper's
school and Florida State University "we will have succeeded in
taking a major part of the leadership of the NASSA."(64) When
Florida State switched its allegiance from NASSA to AASSW,
Harper complained "they are 'biting off' each of our larger and
better institutions one by one." The AASSW even tried to block
a NASSA advertisement from appearing in Survey Midmonthly.(65)

Another tactic of the AASSW had been the creation of the
preprofessional social work education consultation service,
under a paid staff member, in 1945. Over the next few years,
the consultant visited a large number of institutions, caution-
ing them against developing "technical training" programs and
urging them to follow the AASSW model of preprofessional social
work education. The AASSW sponsored meetings and conferences
on the same theme. New schools now often turned to the more
established AASSW for advice. Maxted grudgingly characterized
the consultation service as "a master stroke" on the association's part.(66)

In carrying out these activities, the AASSW acted on a deep
fear of the potential of the undergraduate movement to weaken
the profession. Graduate school educators worried about the
issue of lower standards in NASSA schools. On a more visceral
level, they were threatened by the presence of dissidents in
their midst--"malcontents" who might rouse and unite other
groups dissatisfied with the AASSW's approach.(67)

As the battle intensified, the NASSA used its influence on
the Joint Committee on Accrediting. Partly in response to

NASSA lobbying, the Joint committee made an ominous announce-
ment in November, 1947. Either the two school associations
would settle their differences in two months, or the committee
would declare a moratorium on all accrediting in the field of
social work.(68)
     It was obvious to all concerned that the dual accrediting
system could not continue. The NASSA president, now T. W. Cape
of North Dakota, conferred with Sue Spencer and proposed an
interim joint accrediting plan and eventual merger. The Board
of Directors of the AASSW rejected his proposals.(69) Yet
while the battle continued, the third committee set up to deal
with the problems in social work education gradually made headway toward a resolution. The proposal of an Interim Committee
had been one of the few Joint Committee recommendations
approved by the AASSW. Its membership included both school
organizations, the federal welfare agencies, and the APWA.
Broader committee membership increased the pressure on the two
school associations to compromise.
     The major mechanism used to combat the impasse was, once
again, a comprehensive study of social work education. The
Interim Committee obtained funding from the Carnegie Foundation
for a study to re-examine "the provision and distribution of
educational facilities in relation to present . . . demand for
social service personnel."(70) A study planning committee was
established under Kenneth Pray of the Pennsylvania School of
Social Work. Its members included Harper, Jane Hoey, and
Harriett Bartlett, a respected spokeswoman for social work
practitioners.(71)
     The committee decided early on to seek an outside educa-
tional expert to direct the study. The Carnegie Foundation was
pushing such a move, and committee members felt the Joint Committee on Accrediting would give more credence to a non-social
work evaluation. NASSA representatives hoped an outsider
would be sympathetic to their critique of the social work educational establishment.(72)
     The committee selected Ernest V. Hollis, of the U.S.
Office of Education, to head the study. To balance the team,
they chose social work practitioner and educator Alice Taylor
as his assistant. The two proposed a study which would draw on
reviews of existing material compiled by social work organizations, consultation with individuals in education and practice,
and regional meetings with representatives of educational
institutions and agencies. They aimed to examine social work
employment needs and the programs of training offered by graduate and undergraduate schools to meet those needs. Hollis
hoped the study would "result in the formulation of . . . general principles on which programs of social work education . . .
can be based."(73)
     Both the AASSW and the NASSA had high expectations of the
study's outcome. Harper was enthusiastic about the choice of
Hollis. He viewed him as a "safe" person who would not be
biased against the NASSA point of view.(74) The funding
proposal for the study had emphasized the need to assess educational responses to social service manpower needs. Yet it was
clear that the project had a more important coordinating and
peacemaking function:

The development of a comprehensive structure within which the accrediting bodies, schools of social work, practitioner organizations, and employing agencies could achieve a working agreement on what constitutes acceptable programs of social work education.(75)

Given the divergence in the field, that objective was a very tall order.

As might be expected, Hollis and Taylor were unable to satisfy all demands. To the NASSA's dismay, the completed study did not support the concept of undergraduate social work education as professional training. The report reaffirmed graduate school as the only professional level. Undergraduate training might eventually be used to prepare students for semiprofessional practice, if criteria for such practice could be established. One reason for the graduate school stress was that Hollis and Taylor did not carry out a systematic survey of public welfare needs. Such a survey might have influenced the researchers to suggest undergraduate education as a useful training measure. In addition, AASSW members of the Interim Committee put pressure on Hollis not to legitimize undergraduate training for social work practice.(76)

Hollis did urge the profession to strengthen its undergraduate foundation. He suggested that social work follow the medical model and build a mandatory undergraduate base for further graduate education. This recommendation angered AASSW members, who argued that undergraduate social work programs were not necessarily superior to general preparation in the social sciences.(77)

Hollis and Taylor supported a part of the NASSA philosophy when they recommended the broadening of the concept of social worker to include social welfare personnel. Schools of social work should train people for work in "the social insurances" and public health, as well as in the private agencies. The report noted that "faculty preoccupation with social work education shaped to the needs of private . . . agencies has . . . hindered adoption into the curriculum of new ideas and philosophies of social welfare." It suggested that schools change their emphasis from case work to generic social work. This vision was a broad one. Social work students were to be given a solid generic base, to equip them for practice in a variety of settings. The vision rankled some graduate educators, who felt that a generic approach ignored social work's case work core.(78)

Despite the objections of various factions, the Hollis and Taylor report was accepted by the study committee. Social Work Education in the U.S. was published to a mixed reception in 1951.

While the Hollis and Taylor study was being completed, the Interim Committee continued to work toward a new educational association. The development of a broad council on social work education had been part of the committee's original charge. To move toward such an organization, the committee reconstituted itself as the National Council on Social Work Education, under the chairmanship of the president of the American Association

of Social Workers. The NCSWE was composed of five representatives each from AASSW, NASSA, AASW, and public services,
and one each from the specialized professional groups, Joint
Committee on Accrediting, Association of American
Universities, Association of American Colleges, and National
Social Welfare Assembly.(79)
     The National Council began to plan for the eventual merger
of educational interests in a single organization. The Hollis
and Taylor study supported such a move. The final report had
characterized social work education as the responsibility of
the total profession, and had promoted creation of a single
educational body representing the variety of social work educational and professional interests.(80)
     Even as the two school associations approached a merger,
tensions between them remained. These were felt within the
NCSWE, which conceded that

if the interest of the undergraduate schools is to be maintained
and financial help . . . is to be sought from them, arrangements
will have to be made for membership status and for representation.

But the group hoped to achieve this "without the interference of
approval or accreditation" for undergraduate programs.(81)
     The Council on Social Work Education was formally estab-
lished in 1952. Its purpose was to promote development of
social work education through accreditation, consultation,
research, and publications. The NASSA and AASSW agreed to
renounce their separate identities and merge into a single
accrediting and policy-setting body. The new organization had
a broad membership structure, designed to represent the interests of the two educational associations, practitioner groups,
employing agencies, higher education, the social sciences, and
the general public.(82) Yet within that structure, there was
an unequal balance between AASSW and NASSA concerns. Although
granted some status through an Undergraduate Division within
the council, former NASSA undergraduate programs took a back
seat to graduate school interests. There were ten undergraduate representatives to twenty graduate representatives on the
CSWE governing council. These representatives had to come from
"integrated" undergraduate programs offering courses "intro-
ductory to professional social work." NASSA officials had to
fight for representation on the Commission on Accreditation,
the certifying arm of the CSWE.(83)
     In large measure, the NASSA had simply not been strong
enough to counteract the profession's stress on graduate professional education. Though it had some powerful supporters,
the organization failed to gain the backing of important federal welfare programs. In 1947, Harper wrote of the Children's
Bureau as "still our worst 'enemy.'"(84) The bureau specified
AASSW credits for child welfare workers in state departments.
The Bureau of Public Assistance recognized the usefulness of
undergraduate courses but backed the Hollis-Taylor report's
reaffirmation of graduate education as the correct level for
professional training. The AASSW lobbied successfully with
these agencies to get specific requirements for AASSW training

into certain federal job requirements.(85)

On the state and local levels, public welfare was new and diverse in its goals. It lacked the resources and singleness of purpose to develop and support a comprehensive system of social service training. The public welfare departments of individual states worked with undergraduate social work programs, but the APWA was unable to provide consistent backing to the NASSA cause.(86)

NASSA strength was further sapped from within the profession. The Association of Schools made some accommodation but often fought the undergraduate movement vigorously behind the scenes. Due in part to AASSW lobbying, the Hollis and Taylor study supported graduate education as the basis for professional status. The AASSW stole the NASSA's thunder through consultation services to new programs and increased acknowledgement of the importance of preprofessional training. The organization waged a successful campaign with a number of public institutions, persuading them to accept the AASSW model of social work education. Harper noted, "This 'counter-reformation' on the part of the AASSW has resulted in attaining many of our original objectives, but has also weakened the position of the NASSA."(87)

For the time, at least, the needs of profession-building had won out. Social workers were already ambivalent about the profession's role in public policy. This ambivalence, combined with a stress on selective educational standards as a symbol of professionalism, blocked undergraduate program growth and thus impeded participation in the development of the public social services.

Although the graduate school establishment now had to pay greater attention to generic training and to undergraduate social work programs, the NASSA effort to achieve autonomy for such programs had been derailed. As late as 1963, a skit by graduate educators at the annual CSWE meeting proclaimed "NASSA's in the Cold, Cold Ground."(88) Using tactics of co-optation, lobbying, and negotiation, the Association of Schools countered the attempts of public welfare departments and institutions of higher education to shape manpower training programs in the social services. Yet the issues raised by these external forces, as filtered through the NASSA, were not conclusively resolved by formation of the CSWE. Momentarily quiescent, the undergraduate social work movement would re-emerge with vigor in the late sixties, when forces external to the profession had become powerful enough to challenge professional dominance over social work education.

Notes

Portions of this material were first published by the Council on Social Work Education in the _Journal of Education for Social Work_, vol. 20, no. 3, Fall, 1984.

1. Ernest B. Harper, "Accomplishments and Aims of the National Association of Schools of Social Administration," p. 4, Paper delivered at National Conference of Social Work, April 1948, Council on Social Work Education Records, Record Group I, Box 15, Social Welfare History Archives, University of Minnesota, Minneapolis, Minn.

2. Mildred Mudgett, Report to the Executive Committee of AASSW, 10/35, p. 4, Grace Browning/Mary Houk Papers, Social Welfare History Archives.

3. Minutes, Committee on Technical Requirements, American Association of Social Workers, 11/19/36, 2/8/37, 12/30/37, National Association of Social Workers Records, folder 54, Social Welfare History Archives.

4. Sue Spencer, "Education for Social Work," _Social Work Year Book_ (1949), pp. 173-83.

5. Letter to author from Mattie Cal Maxted, former officer of the NASSA, 4/26/81; Arlien Johnson, "Implications of Type I and Type II Schools of Social Work," _AASSW Newsletter_, V: 15-16 (January, 1939), CSWE Records, I-13; Edith Abbott, "Backgrounds and Foregrounds in Education for Social Work," 1927 address to the AASW, in Abbott, _Social Welfare and Professional Education_ (Chicago: University of Chicago Press, 1942), p. 40.

6. Minutes, Executive Committee, American Association of Schools of Social Work, 3/22-23/41, CSWE Records, I-4; Preliminary Proposal for a Study of Professional Education, Division on Personnel Standards, 4/16/37, NASW Records, folder 63; Minutes, Subcommittee on Technical Requirements, AASW, 5/22/39, NASW Records, folder 54.

7. Mildred Mudgett, "The Four Seasons" (Unpublished autobiography, Mildred Mudgett Papers, Social Welfare History Archives), p. 234; letter from Arlien Johnson to Marion Hathway, 9/10/39, Marion Hathway Papers, folder 9, Social Welfare History Archives.

8. Roy Brown, "Education for Public Welfare and Social Workers: From the Point of View of the State University," _Social Forces_, XVIII: 65-70 (October, 1939); Minutes, Executive Committee, AASSW, 5/26-27/36, CSWE Records, I-4. The school in question, the School of Public Welfare at the University of North Carolina, was the first school of social work to give primary emphasis to public welfare. Its dean was sociologist Howard Odum.

9.   Minutes, Executive Committee, AASSW, 5/23/37; "Notes on Admission Policies Compiled from Minutes of the Executive Committee," AASSW, 6/41, CSWE Records, I-4 and II-10.

10.   "The Problem of Pre-Requisites for Admission to Schools of Social Work," Report by Curriculum Committee, AASSW, 5/26/37, NASW Records, folder 63.

11.   Report   of   Sub-Committee   on   Pre-Social   Work Education, 1/17/44, AASSW Ephemera, Social Welfare History Archives.   See also Report of Committee on Pre-Social Work Education, 1/43, AASSW Ephemera; letter from Hathway to John R. Rademaker (an undergraduate educator), 1/8/40, Hathway Papers, folder 9.

12.   Letter from W. Kumlien to Breckinridge, 7/27/35, CSWE Records, I-1.

13.   Letter from Breckinridge to Kumlien, 11/23/35, CSWE Records, I-1.

14.   Letter from Breckinridge to Wayne McMillen, 1/7/36, CSWE Records, I-1.

15.   Barbara   Kohn   and   Janet   Spector,   "Social   Work   at Washington University: A Look Back," Links (George Warren Brown School of Social Work Alumni Association Newsletter, Spring, 1985), p. 5.

16.   Minutes, Committee on Technical Requirements, AASW, 2/8/37 and 12/30/37, NASW Records, folder 54.

17.   Memo,   Hoey   to   Oscar   Powell,   Executive   Director, Social Security Board, 2/27/39, Records of the Social Security Administration,   Record   Group   47,   folder   631.34,   National Archives, Washington, D.C.

18.   "Report   of   the   BPA   on   Assistance   to   States   in Personnel Training Programs," 11/30/38, pp. 52, 72, Records of the Social Security Administration, folder 631.3.   The BPA also consulted with the AASSW and APWA.

19.   "History   of   the   NASSA-AASSW   Joint   Committee, 9/4/46," CSWE Records, I-15; Minutes, Executive Committee, AASSW, 5/20-22/38, CSWE Records, I-4.

20.   "History of the NASSA-AASSW Joint Committee," p. 2.

21.   Minutes, Advisory Committee on State Universities and Membership Requirements, AASSW, 4/23-24/38, Browning/Houk Papers.

22.   Arthur Evans Wood, "The Fat is in the Fire," The Survey, LXXIV: 313-15 (October, 1938).

23.   Minutes, Subcommittee on Technical Requirements,

AASW, 4/13/38, NASW Records, folder 54; Minutes, Advisory Committee on State University and Membership Requirements, AASSW, 4/23-24/38, Browning/Houk Papers.

24. Eastern Regional Conference, AASSW, 5/7-8/38, p. 22; Memo, Newstetter to Heads of Member Schools, AASSW, 3/29/38, Browning/Houk Papers; Minutes, Executive Committee, AASSW, 11/6-7/38, CSWE Records, I-4.

25. "History of the NASSA-AASSW Joint Committee"; Proceedings of the 26th Annual Meeting of the AASSW, 1/25-27/45, CSWE Records, I-6; Charles S. Levy, "Social Work Education and Practice, 1898-1955," (New York: Wurzweiler School of Social Work, Yeshiva University, 1968, mimeo), pp. 86-94.

26. "History of the NASSA-AASSW Joint Committee."

27. Memo, Newstetter to Heads of Member Schools, AASSW, 3/29/38, Browning/Houk Papers.

28. Education for the Public Social Services (New York: AASSW, 1942), Preface.

29. A Chicago SSSA doctoral recipient of the period, interviewed in 1980, indicated that Abbott and Breckinridge were directly responsible for Hathway's appointment to this post.

30. Eastern Regional Conference, AASSW, 5/7-8/38, p. 22, Browning/Houk Papers.

31. Minutes, Subcommittee on Technical Requirements, AASW, 6/9/38, NASW Records, folder 54.

32. Minutes, Executive Committee, AASSW, 5/20-22/38, CSWE Records, I-4; Minutes, Advisory Committee on State Universities and Membership Requirements, AASSW, 4/23-24/38, Browning/Houk Papers.

33. Minutes, Subcommittee on Technical Requirements, AASW, 4/13/38, p. 12, NASW Records, folder 54; Johnson, "Implications of Type I and Type II Schools of Social Work," p. 5.

34. Education for the Public Social Services, p. 11.

35. Ibid., pp. 9-11, 15.

36. Mattie Cal Maxted Papers, folder 2, Social Welfare History Archives.

37. Letter from Porterfield to Maxted, 3/4/42; Porterfield to Rhyne, 3/10/42 and 5/12/42, Maxted Papers, folder 1.

38. Letter from Porterfield to Maxted, 11/4/42, Maxted Papers, folder 1.

39. "The National Association of Schools of Social Administration, 1942-45," 11/15/45, Maxted Papers, folder 6. See also letter from Maxted to Porterfield, 11/17/42, Maxted Papers, folder 1.

40. Ernest B. Harper, "Accomplishments and Aims of the National Association of Schools of Social Administration," pp. 4-5.

41. Letter from Florence Hutsinpillar to Jean P. Sinnock, 5/8/42, Hathway Papers, folder 12.

42. Letter from Chapin to Hamilton, 1/29/44, CSWE Records, I-15.

43. Minutes, Executive Committee Meeting, AASSW, 1/27-29/43 and 7/17-18/43, CSWE Records, I-3.

44. Minutes, Executive Committee, AASSW, 1/27-29/43, CSWE Records, I-3.

45. Minutes, Executive Committee, AASSW, 9/27-28/41, CSWE Records, I-3; Harper, "Accomplishments and Aims of the NASSA," p. 5.

46. Minutes, Board of Directors (formerly Executive Committee), AASSW, 10/27-28/44, CSWE Records, I-3.

47. Interview with Lucille Barber, February 10, 1982.

48. Minutes, Board of Directors, AASSW, 10/27-28/44, p. 8, CSWE Records, I-3.

49. Harper, "Accomplishments and Aims of the NASSA," p. 6.

50. Letter from Esther Brown to Anna King, President of AASSW, 12/31/45, CSWE Records, I-15; letter from Harper to Maxted, 12/5/45, Maxted Papers, folder 6.

51. "Report of the Joint Committee on Accrediting," 12/16-18/46, CSWE Records, I-15.

52. Minutes, Board of Directors, AASSW, 1/23-26/46, CSWE Records, I-3.

53. Harper, "Accomplishments and Aims of the NASSA," p. 6; letter from Maxted to Harper, 6/15/45; Harper to Maxted, 6/23/45, Maxted Papers, folder 6.

54. Letter from Harper to Charles E. Fryley, Iowa State College, 1/30/46, Maxted Papers, folder 7; Letter from Harper to Anna King, 2/7/46, CSWE Records, I-15.

55. "Report of Joint Committee on Accrediting," 4/26-27/46, CSWE Records, I-15; Letter from Tigert to Harper, 2/9/46; Maxted to Harper, 2/12/46, Maxted Papers, folder 7.

56. W. I. Newstetter, Report to Executive Committee, AASSW, 5/40, CSWE Records, I-15.

57. Minutes, Board of Directors, AASSW, 1/23-26/46, CSWE Records, I-3.

58. "Resume of Address by Ernest B. Harper, Director Emeritus," Michigan State University School of Social Work, 5/13/64, mimeo.

59. Harper, "Accomplishments and Aims of the NASSA," p. 10.

60. "The NASSA; 1942-1945" (pamphlet, 1945), Maxted Papers, folder 6; NASSA Constitution and By-Laws, 4/22/44, Revised, 4/48, Maxted Papers, folder 2; letter from Sue Spencer to Ben Youngdahl, 1/5/48, CSWE Records, I-15.

61. Letter from Mereb Mossman to Sue Spencer, 10/14/47, CSWE Records, I-15.

62. Letter from Harper to Maxted, 2/26/46, Maxted Papers, folder 7.

63. Letter from Maxted to Harper, 11/10/44, Maxted Papers, folder 6.

64. Letter from Maxted to Harper, 6/15/45; Harper to Maxted, 6/23/45, Maxted Papers, folder 6; Youngdahl to Spencer, 7/18/47; Spencer to Youngdahl, 9/10/47, CSWE Records, I-15. Florida State was the home of one of the NASSA officers.

65. Harper to Coyle Moore, 1/10/48, Maxted Papers, folder 9; Youngdahl to Bradley Buell, Editor of The Survey, 7/18/47, CSWE Records, I-15.

66. Letter from Maxted to Harper, 6/15/45, Maxted Papers, folder 6; "Report on Activities of Pre-professional Consultant," 1/5/48-4/1/48, Maxted Papers, folder 9; Minutes, Board of Directors, AASSW, 9/21-22/45, CSWE Records, I-3.

67. See, e.g., letter from Youngdahl to Buell, 7/18/47, CSWE Records, I-15.

68. Confidential Memo, Spencer to Deans and Directors, AASSW Schools, 11/12/47, CSWE Records, I-15.

69. Ibid., p. 8.

70. Memo, Sue Spencer to Members, NCSWE, n.d., Maxted Papers, folder 8.

71. Bartlett took over the chairmanship after Pray's death. Minutes, National Council on Education for Social Work, 8/26-27/46, Maxted Papers, folder 7.

72. Letter from Harper to Cape, 2/17/48, Maxted Papers, folder 9.

73. Minutes, National Council on Social Work Education, 10/30/48, Records of Study of Social Work Education, folder 2, Social Welfare History Archives.

74. Letter from Harper to Cape, 2/17/48, Maxted Papers, folder 10.

75. Ernest V. Hollis and Alice L. Taylor, _Social Work Education in the U.S._ (New York: Columbia University Press, 1951), p. viii.

76. Letter from Harper to Wetzel, 4/17/49; Wetzel to Harper, 4/26/49, Maxted Papers, folder 12.

77. Minutes, NCSWE Meeting, 10/14/49, Records of Study of Social Work Education, folder 2.

78. Ibid.; Hollis and Taylor, p. 213; letter from Helen Wright to Hollis, 12/48; Wright to Bartlett, 4/7/50; Towle to Hollis, 4/4/50; Wright to Hollis, 4/3/50, Records of Study of Social Work Education, folder, Miscellaneous Correspondence.

79. NCSWE, Articles of By-Laws, n.d., CSWE Records, I-16.

80. Hollis and Taylor, pp. 345-46.

81. "Report on Proposed Organizational Plan for Council on Social Work Education," 3/28/50, CSWE Records, Box I-19.

82. By-Laws, CSWE, 12/8-9/50, CSWE Records, Box I-19.

83. Pencilled note, Wetzel to Maxted on List of Nominations for Commissions, 11/4/55, Maxted Papers, folder 26; By-Laws, CSWE, as revised 4/28/51, CSWE Records, Box I-1.

84. Letter from Harper to Maxted, 4/17/47, Maxted Papers, folder 8.

85. Letter from Hoey to Fred Steiniger, 1/3/52, Maxted Papers, folder 16; Wetzel to Cape, 6/23/48, Maxted Papers, folder 10; Harper to Gustavson, Chair of Joint Committee on Accrediting, 10/30/47, Maxted Papers, folder 8.

86. Letter from Wetzel to Harper, 4/26/49, Maxted Papers, folder 12.

87. Letter from Harper to Gustavson, Maxted Papers, folder 8.

    88.   CSWE, Annual Program Meeting, Boston, Mass., 1963,
CSWE Records.

8

Broadening the Knowledge Base: Social Work's Use of Social Science in the 1950s

In 1947, the Russell Sage Foundation announced a new emphasis in funding. Instead of investing in a large research staff and in general grants to social work agencies, the charitable organization would now promote interdisciplinary efforts to develop "a closer and more effective relationship between social welfare practice and the social sciences." Such efforts were important, the foundation decided, because while knowledge of human behavior had recently expanded, practitioners and social scientists had grown farther and farther apart. In an attempt to close the gap, the foundation planned a new role for itself as liaison between research and practice.[1]

The policy shift at Russell Sage was part of a general move to broaden social work knowledge and practice in the 1950s. The foundation's activities, under the chairmanship of Donald Young, were an important catalyst in this process. Other groups played a part: social group workers, social work researchers, and educators seeking to develop doctoral programs in social work. Two trends influenced these efforts: a growing sense of interrelatedness between the social sciences and psychiatry, and the perception of many social work educators that the profession needed to ground itself more thoroughly in a scientific base. In addition, the attempt to broaden social work knowledge in the fifties drew on earlier developments in social work practice and the relationship between social workers and social scientists.

Shifts in social work knowledge were related to changes in the scope and focus of practice from the 1930s on. The rise of public welfare and an undergraduate training movement, the refinement of group work theories and techniques, the growth of the functional school of case work, the development of federal involvement in mental health training and research--these and other factors pushed social work away from a focus on case work as traditionally defined. Changes in practice were accompanied by changes in the knowledge base. Taking place simultaneously, each affected the shape of the other. Both sets of changes occurred within the context of continued professionalization. They brought new versions of the ongoing debates over broad versus narrow professionalism, the importance of achieving professional status, and the degree to which social work should maintain autonomy in developing its own knowledge and training. Social workers sought a broader, more scientific knowledge base to bolster the profession. Yet,

ironically, pursuit of this base entailed movement beyond narrow professional boundaries.

To evaluate these changes, we should recall the shape of
social work knowledge and practice in the early forties.
Social work had emerged from the Depression period with a strong
interest in psychoanalytic theory. The war years accelerated
this interest, in part because the shortage of psychiatrists at
home encouraged use of social case workers in psychiatric services.(2)   Despite some attention to principles of economics,
social work's major theoretical thrust was now an attempt to
master Freudian precepts and translate them into practice. The
functional school, drawing on the work of Otto Rank, represented the same theme in a minor key. The functional and diagnostic schools differed in their views on the importance of
agency function, the usefulness of personal histories, and the
proper length of treatment. The functionalists, in their
stress on the individual's inborn will, gave more credence to
client autonomy and responsibility for change. Yet both
schools emphasized emotional adjustment and the key role of
personality structure in mediating between inner needs and
environmental realities. They saw the relationship between
worker and client as a major factor in treatment. Both schools
of thought rested somewhat uneasily on the more sociological
base developed earlier by Mary Richmond in Social Diagnosis.(3)

Social work education and practice in the early forties
continued to stress case work as the basic helping method.
Group work techniques were being developed, and in 1944 the
Association of Schools established a "Basic Eight" curriculum
for graduate schools which included group work along with community organization and social administration. Yet schools
gave differential emphasis to the subjects specified in the
Basic Eight, and the primacy of case work was not seriously
challenged.(4)

Freed from their traditional relief-giving functions during the New Deal, private social work agencies could concentrate on improving individual functioning. The diagnostic-
functional debate furthered workers' interest in psychiatric
influences on practice. The resulting case work was an amalgam
of Richmond's stress on study and diagnosis of social situations and the newer psychoanalytic emphasis on the individual's
emotional adjustment. Now social workers in cities like New
York and Chicago had to know both "Street Marxism" and "Street
Psychoanalysis." Social workers may have talked more about the
new emphasis than they practiced it, but the model had become an
ideal for which to strive.(5)

Gordon Hamilton, of the New York School, was a major figure
in the development of this model. Her text, Theory and Practice of Social Case Work, published in 1940, revised in 1951,
and reprinted numerous times, was widely read and praised. One
educator acclaimed it as a pioneering effort to bring together
all the parts of case work into a significant whole.(6) The
book described a psycho-social approach to social work practice, but the emphasis was more clearly on the "psycho" than the
social. Hamilton argued that psychiatry could make a greater
contribution to social work than any other discipline.(7)
Though she referred to the uses of anthropology and the rela-

tionship between psychiatry and sociology in both editions, her model of case work drew predominantly on such psychoanalytic concepts as the client-therapist relationship, transference, and interpretation. Hamilton assured her readers that "at the center of the case work process is the conscious and controlled use of the worker-client relationship to achieve the ends of treatment."(8)

Charlotte Towle reinforced the idea of a psychiatrically informed case work. Edith Abbott persuaded Towle to join the SSSA faculty in 1932, "to teach psychiatric concepts [and] to develop psychiatric field placements." In light of the new emphasis within case work, Abbott felt that Towle would be a prestigious addition to the school. Towle had received her certificate in psychiatric social work from the New York School and was influenced by work with Dr. Marion Kenworthy and with psychiatrists at the New York City Institute for Child Guidance. She sought to infuse all of social work with psychiatric understandings. Her writings and teaching had a profound effect on case work.(9)

Despite the institutionalization of the case work point of view in social work education and practice, this approach was challenged in the late 1940s. Sources inside and outside the field called upon social work to develop a firmer conceptual base and to expand the practice repertoire.

The Hollis-Taylor report of 1951 played a major role in encouraging social work to re-examine and strengthen its knowledge. The report noted that the roots of social work education lay more in practice than in the academic setting. Although it drew initially from the social sciences, social work had separated itself more and more from them. This had resulted in a narrowing of curriculum and decreased attention to research. The use of case workers as faculty perpetuated "the emphasis on therapeutically oriented services to individuals" as the major area of social work practice. Hollis and Taylor envisioned an expanded practice, based on a broader, more scientific, and more carefully conceptualized body of knowledge. Such knowledge would draw in part on insights from the social sciences and other disciplines, in part on social work's own systematic development of concepts and data. Social work could now "seize the opportunity of being the group that leads research and study in [social] problems."(10)

Ralph Tyler was another important figure in the movement toward a more scientific social work. Tyler was a professor of education and dean of the Division of Social Sciences at the University of Chicago. An expert in curriculum development and evaluation, he played a role similar to that of Abraham Flexner in advising social work on furthering its professional development. Tyler consulted with Abbott and Breckinridge at the Chicago School and wrote the foreward to Charlotte Towle's The Learner in Education for the Professions.(11) In an address to the annual meeting of the Association of Schools in 1952, he asserted that "true professions" were distinguished by possession of a code of ethics and by use of techniques based on principles rather than on routine skills or rule-of-thumb. "As a profession becomes more mature," Tyler explained,

it recognizes that the principles used in the profession must be
viewed in an increasingly larger context and that correspond-
ingly the science needed for the profession must be critically
expanded to more basic content.(12)

Leading social work educators agreed with Tyler on the
need for clearly defined, scientifically based principles of
practice.(13) They were impressed by arguments that professional status depended on scientific development. This
seemed to make sense in a country where science is often viewed
as a legitimator of professionalism.(14) In addition, social
workers tended to believe that professional status would only
be obtained if the "science of social work" was developed by
social workers themselves, rather than outsiders. Alfred
Kahn, of the New York School, expressed this conviction in his
essay in an important book on the future of social work. Kahn
explained:

Social work . . . either must formulate and test its own knowledge . . ., supplementing it with critical use of social science
knowledge, or it must surrender its professional functions to
new and more rigorous disciplines, thereby assigning its
practitioners to the role of useful technicians and abandoning
the hope of attaining full professional status for the
field.(15)

The scientific approach to social work meant different
things to different people. To some, it was systematic gathering and analysis of data, to others, the testing of theory, and
to still others, the incorporation of principles from the
social and behavioral sciences. The range of conceptions suggests that "science," like "standards," was more a symbolic
term associated with professionalism than a tightly defined set
of ideas.

Underlying the varied approaches to science was the conviction that social work needed to define its conceptual base.
A number of writers noted the confused state of social work
knowledge and the haphazard use of theory and data from other
disciplines. They described the pressing need to identify the
basic content of social work and to systematize the use of
knowledge from other sources.(16)

Several trends in social work encouraged greater attention
to the social and behavioral sciences as part of social work's
conceptual base. Proponents of professional training in public welfare stressed the importance of social science in that
training. Undergraduate social workers concurred, laying particular stress on sociology. Their programs made much greater
use of the social sciences than did the graduate schools. At
the same time, postwar developments in international social
work led to growing awareness that American social work had been
confined largely to psychological theories, while British and
European social workers drew from a variety of disciplines.(17)

Pressures to revise social work knowledge were paralleled
by pressures to change its practice. The Hollis-Taylor report
played a crucial role, urging social workers to move beyond the
confines of case work and to expand their expertise in group

work, research, community organization, and administration.
The commonalities of all these methods could be taught in a
generic social work curriculum. Social workers would then
develop basic competence in a broad range of skills, applicable
in a variety of settings.(18)

Trends in public welfare and in international social work
also reinforced the call for a broader practice base. Public
welfare work demanded administrative and organizational, as
well as therapeutic, skills. International social work
stressed community planning and involvement in social policy.

Forces for change existed even within case work. The
lengthy debate between the functional and diagnostic schools
led to a re-examination of case work principles. The functionalist approach, with its emphasis on agency setting and on
present-oriented treatment, helped to broaden the scope of case
work practice. Another source of change, initially affecting
case work but gradually extending to the field as a whole, was
the inauguration of U.S. Public Health Service fellowships in
psychiatric social work. The National Mental Health Act of
1946 established federal support for mental health research and
training. Grants were given first by the USPHS, later by the
National Institute for Mental Health. Although initially the
grants were used to support clinical training, their scope was
soon expanded to cover education for positions in administration, research, and mental health planning.(19)

Perhaps the greatest impetus for change in social work
practice was the growth of social group work in the 1940s. The
field had an important effect on social work knowledge as well.
Group workers in the twenties and thirties had been a diverse
lot, struggling with issues of training, professional identification, and definition of group work goals. By the forties,
many of these issues had been at least partially resolved. An
expanded and more unified field, group work was an area of practice which case workers could no longer ignore. It offered not
only alternate skills, but also different theoretical perspectives.(20)

The American Association for the Study of Group Work was
formed in 1936. It grew out of a national meeting organized by
the New York Conference on Group Work in 1934. The AASGW represented group workers in settlements, youth service agencies
such as the YMCA and the Girl Scouts, recreational organizations, and mental hygiene settings. The association promoted
the study of group work and increased interaction among practitioners.(21)

Because these practitioners came from a variety of
backgrounds, including social work, education, and recreation,
the problem of group identity was a serious one. For a number
of years the AASGW followed a broad membership policy, envi-
sioning group work as a field cutting across professional
boundaries. By the mid-1940s, however, many group workers
wanted a more definite professional status. Despite some
opposition within the organization, the AASGW moved to seek
that status through a closer alliance with social work. In
1946, the association became the American Association of Group
Workers, an organization of "professional workers."(22) It
had over 2,000 members. Nine years later, the new association

joined with the AASW and other professional social work groups to form the National Association of Social Workers.(23)

As group workers developed a stronger professional organization, they also improved their educational preparation. Group work education began as agency-based training for youth service and recreation workers. It gradually evolved into a more academically respectable university-based curriculum.

The first graduate course on group work was developed by Wilbur Newstetter and Clara Kaiser at the Western Reserve University School of Applied Social Sciences (SASS). The course was organized in 1923 in response to a request by local recreational agencies. Aided by a grant from the Laura Spelman Rockefeller Fund, the Western Reserve School strengthened and expanded group work training over the next several years.(24) In 1934, Kaiser left to develop group training at the New York School of Social Work. To replace her, SASS hired Grace Coyle, an executive in the research division of the National Board of the YWCA.

When Coyle came to SASS, its group work curriculum was already becoming nationally known. Newstetter, who sparked the initial program at SASS, promoted group work education at professional meetings and engaged in his own small group research. His presentation "What is Social Group Work?" at the National Conference of Social Work in 1935 was one of the first comprehensive descriptions of the field.(25) Kaiser, a former YWCA executive, joined the SASS faculty full-time in 1927. Working with other instructors and local group workers, she published a set of sample group records in 1930.(26)

Grace Coyle was a strong addition to the Western Reserve program. She was a Wellesley graduate with a certificate from the New York School of Philanthropy and both an M.A. in economics and a Ph.D. in sociology from Columbia University. At Columbia, the noted sociologist Robert MacIver was her advisor. MacIver described Coyle as maintaining "the highest standards of scholarship." Working first in settlement houses and then in the YWCA, Coyle was both theorist and practitioner. She was often sought out for consultation on group work training and practice. She belonged to the American Sociological Society and was active in the American Association of Social Workers. She published extensively in small group theory and group work practice, beginning with <u>Social Process in Organized Groups</u> in 1930. Her work was recognized by sociologists as well as social workers. Her thirty-year leadership in group work education was an important factor in the growing acceptance of the field.(27)

Coyle, Kaiser, Newstetter, and others described the group work method as

an educational process emphasizing (1) the development and social adjustment of an individual through voluntary group association; and (2) the use of this association as a means of furthering other socially desirable ends.

The role of the worker was to guide "the adjustive efforts of the group in its acceptance of each individual member," and to assist in the achievement of group objectives.(28) While

skills in recreation and handicrafts were among the "tricks of
the trade," the new social group workers used these as a means
to an end--that end being the growth of the individual and the
achievement of desirable social goals. The new group work process drew heavily upon John Dewey's philosophy of progressive
education. Dewey described education as preparation for
democracy and as part of a child's general growth and development. Influenced by Dewey's writings, group workers like Coyle
moved the field away from its earlier emphasis on "building
character" and toward an emphasis "that was educational in nature and related to the development of personality through group
experience."(29)

By 1935, twenty-one schools offered a specialized program
in group work.(30) The AASGW had a committee on professional
education, and a Conference of Professional Schools of Recreation and Group Work was established in 1941. In 1940, the American Association of Schools of Social Work recognized group
work "as one of the four basic methods of social work practice"
and established a subcommittee on the group work curriculum.
By the end of the decade, the AASSW had accredited group work
programs in twenty-one universities and colleges.(31)

Not all social workers welcomed the new field. Some,
including leaders in the professional schools and associations,
questioned the quality of group education and standards for
practice. Group work's heritage of recreation and character-
building was difficult to shake off. Edith Abbott thought the
settlement movement should realize sooner or later "that games,
gymnastics, dramatics, and sewing are not social work." Grace
Marcus warned her colleagues, "I don't think we can assume group
work education is social work education." Charlotte Towle told
a friend, "They have never had anything that was worth much at
Western Reserve."(32)

These criticisms slowed group work's acceptance by particular schools and by the AASW. In 1944, the Chicago School consulted Coyle about starting a group work sequence, but delayed
development of a program until 1957.(33) During the debates
about membership requirements for the professional association, Walter West argued against extending membership to group
workers who had received their training outside of a school of
social work. West felt the field lacked clear-cut standards.
He also viewed development of a group work specialization as a
threat to professional unity. He believed in a generic education for all social workers and warned that "the School at Western Reserve has always kept up this separatist thing."(34)

In response to criticism, group workers continued to promote the professional legitimacy of their field. Their pressure on the AASW to broaden its membership policies led the
organization to call an important meeting of representatives of
several emerging specialties in 1945. The group work issue had
stimulated the AASW to consider the needs of other fields of
practice. The 1945 conference included representatives from
group work, community organization, public welfare, and probation and parole. While only a tentative discussion of the possibility of broadening membership took place, the meeting nevertheless signified a move toward a wider practice base and away
from emphasis on a single method--case work.(35)

Group work's prestige was enhanced by new theoretical developments in the forties and fifties. The field had always had an eclectic approach to knowledge and was receptive early on to social science contributions to small group theory. Prior to the mid-1930s, group workers attempted to integrate the ideas of progressive education with the concepts of early social psychologists like Charles Horton Cooley. By the forties, they had discovered the work of social psychologist Muzafer Sherif and psychiatrist J. L. Moreno, who developed the sociogram and psychodrama, a form of therapeutic group practice. But by far the greatest impact on group work's intellectual development came from exposure to the theories of group dynamics developed by Kurt Lewin and his associates and later put into practice at the National Training Laboratory in Bethel, Maine.(36)

The intellectual leader of a group which included Ronald Lippitt, Leon Festinger, R. K. White, and others, Lewin combined a broad theoretical focus with careful laboratory study of the effects of group composition on behavior. His work "showed it was possible to use social conditions in a laboratory setting to change the psychological states of persons participating in a group situation." After Lewin's death in 1947, the research center he had founded at MIT moved to the University of Michigan. In addition, the National Training Laboratory was established under Leland Bradford to apply the concepts of group dynamics developed by Lewin and others. At Harvard, another set of theorists was at work. This group, basing its work in the laboratory of small group research, engaged in more sociologically oriented small group studies led by Robert F. Bales and including Edgar Borgatta, Paul Hare, and others. With a less experimental approach, the work of George C. Homans represented another influential thrust from Harvard.(37)

Social group workers followed these new theoretical developments closely. Coyle corresponded with Bales and Borgatta, who also expressed interest in her work. Gisela Konopka, a group work leader on the faculty at the University of Minnesota School of Social Work, read extensively in the research on small groups. A committee on the relationship of group work to the social sciences was set up by the AAGW in 1950. As a first activity, the group discussed a conference "to bring together people doing research in group relations with group workers." The proposed list of participants included Lippitt, Bales, and Helen Jennings, the editor of Sociometry, a journal founded by Moreno.(38)

Group workers were particularly affected by the work and growing reputation of the National Training Lab. NTL staff actively promoted their ideas to leaders in business, education, and social welfare. Coyle was invited to attend a series of group sessions at the NTL in the summer of 1948. Over the next few years, other group workers and social agency executives journeyed to Bethel to participate in small group situations aimed at changing individual behavior and beliefs through group confrontation and interaction.

While impressed with NTL's scientific foundation and its development of skills, social group workers were uneasy about its messianic qualities and its attempt to reduce all group the-

ory to a single approach. One visitor to Bethel characterized
NTL's framework as "an ill-integrated blend of two schools of
theory: a field theory of tensions in social situations, and a
clinical theory stemming apparently from Carl Roger's
Client-Centered Therapy." Fritz Redl, a psychologist and
group theorist at Wayne State School of Social Work, wrote Coyle
that in his summer at Bethel he "got so goddam mad" at their
single-mindedness that he bought a target pistol and shot tin
cans.(39)

Coyle criticized the Bethel group for neglecting individual theory and making the group an end in itself. While she
felt the NTL offered productive ideas and techniques, she
warned her colleagues: "They are a very enterprising group and
are spreading a kind of doctrine all over the country." Their
ideas lacked "critical evaluation . . . and the result is a good
many half-baked promotional schemes [which] might lead people
to believe that they had the final answer."(40)

One senses in these criticisms a feeling that the NTL had
stolen the limelight from social group workers and was promoting as "brand-new" a method and theoretical approach which had
already been developed. As one group worker noted,

Much that appears today as research findings in group dynamics
was known to group workers, at least on an intuitive and non-
theoretically sophisticated level, but . . . we never tested our
insights.(41)

Social group workers sought recognition for their development
of a unique theoretical base.

Yet despite the desire for "ownership" of ideas, this
resentment probably served a positive function. Aware of the
research activity underlying group dynamics and the public
interest in the NTL model, group workers were spurred to expand
their own research and theory base. In doing so, they drew from
a variety of sources of knowledge, including psychiatry as well
as the social sciences. Major products of this work were the
writings of Coyle, Newstetter, Konopka, Redl, and Harleigh B.
Trecker of the University of California. A particularly influential book was Social Group Work Practice, written by
University of Pittsburgh faculty members Gertrude Wilson and
Gladys Ryland. Wilson and Ryland's comprehensive text brought
together knowledge from psychiatry, social work, and the social
sciences.(42)

These developments in group work theory and practice
increased the field's respectability in the eyes of social work
leaders. Group work methods were added to the practice repertoire. Social psychological theory used by group workers filtered into the social work mainstream.

At the same time, other forces prompted a renewed look at
the social and behavioral sciences. Some of these, such as the
developing fields of community organization and international
social work, were primarily concerned with the use of social
science insights by social workers to broaden their theoretical
framework and improve their practice.(43) Others, however,
called for more active collaboration between social workers and
social scientists. The Russell Sage Foundation was the chief

catalyst in promoting such a partnership.

The idea of collaboration between social workers and social scientists was not new. In the late 1800s, practitioners and theorists were united by a concern for social reform based on the scientific study of man. Charity workers, social reformers, and social scientists had together founded the American Social Science Association in 1865. Many early sociologists were also social workers.(44) In 1874, however, the National Conference of Charities and Corrections separated from its parent organization, the ASSA. Up through the 1920s, social workers and academic social scientists concentrated on defining specialized fields, developing knowledge,and forging separate professional identities. In the 1920s, social workers looked more to psychiatry for their theoretical base than to the emerging social science disciplines.(45)

At the end of the decade, a brief rapprochement flowered between social workers and social scientists, especially sociologists. This was based in part on sociologists' discovery of social work case records as data. Interest in collaboration sparked the founding of a Section on Sociology and Social Work within the American Sociological Society in 1928.(46) Robert MacIver analyzed the potential of this relationship in The Contribution of Sociology to Social Work. MacIver posited an "art/science" dichotomy to characterize the boundaries between the two groups and argued the usefulness of each to the other. His thesis was applauded by social workers interested in interaction between the fields.(47)

MacIver's counterpart in social work was Maurice Karpf, a leading figure in Jewish social services. Karpf was actively involved in the movement for professionalization in social work. He argued that this necessitated development of an intellectual and scientific foundation. In The Scientific Basis of Case Work (1931), Karpf promoted the usefulness of psychology, sociology, and social psychology in building that foundation. He encouraged interaction between social workers and social scientists, but he saw difficulties in bringing this about. Sociologists tended to look down on social workers; some social workers viewed sociologists as people "who clothe the simplest ideas in the most cumbersome language." Karpf noted:

To my mind there is a very close and distinct relationship between sociology and social work. It is only between sociologists and social workers that there is no relation, unless it is a negative one.(48)

Where Karpf was skeptical, other social workers were downright negative about the social worker-sociologist relationship. Edith Abbott and Sophonisba Breckinridge had little interaction with the prominent Department of Sociology at the University of Chicago. They saw sociologists as rivals in the development of social work education and as impediments to creation of a distinct social work identity. Other leaders in the Association of Schools shared their distrust.(49) Social workers also had mixed feelings about the value and ethics of sociological research. Charlotte Towle, for example, deplored "ruthlessness" in sociologists who studied people rather than treating them.(50)   For their part, sociologists became increasingly concerned with achieving scientific respectability--a respectability that seemed to demand strict separation between scholarship and social action.   The two groups drifted apart again in the thirties, despite the urgent need for researchers and practitioners to cooperate on addressing the social problems of the Depression.(51)   During the forties, the controversy between undergraduate social work programs and the AASSW tended to pit sociologists and graduate social work educators against each other, further widening the gap.

At the end of the 1940s, however, interest in collaboration reappeared.   Articles on social work-social science interaction began to crop up in social work journals; speakers at professional conferences again addressed the subject.   Stanley Davies, for example, spoke on "The Relationship of Social Science to Social Welfare" at the National Welfare Assembly of 1949.(52)   That same year, the Social Work Journal offered awards for the best articles on "The Contribution of the Human Sciences to Social Work Practice."(53)   Henry Maas won first prize with a piece on "Collaboration between Social Work and the Social Sciences."   Several articles on the implications of the concept of culture for case work practice were published in 1950.(54)   From 1932 to 1946, there were no articles on social science theory and data in the Social Service Review; in the next five years, there were four.(55)

Several factors within the profession influenced the turn toward social science--desire to improve the knowledge base, the perceived connection between science and professionalism, and the growth of group work, public welfare, and other fields. Equally important were significant changes within the social and behavioral sciences. Old barriers were fast disappearing. Psychiatrists and anthropologists had begun a fruitful collaboration, in which concepts of cultural anthropology enlarged the understanding of personality, and psychoanalytic theory shed light on anthropological studies of human behavior.(56)   This cross-fertilization soon spread to sociology, which joined in multidisciplinary studies of child rearing and the internal structure of the family.   The formation of the Department of Social Relations at Harvard in 1948 brought together Talcott Parsons, Clyde Kluckhohn, Gordon Allport, and others in an attempt to coordinate knowledge from psychology, psychiatry, social and cultural anthropology, and sociology.(57)

In addition, sociology had again become interested in applied work.   Sociologists had concentrated largely on scientific development of the discipline in the twenties and thirties, but their involvement in national planning during World War II spurred a rediscovery of the relation between scholarship and social policy.   Sociologists like Robert Lynd encouraged a reexamination of the place of values in a scientific discipline. Promoting value-oriented "action research," the Society for the Study of Social Problems was founded by sociologists and other social scientists in 1951.   The group sought ties with social workers and other practitioners.(58)

An important area of applied research was race relations. Discrimination against black Americans was an obvious blot on the record of a country which fought "to make the world safe for democracy." The forties saw progress in the expansion of civil rights, particularly at the state and local levels. Sociologists and other social scientists contributed to the civil rights movement through studies on the dynamics of prejudice and the status of blacks in postwar America. Attention to the situation of blacks was part of a larger interest in ethnic groups and the importance of cultural dynamics in shaping attitudes and behavior.(59)

These trends in the social sciences increased their appeal to social work. Interdisciplinary efforts broadened the range of social inquiry and put theorists and practitioners in touch with one another. Psychiatry's interest in cultural anthropology brought the concept of culture to social work's attention.(60)

Social workers joined social scientists in their concern for the problems of blacks in America. This concern was consistent with the profession's traditional focus on ethnic groups and the plight of minorities. Social work courses on Americanization gradually gave way to ones on nationality and racial backgrounds and then to study of the "cultural aspects of social work practice."(61)

Thus potential for social science-social work collaboration already existed when the Russell Sage Foundation entered the picture in 1947. Founded forty years earlier by Mrs. Russell Sage, the foundation sought to use research and education "for the improvement of social and living conditions in the United States."(62) For many years the foundation supported major research departments and provided grants to social welfare agencies. A combination of financial difficulties and staff changeovers promoted a basic program review in the late forties. This reconsideration was greatly affected by a new presence in the organization. Donald Young was a sociologist interested in applied work and the former executive director of the Social Science Research Council. He became general director of Russell Sage in 1948.(63)

Young believed strongly in sociology's obligation "to pay its own way by contributions to knowledge of recognized social utility." He felt sociologists had made a serious mistake in not collaborating more closely with professionals in social work, law, and the health field, and in not giving practical help on problems of joint interest.(64) In his first annual report for Russell Sage, Young noted:

[Social science] needs to be kept realistic by contact with the practitioners who use its results; the practitioners need to keep informed about the frontiers of research knowledge bearing on their techniques.(65)

The Russell Sage Foundation had particular ties with social work. This was a field about which Young had specific concerns. Young criticized the profession for its narrow, case work focus, and believed that a useful social science-social work partnership called for a shift in the profession's intellectual perspective and practice.(66)

Young's interests, coupled with the foundation's financial straits, produced decisive changes. Young added Leonard Cottrell, a social psychologist, to his staff. Over the next two years, Sage sold its building, made its terminal grants to agencies, and disbanded its research departments. It handed over publication of the Social Work Year Book to the AASW, and transferred its extensive social work library to the New York School of Social Work. One observer has described the transfer as a deliberate attempt to "get rid of this [narrow] social work stuff" and to broaden the foundation's approach.(67) These changes symbol-ized a decision to stop direct production of social welfare research and support of social work activities and to take on a more facilitative, social science-oriented role instead.

Under Young's directorship, the Board of Trustees decided to focus primarily on building a more effective relationship between the social sciences and social practice. The founda-tion would act as liaison and fund experimental ventures which brought researchers and practitioners together.(68)

The foundation expected resistance to its new interdisci-plinary thrust, particularly from social work. The pro-fession's stress on autonomy might well clash with moves toward collaboration. Young decided to proceed slowly, looking for situations where the foundation could place social scientists in teaching positions in professional schools. Schools of medicine and public health were the most immediately receptive to this idea.(69)

Another early project involved exploring "the con-tributions of the behavioral sciences to practice in a psycho-analytically-oriented child guidance clinic." Otto Pollak, a sociologist, was placed at the New York Jewish Board of Guard-ians in 1949. Out of Pollak's collaboration with the clinic's staff came the influential book Social Science and Psycho-therapy for Children (1952).(70)

The foundation achieved its first entry into professional social work education with the appointment of Katharine Spencer as a consulting anthropologist at the New York School for 1950-51. Spencer was to help expand that part of the curriculum dealing with "the relation of cultural factors to social work theory and practice."(71) This project underscored social work's growing interest in cultural anthropology, which was shown by the formation of a special committee on cultural dynam-ics within the AASSW and a growing literature on the importance of cultural elements in case work. The NYSSW project culmin-ated in publication of a casebook of seven ethnic case studies in 1955.(72)

By 1952, the foundation had achieved a fair degree of suc-cess in promoting social science-practitioner collaboration. Yet most of its work was in the areas of psychiatry, medicine, and public health. Social work, Young complained, showed a "virtual absence of a generally accepted pattern of interdisci-plinary collaboration . . . except with psychiatry."(73) In that year, however, Sage launched two significant projects within the field--a program of curriculum revision, under the direction of a sociologist, at Western Reserve's School of

Applied Social Sciences (SASS), and an interdisciplinary faculty seminar at the University of Michigan.

The University of Michigan project was the more extensive of the two. Its initiation had much to do with the creativity and fervor of David French and his interaction with Donald Young. French was a social worker interested in research. In 1952 he resigned as editor of the Social Work Journal and assistant executive secretary of the AASW in order to carry out a two-year study of the place of research in social work. French had conferred with Young about this work. When he moved to the University of Michigan to carry out his project, French "brought the Young philosophy" with him.(74)

The University of Michigan provided fertile ground for this philosophy. The university had a tradition of interdisciplinary work, including the interdepartmental social psychology program established by Theodore Newcomb in the late forties. The School of Social Work was a newer, less prestigious school than the NYSSW or Chicago's SSSA. Sage would find it easier to promote the use of social science faculty at Michigan than in the older, more well established programs. The school's dean, Fedele Fauri, while not himself a social scientist, had "an instinct that the social science collaboration was the right way to go." Fauri, French, and Young worked well together.(75)

In 1952, as part of his research project, French organized an interdisciplinary faculty seminar at the university. Three years later, Sage supported continuation of this committee through funds for the position of executive secretary, to be filled by French. The Coordinating Committee on Social Welfare Research brought together a notable group of faculty from public health, social work, education, and the social sciences. Its members included Kenneth Boulding, Robert Angell, Amos Hawley, Morris Janowitz, and Ronald Lippitt. Robert Vinter and Eleanor Cranefield represented the School of Social Work. Cranefield was a clinical social worker. Vinter, a group worker with an interdisciplinary degree in sociology and social psychology from Columbia, had just been added to the social work faculty.(76)

The committee sought "to develop ways and means for effecting a more productive relation between social science research and social work training and practice." It served as a research clearinghouse within the university, placed university researchers in social agencies, and sponsored a study on ADC mothers. To the committee's surprise, however, working together was not easy. As Angell noted, "We just didn't talk each other's language." The social scientists dealt with abstractions which would lead to prediction; the social workers were caught up in the concrete complexity of "real" problems. While the social scientists were careful to keep value premises separate from scientific theories, the social workers took for granted the values current in the profession. French served as "a perpetual trouble-shooter," according to Angell. "We were astonished at how deep-seated our differences in orientation were."(77)

Through conscious efforts at interaction, the barriers gradually wore away. Sage regarded the committee's work as a

significant interdisciplinary endeavor. Encouraged to suggest
new projects for funding after the initial grant had expired,
the committee came up with the innovative idea of a combined
doctorate in social work and the social sciences. Unlike other
social work doctoral programs, this one would require students
to meet Ph.D. requirements both in social work and in a selected
social science. Young liked the idea; French wrote the grant
proposal; and Fauri engineered its approval by the university.
In 1956, Russell Sage granted the project $250,000 for a five-
year period.(78)
     Development of the grant proposal involved resolving
issues about the degree of autonomy to be afforded the School of
Social Work and the purposes of a combined doctoral program.
The committee at first contemplated training for a wide range of
roles, including practice, but eventually decided that the program should prepare for leadership in research, teaching, and
social work administration. The program's goal would be to
advance utilization of the social sciences in social welfare.
The committee discussed two options for doing this: an
interdepartmental doctorate granted by the Graduate School and
a "professional doctorate" with a social science minor, centered in the School of Social Work. The first plan stressed a
balance between social work and social science; applicants need
not have an M.S.W. The second option gave more authority to the
School of Social Work and required the professional degree.(79)
     Fauri and most of the Coordinating Committee favored the
interdepartmental doctorate. School of Social Work faculty
members not on the committee criticized this option for its lack
of stress on development of a "professional self." They were
particularly troubled by inclusion of students lacking the
M.S.W. One instructor argued "there is need to be on guard
against a person who has a Ph.D. thinking he can go out and
teach case work."(80)
     Desire for professional autonomy thus colored the debate
over whether to accept a social work-social science doctorate.
In the end, due in part to Fauri's influence, the School of
Social Work faculty did endorse the program. In a gesture of
independence, however, they also voted to develop an additional
doctorate within the professional school.(81)
     The Coordinating Committee based its final proposal on the
belief that training in both social science and social work was
necessary for competent social welfare research. Existing
social work doctoral programs seemed to be doing an inadequate
job in this area. Young strongly supported the interdepartmental plan, criticizing the committee only for making too many
concessions to social work in developing the proposal.(82)
     The program established by the committee and funded by
Sage was intellectually and structurally an interdisciplinary
one. It was administered through the School of Social Work,
but directed by an interdepartmental committee appointed by the
dean of the university's Graduate School. This supervisory
committee controlled the admissions process. Degrees were
granted by the Graduate School rather than the School of Social
Work. Henry Meyer, a sociologist at New York University who
had since 1952 collaborated in research with social workers in
several agencies and was involved in a study of social work

effectiveness, was brought in to head the program. The university cooperated in Sage's objective by placing other social scientists on the social work faculty.(83)
     The new program was a departure from existing social work doctorates. It met with a degree of criticism within the profession. Rachel Marks editorialized in the Social Service Review:

The Michigan plan presents what seems to be a very heavy integrative task for the student. . . . The new combined degree will apparently provide somewhat more than a Master's Degree in each of the two fields, but does it provide enough advanced work in either to give the student real command of his field?(84)

Yet the Michigan program succeeded in its goal of producing qualified researchers, teachers, and administrators. Its early graduates included Phillip Fellin, Rosemary Sarri, Aaron Rosen, Arnold Gurin, Eileen Gambrill, and others who went on to become prominent in the field. The program contributed to recruitment of faculty with strong credentials in research and the social sciences. Another important product was publication of Behavioral Science for Social Workers, which featured articles by program faculty and students.(85)
     The program had more difficulty meeting a secondary goal--Young's plan that the presence of social scientists in a school of social work would have a "trickle down" effect on other faculty and on curriculum.(86) Though they hoped to have a broadening influence on the M.S.W. program, doctoral faculty were at first used primarily in the master's level research courses. Social science content only gradually filtered down to the master's level, as content of the doctoral seminars was brought into other M.S.W. courses taught by doctoral faculty. It was not until 1965 that the influence of the social science group was sufficient to incorporate group work with case work as the social treatment component and to confirm the equal status of community organization, administration, and policy in the M.S.W. curriculum.(87)
     The Sage project at the University of Michigan was the foundation's most sustained and successful attempt to influence the shape of social work education.(88) Even here, the program was hindered by social work faculty's hesitations and concerns about undermining "professional socialization." Elsewhere, attempts at collaboration between social work and social science faculty went much less smoothly. Russell Sage persuaded the New York School of Social Work to hire several social scientists, and the school had social science-trained welfare policy figures like Eveline Burns and Nathan Cohen on its faculty.(89) Burns, an economist by training, was a strong proponent of an emphasis on the social sciences in social work doctoral programs, including the one at New York, which she headed. Yet there was much friction between case work faculty and the newcomers. Gordon Hamilton reported great concern over "the influx of social issues . . . with no respect for social work education." Charlotte Towle, sympathizing with her New York colleagues, characterized the newer faculty as that "gang of social pseudo scientists."(90)

Similarly, Russell Sage's project at Western Reserve encountered difficulties in interdisciplinary collaboration and a preoccupation of social workers with the professional autonomy issue. A more traditional approach to interdisciplinary work than that at Michigan, the project at SASS involved placing sociologist Joseph Eaton at the school to direct faculty in a curriculum review beginning in 1953.(91)   Eaton was to help the school develop a stronger social science orientation. The plan grew out of the school's consultation with Young and Cottrell. Cottrell felt placing Eaton at SASS would put "the carrier of the social science culture into the professional tribal group."(92)

SASS in the fifties seemed a good place for such an experiment. Coyle and her protegee, Margaret Hartford, had a strong interest in the application of social science concepts. In 1950 they had developed a course on Dynamics of Community Life which included material on the nature of culture and the social and economic structure of the community. Not only was the school embarking on an extensive curriculum review, but it was also planning to initiate a doctoral program.(93)

During the project (1953-56), Eaton participated in discussions of curriculum and taught seminars to doctoral students. But when the faculty evaluated the experiment, they concluded that he had not really facilitated the addition of social science content at the school.(94)   They saw Eaton as an outsider whose knowledge of social work was more superficial than he realized. They questioned his assumption that "support for social work generalizations [was to] be found only in the social sciences." Some criticized his exclusion of psychoanalytic insights.(95)

Eaton, for his part, commented on social work's preoccupation with developing its "own science" and its "own field of knowledge." He felt this was part of an attempt to achieve autonomy as a profession. Writing in Social Work in 1956, Eaton observed:

[Social work's] present clamor for the development of a . . . social work science is probably more related to the profession's struggle for recognition than for new knowledge. . . . [This may be] a ritualistic assertion to cut the umbilical cord from those other applied behavioral sciences which at present enjoy more public prestige.(96)

By and large, the SASS faculty followed an approach more typical in social work than that adopted at the University of Michigan. Rather than utilize the resources of an outside consultant, they sought to develop their own expertise in the social science realm, and to maintain control over the selection and application of social science concepts. When the SASS faculty first discovered the new "cultural content," for example, they decided to become prepared, through summer reading and other re-education, to teach this material themselves. It is perhaps not surprising that the most notable product of the Sage project at SASS was not Eaton's work, but a monograph by Coyle on Social Science in the Professional Education of Social Workers.(97)

Coyle's work was one of the fullest descriptions to date of the problems and potential in the theory-practice relationship. It drew not only on the SASS experience, but also on the results of a survey of the fifty-two other schools of social work in the U.S. The survey demonstrated that many schools were attempting to incorporate social science material into the curriculum. Coyle offered a thoughtful analysis of the difficulties in this endeavor. Major barriers were the abstract nature of much of social science knowledge and the different stances of theorist and practitioner toward values. In addition, there was social work's desire for control over its knowledge base. Coyle agreed with many of her respondents that social work educators should take major responsibility for the presentation of social science concepts, either teaching the material themselves, or coordinating and directing its presentation by others.(98)

Sage's attempts to broaden the social work profession thus produced mixed results. While widespread collaboration between social workers and social scientists did not occur, the fifties witnessed a slow but steady influx of social science into the social work curriculum. Coyle's survey documented use of social science knowledge in many graduate schools. The social work literature of the period paid increasing attention to the relevance of social science concepts and to the nature of the theorist-practitioner relationship.(99)

Many forces contributed to these developments, but Sage projects at Michigan, Western Reserve, and other schools were important catalysts. Equally influential were the interdisciplinary studies sponsored by Sage, including Pollak's Social Science and Psychotherapy for Children, Harold Wilensky and Charles Lebeaux's classic Industrial Society and Social Welfare (initially commissioned by Sage for presentation at the International Conference of Social Work), Howard Polsky's Cottage Six, and Richard Cloward and Lloyd Ohlin's work on juvenile delinquency.(100)

While pleased with the success of their projects, the Sage staff recognized that attempts at theorist-practitioner collaboration created a number of strains. They attributed these to status differentials, differences in professional "cultures," the inability of psychoanalytically trained social workers to understand the significance of culture, and the differences in work setting between social work and social scientist.(101) For their part, social workers spoke of difficulties in deciding which social science concepts to use and how best to integrate them into social work practice. The "value-free" stance of some social scientists was also a problem. As Alfred Kahn put it:

The social worker who is on the front line of service finds the social scientist somewhat silent on subjects of major concern, and also inclined to conceptualize the obvious and complicate the simple.(102)

But perhaps the most important issue raised by the attempt to use the social sciences was the degree to which social work could maintain autonomy and professional identity while borrow-

ing from and collaborating with others. Towle described the
problem clearly:

Social work is, to a large extent, at a stage of being engulfed
in its borrowings and enmeshed in its identification with others. Confused identity has led to unsound professional practices . . . social work does not have the problem of inbredness
of the older . . . professions. Instead it has the problem of
promiscuity.(103)

     Social work researchers and doctoral faculty found this
issue of autonomy particularly troublesome. A Social Work
Research Group had been formed in 1949 to further social work
research and provide a channel of communication among researchers.(104) One of the group's major concerns was how to
differentiate social work research from that of the social scientist, from whom social work had borrowed many research
methods and skills. William Gordon, of the Washington
University School of Social Work, was a leading figure in the
research movement. A biologist by training, Gordon argued the
need for social work "to perform the essential and traditional
scholarly and scientific task of actively . . . developing the
knowledge on which its practice is based."(105) He and others
would have regarded as heresy David French's contention that
"what we've thought of as social work's theoretical foundation
is to be located in the sciences and not in an independent body
of social work theory."(106)
     The feeling that social work should create its own knowl-
edge was also strong within doctoral programs. Although
several of these had been started in the twenties, significant
growth in post-master's training did not occur until the 1950s.
In 1950, five schools offered doctoral degrees in social work;
in 1958, twelve were doing so. Few programs followed the
Michigan model of close collaboration with social science
departments.(107) Instead, they sought "to advance the status
of social work as a learned profession" and to encourage the
learner's identification with mentors in social work.(108)
The AASSW Committee on Advanced Education encouraged "meaningful communication with specialists" in other disciplines, but
felt strongly that the integration of knowledge from these
disciplines should be carried out by the social work faculty.(109)
     Social work leaders saw the development of doctoral
programs and an indigenous research as important ways to further the science of the profession. Both "would enhance the . .
. status of social work in an increasingly science-conscious
society."(110) As a result, members of the profession would be
able to present themselves as the scholarly peers of those in
related disciplines. Yet the path to professional status
through science and scholarship contained a built-in dilemma:
how to develop a knowledge base without over-reliance on the
social scientist. Aware of their tenuous professional status,
social workers did not wish to exchange one dependent
relationship--that with psychiatrists and physicians--for
another.(111) This fear of domination by other disciplines

prevented social workers from achieving a truly broad and flexible theory base and moving beyond a primary focus on the individual in practice.

Yet despite this failure, social workers in the fifties
did make some progress toward integration of new intellectual
concepts and practice methods. The model of case work which
emerged at the end of the decade was broader and more
definitive. A major figure in this development was Helen
Harris Perlman, a case worker on the faculty of the Chicago
School. Perlman was a student of Gordon Hamilton and a close
colleague of Charlotte Towle. In her work, she pulled together
insights from the diagnostic and functional schools, as well as
from the social and behavioral sciences. In 1957, she published Social Casework: A Problem Solving Process. This text,
influential for years to come, presented a coherent practice
model based on environmental, cultural, and psychological
determinants of behavior.(112)

Broadening of the practice base was also evident in the
growth of a generic program of education in many schools of
social work. Employing a new meaning for the term "generic,"
these programs emphasized a common core of knowledge and a mastery of principles basic to all the methods used in social
work.(113)

Although social workers and social scientists did not
become close allies, social science concepts were slowly
absorbed in the graduate curriculum. Many schools attempted to
integrate knowledge in a new course on human behavior and the
social environment. Integration and autonomy were the key concepts in the profession's use of the social sciences. By the
end of the fifties, social workers had begun to look for a new,
all-inclusive theoretical framework which would pull together
various sources of knowledge and provide the base for autonomous professional practice.(114)

Notes

1. Russell Sage Foundation, Annual Report, 1947-48, pp. 12-14.

2. Letter from Charlotte Towle to Kathleen Woodroofe, 10/17/58, Papers of Charlotte Towle, Box 2, folder 4, Regenstein Library, University of Chicago, Chicago, Ill.

3. Virginia Robinson, A Changing Psychology in Social Case Work (Chapel Hill: University of North Carolina Press, 1930); Robinson, The Development of a Professional Self: Teaching and Learning in Professional Helping Processes (New York: AMS Press, 1978); Cora Kasius, ed., A Comparison of Diagnostic and Functional Case Work Concepts (New York: Family Service Association of America, 1950); Carel Germaine, "Casework and Science: A Historical Encounter," in Robert W. Roberts and Robert H. Nee, eds., Theories of Social Casework (Chicago: University of Chicago Press, 1970), p. 13.

4. Interview with Mary Burns, April 10, 1979; Interview with Milton Chernin, October 13, 1977; Helen Wright, "Social Work Education: Problems for the Future," in Cora Kasius, ed., New Directions in Social Work (New York: Harper, 1954), pp. 184-85; Minutes, Board of Directors, American Association of Schools of Social Work, 10/15-16/48, Council on Social Work Education Records, Record Group I, Box 3, Social Welfare History Archives, University of Minnesota, Minneapolis, Minn.

5. Recent historians have questioned the extent of the "psychiatric deluge" posited by Kathleen Woodroofe, From Charity to Social Work, (London: Routledge and Kegan Paul, 1968), and Roy Lubove, The Professional Altruist (New York: Atheneum, 1969). See Leslie Alexander, "Social Work's Freudian Deluge: Myth or Reality?" Social Service Review, XLVI: 517-38 (December, 1972), and Martha Heineman Field, "Social Casework Practice During the 'Psychiatric Deluge,'" Social Service Review, LIV: 482-507 (December, 1980). Yet while social workers may not have consistently practiced Freudian case work, they certainly talked and wrote a good deal about it. Letter from Grace Coyle to Ernest Hollis, 10/3/49, Grace Coyle Papers, Box 4, Case Western Reserve University Archives, Cleveland, Ohio; Annette Garrett, "Historical Survey of the Evolution of Case Work," Journal of Social Casework, XXX: 219-28 (June, 1949).

6. Florence Sytz, "Social Casework," Social Work Year Book (1951), p. 463. See also F. J. Bruno, review of Theory and Practice of Social Case Work, by Gordon Hamilton, Annals of American Academy of Political and Social Science, CCXI: 240 (September, 1940); Jeannette Regensburg, review of Theory and Practice of Social Case Work, The Survey, LVI: 278 (September, 1940); Germaine, pp. 18-20.

7. Gordon Hamilton, Theory and Practice of Social Case Work (New York: Columbia University Press, 1940), pp. 344-45.

8. Gordon Hamilton, Theory and Practice of Social Case Work, 2nd ed. (New York: Columbia University Press, 1951), p. 22. In the first edition, Hamilton cites Ruth Benedict, Karen Horney, S. R. Slavson, John Dollard, and Abram Kardiner, but rarely discusses the usefulness of particular social science concepts in social work practice. The second edition has few references to the social sciences.

9. Helen Harris Perlman, "Charlotte Towle: An Appreciation," in Perlman, ed., Helping: Charlotte Towle on Social Work and Social Casework (Chicago: University of Chicago Press, 1969), pp. 8-9. In Towle's writings see, e.g., "Factors in Treatment," National Conference of Social Work, Proceedings (1936), pp. 171-91; "Teaching Psychiatry in Social Case Work," The Family, XX: 324-31 (February, 1940); "Underlying Skills of Case Work Today," Social Service Review, XV: 456-71 (September, 1941); and "Helping the Client to Use His Capacities and Resources," NCSW, Proceedings (1948), pp. 259-70.

10. Ernest V. Hollis and Alice L. Taylor, Social Work Education in the U.S. (New York: Columbia University Press, 1951), pp. 21, 46, 144, and 213.

11. Charlotte Towle, The Learner in Education for the Profession (Chicago: Univ. of Chicago Press, 1954). Ironically, Towle was rather skeptical of Tyler's work. His contribution to her book was urged on her by Helen Wright, dean of the SSSA, to show interdepartmental cooperation at the University of Chicago. Letters from Towle to Eileen Younghusband, 2/5/58 and 2/14/58, Dame Eileen Younghusband Papers, Correspondence, National Institute for Social Work, London, England.

12. Ralph Tyler, "Distinctive Characteristics of Education for the Professions," Social Work Journal, XXIII: 55-62 (April, 1951). Tyler had published a major work on setting educational objectives, Basic Principles of Curriculum and Instruction (Chicago: University of Chicago Press) in 1950. His framework on learning objectives was used in the 1959 CSWE Curriculum Study.

13. See, e.g., Grace Coyle, "The Place of the Social Sciences in the Doctoral Program for Social Work Students," in Council on Social Work Education, Social Work Education in the Post-Master's Program, no. 2 (New York: CSWE, 1954), pp. 67-81; Alfred Kahn, "The Nature of Social Work Knowledge," in Kasius, New Directions in Social Work, p. 205; Katherine A. Kendall, "Education for Social Work," Social Work Year Book (1954), p. 170.

14. Cf Great Britain, where the scientific basis of professionalism receives less stress. L. J. Sharpe, "The Social Scientist and Policy-Making," in A. H. Halsey, ed., Traditions of Social Policy (Oxford: Blackwell, 1976), pp.

216-45; Philip Elliott, The Sociology of the Professions (London: Macmillan, 1972), pp. 42-55.

15. Kahn, pp. 210-11; see also Arlien Johnson, "Science and Social Work," Presidential Address to NCSW, Social Service Review, XXI: 308 (September, 1947).

16. See, e.g., Kasius, New Directions in Social Work, "Introduction," p. xix; Kahn, p. 194.

17. Kasius, New Directions in Social Work, p. 19; Jane Hoey, "International Social Work Developments," in Kasius, New Directions in Social Work, pp. 87-109; Katherine Kendall, "International Developments in Social Work Education," Social Work Journal, XXXII: 70-77 (April, 1951); Jan F. de Jonge, "A European View of American Social Work," Social Casework, XXXI: 150-55 (April, 1950); UNESCO, The Contribution of Social Sciences in Social Work Training (New York: U.N., 1961).

18. Hollis and Taylor, pp. 47 and 228; Minutes, Board of Directors, AASSW (discussion with Hollis), 1/26/49, p. 9, CSWE Records, I-3.

19. "Social Work Fellowships and Scholarships" (Pamphlet, American Association of Social Workers, 10/47), in CSWE Records, XI-2; Sue Spencer, Progress Report, AASSW Doctoral and Advanced Third Year Programs, 7/1/48-2/28/49, and Progress Report, Committees, 7/1/48-2/28/50, p. 1, CSWE Records, XXII-236.

20. A concise history of the development of social group work in the U.S. can be found in Kenneth Reid's From Character Building to Social Treatment (Westport, Conn.: Greenwood Press, 1981).

21. Ibid., pp. 140-42.

22. American Association of Group Workers, Toward Professional Standards (New York: Association Press, 1947), p. 169.

23. See, e.g., Minutes, Ad Interim Committee, American Association of Social Workers, 6/19/37, pp. 11-15, folder 22, and folders 804 and 806: "Annual Business Meetings, AAGW, 1937-46" and "Central Committee, AAGW, 1938-46," National Association of Social Workers Records, Social Welfare History Archives. The history of the attempts of group workers to join the AASW will be discussed in chapter 9.

24. Annual Meeting, Group Work Committee, 4/8/29 and 6/1/32; Minutes, Group Work Committee, 1/13/30, School of Applied Social Sciences, Western Reserve University Records, folder: Group Work Faculty Minutes (1926-34), 28 F, Case Western Reserve University Archives.

25. According to Newstetter, the term "group work" was

first used at Western Reserve. Minutes, Group Work Committee,
1/3/30; Annual Meeting, Group Work Committee, 6/1/32, SASS
Records, folder: Group Work Faculty Minutes (1926-34); Wilbur
Newstetter, Wawo-Kuje Camp, A Research Project in Group Work
(Cleveland: SASS, Western Reserve University, 1930).
Newstetter was later joined in this research by Theodore
Newcomb. See also Reid, p. 120; Newstetter, "What is Social
Group Work?" NCSW, Proceedings (1935), pp. 291-99.

26. Clara Kaiser, The Group Records of Four Clubs at
University Neighborhood Centers (Cleveland: SASS, Western
Reserve University, 1930), described in Reid, p. 120.

27. "Grace Coyle," Encyclopedia of Social Work (New York:
NASW, 1971), pp. 161-62; reference letter from Robert MacIver,
1/16/29, Coyle Papers, Box 4, 3 HC 3; letter from Helen Wright
to Coyle, 4/13/44; W. L. Mitchell, Deputy Commissioner, Bureau
of Public Assistance, to Coyle, 3/8/51; Coyle to Kathryn Close,
Assoc. Ed., The Survey, 2/3/44, Coyle Papers, Box 4. Coyle's
publications included Social Process in Organized Groups (New
York: Richard R. Smith, 1930), Group Experience and Democratic
Values (New York: Woman's Press, 1947), and Group Work and
American Youth (New York: Harper, 1948). She was cited by
sociologists and social psychologists (e.g. Emory Bogardus, in
Fundamentals of Social Psychology (New York: Appleton-Century
Crofts, 1950), p. 489, and A. Paul Hare, Handbook of Small Group
Research (New York: The Free Press, 1962), p. 3. She took
important leadership roles in the AASW and was one of the people
suggested for executive secretary when West resigned in 1942.
Letter from Frank Bruno to Walter West, 3/18/42, NASW Records,
folder 15.

28. Newstetter, "What is Social Group Work?" pp. 291,
294.

29. Coyle, "Social Group Work," Social Work Year Book
(1951), pp. 466-72; Reid, p. 115.

30. Edith Abbott, "Education for Social Work," Social
Work Year Book (1935), p. 162.

31. Coyle, "Social Group Work," pp. 468-69; Letter from
Clara Kaiser to Chester Bower (SASS), 6/24/40, Coyle Papers,
Box 5.

32. Minutes, Curriculum Committee, AASSW, 11/6/32, AASSW
Files in Grace Browning/Mary Houk Papers, Social Welfare
History Archives. Minutes, Ad Interim Committee, AASW,
6/19/37, p. 20, NASW Records, folder 22; Letter from Towle to
Younghusband, 11/19/57, Younghusband Papers.

33. Letter from Helen Wright (Dean of SSSA) to Coyle,
4/13/44; Alton Linford (Dean, SSSA) to Coyle, 1/15/57, Coyle
Papers, Box 4.

34. Minutes, Ad Interim Committee, AASW, 6/19/37, p. 20,

NASW Records, Folder 22, pp. 11-19.

35. Letter from Joe Anderson to Coyle, 12/7/44; Anderson to David Dressler (Division of Parole, Albany, New York), 12/6/44, NASW Records, folder 17; "Report of Conference with Representatives of Group Work, Community Organization, Public Welfare, and Probation and Parole," 1/45, NASW Records, folder 18.

36. Reid, p. 115; letter from W. L. Kindelsperger, Tulane University, to Coyle, 11/12/56; Gisela Konopka to Coyle, 12/15/55; Vilona P. Cutler, University of Oklahoma, to Coyle, 10/31/56, Coyle Papers, Box 8. Cutler was at the same university as Sherif, and used him as a guest lecturer in her group work class.

37. Nicholas C. Mullins, Theories and Theory Groups in Contemporary American Sociology (New York: Harper and Row, 1973), pp. 108-13; Reid, pp. 153-54. Hare, Borgatta, and Bales edited Small Groups: Studies in Social Interaction (New York: Alfred A. Knopf, 1955), which became a standard reference for social group work courses.

38. Letter from Edgar Borgatta to Coyle, 4/16/54; Robert Bales to Coyle, 1/50, Coyle Papers, Box 4; Konopka to Coyle, 12/15/55, and other correspondence from schools responding to a survey by Coyle on the use of social science material in group work courses, 1955 and 1956, Coyle Papers, Box 8; Coyle to Jennings, 5/11/50, Coyle Papers, Box 4.

39. Letter from Al Sheffield to Coyle, 8/3/52; Redl to Coyle, n.d., but ca 11/50, Coyle Papers, Box 4.

40. Letter from Coyle to Donald VanValen, 9/10/48; Coyle to Frank Hertel, FSAA, 12/13/48; Coyle to Sheffield, 10/2/52, Coyle Papers, Box 4. See also Konopka to Coyle, 12/15/55, Coyle Papers, Box 8.

41. Letter from Alan F. Klein to Coyle, 12/9/55, Coyle Papers, Box 8.

42. For examples of group work literature, see Gisela Konopka, Therapeutic Group Work with Children (Minneapolis: University of Minnesota Press, 1949); Fritz Redl, "The Phenomenon of Contagion and Shock Effect in Group Therapy," in K. R. Eissler, Searchlights on Delinquency (New York: Inter-national Universities Press, 1949), pp. 315-28; Harleigh B. Trecker, Social Group Work Principles and Practices (New York: Woman's Press, 1948); Gertrude Wilson and Gladys Ryland, Social Group Work Practice (Boston: Houghton Mifflin, 1949); Reid, pp. 161-62. Konopka was a student of Wilson and Ryland at Pittsburgh.

43. The field of community organization had begun to develop in the late forties. It recognized the usefulness of social science material, but did not explore that material

fully until the sixties. See Lloyd E. Ohlin, "The Development of Social Action Theories in Social Work," Council on Social Work Education, Annual Program Meeting (1958); "New Developments in Community Organization Practice and Their Significance," Workshop Report, CSWE, APM (1961), CSWE Records, Ephemera.

44. For an informative history of the ASSA and the interaction between professional and "amateur" social scientists, see Thomas L. Haskell, The Emergence of Professional Social Science (Urbana: University of Illinois Press, 1972). Sociologists who were also social workers included Stuart Queen, Charles Ellwood, Jesse Steiner, John Gillin, and Henry Pratt Fairchild. Howard Odum, American Sociology (New York: Longmans, Green, 1951), pp. 136, 158, 177, 198-206, and 374-75. Jane Addams, Mary McDowell, and Robert Woods were charter members of the American Sociological Society, founded in 1906.

45. Roscoe C. Hinkle and Gisela Hinkle, The Development of Modern Sociology (Garden City, N.J.: Doubleday, 1954), pp. 1-43; James T. Carey, Sociology and Public Affairs (Beverly Hills, Calif.: Sage, 1975), pp. 35-36.

46. Helen I. Clark, "Cooperative Research and Student Training," The Family, XII: 22-25 (March, 1931); L. Guy Brown, "Possible Contributions of Social Case Work to Sociology," American Sociological Society, Proceedings, (1933), pp. 130-35; Ernest Burgess, "What Social Case Records Should Contain to be Useful for Sociological Interpretation," Social Forces, VI: 524-32 (September, 1927); Maurice Karpf, "Sociology and Social Work," The Family, X: 67-73 (May, 1929); Helen Riddich, "The Relation of Sociology to Social Work," The Family, VIII: 353-59 (February, 1928); "Notes and Comments," Social Service Review, II: 116-17 (March, 1928).

47. Robert MacIver, The Contribution of Sociology to Social Work (New York: Columbia University Press, 1931); MacIver, "Sociology and Social Work," Social Work Year Book (1933), pp. 497-500; Joanna C. Colcord, "The Theory Back of Us," review of The Contribution of Sociology to Social Work, by Robert MacIver, The Survey, LVII: 216 (November 15, 1931). For a discussion of MacIver's notion of the art/science dichotomy, see Robert D. Leighninger, Leslie Leighninger, and Robert Pankin, "Sociology and Social Work: Science and Art?" Journal of Sociology and Social Welfare, II: 81-89 (Winter, 1974).

48. Maurice Karpf, Scientific Basis of Case Work (New York: Columbia University Press, 1931), pp. 51-56; Karpf, "The Relation between Sociology and Social Work," Journal of Social Forces, III: 419-27 (March, 1925). Other social workers encouraging collaboration included Ada Sheffield, who used the notion of "gestalt" to develop a new concept of the client's "situation." Sheffield, Social Insight into Case Situations (New York: D. Appleton-Century, 1937). See also Maurine

Boie, "The Case Worker's Need for Orientation to the Culture of the Client," NCSW, Proceedings (1937), pp. 112-23, and Neva R. Deardorff, "The Relation of Applied Sociology to Social Work," Social Forces, XI: 190-93 (December, 1932).

49. Letter from Breckinridge to W. Kumlien, 11/23/35; Minutes, Executive Committee, AASSW, 10/15/32, CSWE Records, Box I-1, 4; interview with Henry Meyer, April 9, 1981; Hathway to Breckinridge, 8/5/33; Johnson to Hathway, 9/10/39, Marion Hathway Papers, folders 7 and 9, Social Welfare History Archives; Carey, pp. 88-89; interview with Harriett Bartlett, August 20, 1979.

50. Letter from Towle to Kathleen Woodroofe, 10/17/58, Towle Papers, Box 2, folder 4.

51. Howard Odum, "The Errors of Sociology," Social Forces, XV: 327-42 (March, 1937); Mark A. May, "Is There a Science of Human Relations?" The Family, XVII: 139-44 (July, 1936); and H. G. Duncan and Winnie L. Duncan, "Shifts in Interests of American Sociologists," Social Forces, XII: 209-12 (November, 1933).

52. Stanley Davies, "The Relationship of Social Science to Social Welfare," Social Work Journal, XXXI: 20-26 (January, 1950).

53. "Social Work Journal Awards," Social Work Journal, XXX: 164 (October, 1949).

54. Henry Maas, "Collaboration between Social Work and the Social Sciences," Social Work Journal, XXXI: 104-9 (July, 1950); Davies, "The Relationship of Social Science to Social Welfare"; Dorothy Lee, "Some Implications of Culture for Interpersonal Relations," Social Casework, XXXI: 355-60 (November, 1950); Anne F. Fenlason, "Anthropology and the Concepts of Culture," Social Work Journal, XXXI: 178-82 (October, 1950). Fenlason's article won second prize in the Journal contest.

55. Steven J. Diner, "Scholarship in the Quest for Social Welfare A Fifty-Year History of the Social Service Review," Social Service Review, LI: 22 (March, 1977).

56. See, e.g., Ralph Linton, The Cultural Background of Personality (New York: D. Appleton-Century, 1945); Ruth Benedict, The Chrysanthemum and the Sword (Boston: Houghton Mifflin, 1947); Edward Sapir, Culture, Language, and Personality, ed. David G. Mandelbaum (Berkeley: University of California Press, 1956).

57. Edward Shils, The Present State of American Sociology (Glencoe, Ill.: Free Press, 1948), pp. 32-33, 59; Howard Odum, American Sociology, pp. 241, 388. Psychoanalytic concepts were introduced to sociology by Harold Lasswell in Psychopathology and Politics (Chicago: University of Chicago

Press, 1935). See also Abram Kardiner, The Psychological Frontier of Society (New York: Columbia University Press, 1945). The entire November 1939 issue of American Journal of Sociology (vol. 45) was devoted to the influence of Freud on sociology.

58. Robert Lynd, Knowledge for What? (Princeton: Princeton University Press, 1946); Barry Skura, "Constraints on a Reform Movement: Relationships between SSSP and ASA, 1951-70," Social Problems, XXIV: 15-36 (October, 1976); Elizabeth Briant Lee and Alfred McClung Lee, "The Society for the Study of Social Problems: Parental Recollection and Hopes," Social Problems, XXIV: 4-14 (October, 1976).

59. Edwin J. Lukas and Theodore Leskes, "Civil Rights and Civil Liberties," Social Work Year Book (1954), pp. 105-15; Thomas F. Pettigrow and Kurt W. Back, "Sociology in the Desegregation Process: Its Use and Disuse," in Paul F. Lazarsfeld, William H. Sewell, and Harold L. Wilensky, eds., The Uses of Sociology (New York: Basic Books, 1957), pp. 692-722. See also E. Franklin Frazier, The Negro in the U.S. (New York: Macmillan, 1949); Morton Deutsch and Mary Evans Collins, Interracial Housing (Minneapolis: University of Minnesota Press, 1951); Gordon Allport, The Nature of Prejudice (Cambridge, Mass.: Addison and Wesley, 1954); and Gunnar Myrdal, An American Dilemma (New York: Harper, 1944).

60. The works of Otto Pollak and Erik Erickson, which drew both on the Freudian tradition and on anthropological insights, were popular among social workers. Letter from Konopka to Coyle, 12/15/55, Coyle Papers, Box 8; Coyle, "New Insights Available to Social Work from the Social Sciences," Social Service Review, XXVI: 291 (September, 1952); Otto Pollak, Social Science and Psychotherapy for Children (New York: Russell Sage, 1952), and "Cultural Dynamics in Casework," Social Casework, XXXIV: 279-84 (July, 1953).

61. Minutes, Curriculum Committee, 1/16/50, SASS Records, Box 5.

62. John M. Glenn et al., Russell Sage Foundation: 1907-1946 (New York: Russell Sage, 1947), pp. 1-16.

63. Russell Sage Foundation, Annual Report (hereafter referred to as AR), 1947-48, pp. 1-19. Young wrote American Minority Peoples (New York: Harper, 1932), and Research Memorandum on Minority Peoples in the Depression (New York: Social Science Research Council, 1937).

64. Donald Young, "Sociology and the Practicing Professions," American Sociological Review, XX: 641-48 (December, 1955).

65. Russell Sage, AR, 1947-48, p. 14.

66. Interview with Henry Meyer, April 8, 1981.

67. Ibid.; "Russell Sage Foundation," American
Foundation News Service, March 22, 1950; "Income Drop Listed by
Sage Foundation," New York Times, SCVIII (February 2, 1949);
"Sage Foundation to Sell Its Home," New York Times, XCVIII: 1,
25 (May 4, 1949); "Library to Lose Russell Sage Aid," New York
Times, SCVIII: 19 (January 21, 1949).

68. Russell Sage, AR, 1947-48, "Report of the General
Director," pp. 12-14.

69. Sage placed social scientists in the Departments of
Medicine and Nursing at Cornell University and at the Harvard
School of Public Health. Russell Sage, AR, 1948-49, pp. 9-12,
18, and 1949-50, p. 22; Eveline Burns, "The Doctoral Program,
Progress and Problems," in Social Work Education in the
post-Master's Program, no. 2, p. 58.

70. The book was published by Russell Sage and cited by a
number of social workers.

71. Russell Sage, AR, 1949-50, p. 25.

72. Annual Meeting, AASSW, 1950, NASW Records, Ephemera.
Sage underwrote publication of Socio-Cultural Elements in
Casework: A Case Book of Seven Ethnic Case Studies (New York:
CSWE, 1955). For examples of the literature on culture and
case work, see Dorothy Lee; Fenlason; William Gioseffi, "The
Relation of Culture to the Principles of Casework," Social Case
Work, XXXII: 190-95 (May, 1951); Boie; and Mary A. Young,
"Cultural Factors and Family Case Work," The Family, XIX: 76-
79 (May, 1938).

73. Russell Sage, AR, 1952-53, "Report of the General
Director," p. 12.

74. Interview with Meyer, April 9, 1981. French published An Approach to Measuring Results in Social Work (New
York: Columbia University Press) in 1952.

75. Interview with Meyer, April 9, 1981; Russell Sage,
AR, 1951-52, p. 16; Minutes, Coordinating Committee on Social
Welfare Research (hereafter referred to as CCSWR), 7/27/55, p.
2, University of Michigan School of Social Work Records, Ann
Arbor, Michigan.

76. Solomon Axelrod was the representative from public
health. Interview with Meyer, April 9, 1981. Hawley was the
committee's first chairman; Angell succeeded him. Russell
Sage, AR, 1953-54, pp. 20-22; Minutes, CCSWR, 7/27/55,
University of Mich. SSW Records.

77. Robert C. Angell, "A Research Basis for Welfare
Practice," Social Work Journal, XXXV: 145-52 (October, 1954).
Angell's paper was delivered at the NCSW, 1954.

78. Interview with Meyer, April 9, 1981; Russell Sage, AR, 1953-54, pp. 20-22; 1954-55, pp. 18-20; Memo from French to CCSWR, 5/14/56, University of Mich. SSW Records.

79. Different tracks were suggested for M.S.W. and non-M.S.W. applicants in option 1. Minutes, CCSWR, 10/28/55; CCSWR, "Memorandum Outlining Proposal for Submission to Russell Sage Foundation," 10/27/55, University of Mich. SSW Records.

80. Minutes, CCSWR, 10/28/55, 11/18/55; Summary of Discussion of Program of Advanced Training and Research, 2/16/56, University of Mich. SSW Records.

81. Summary of Discussion of Program of Advanced Training and Research, 2/16/56. This doctorate was never established.

82. CCSWR, "Proposal for Advanced Training in Social Welfare, First Draft," 12/21/55; Minutes, CCSWR (meeting with Donald Young), 1/12/56, University of Mich. SSW Records.

83. Meyer had a joint appointment with Sociology. His research had been sponsored by Sage and involved collaboration with Borgatta and Wyatt C. Jones. Their report, Girls at Vocational High, was published by Sage in 1965. Its findings cast doubt on social work effectiveness, although these outcomes were not yet known when Meyer joined the social work faculty. Interview with Meyer, April 9, 1981; CCSWR, Proposed Agenda, 7/19/56, University of Mich. SSW Records.

84. Rachel Marks, "Notes and Comments," Social Service Review, XXXI: 215-16 (June, 1957).

85. Edwin Thomas, ed., Behavioral Science for Social Workers (New York: Free Press, 1967). The program's faculty included Thomas (who had a joint appointment with Psychology and had both an M.S.W. from Wayne State and a Ph.D. in social psychology from Michigan), Eugene Litwak (who had a Ph.D. in sociology from Columbia University), Jack Rothman (a community organization specialist with a social psychology degree from Columbia), and Paul Glasser (who had an M.S.W. from Columbia and a Ph.D. in sociology from the University of North Carolina).

86. CCSWR, Draft, "Relation of Advanced Degree Program and Professional Training Program in Social Work," ca 1/56, University of Mich. SSW Records.

87. Minutes, CCSWR, 3/28/58, University of Mich. SSW Records; interview with Meyer, April 9, 1981.

88. The Sage grant was renewed in 1960.

89. Sage provided funds for the development of the doctoral program at the NYSSW. Three social scientists (Robert R. Bush, Lloyd Ohlin, and James Bieri) were placed on the doctoral faculty. Russell Sage, AR, 1956-57, pp. 12-13.

90. Hamilton, quoted in letter from Towle to Younghusband, 5/18/57; Towle to Younghusband, 2/5/58, Younghusband Papers.

91. Coyle was made head of the project. Minutes, Faculty Meeting, 11/13/53; SASS Records, Box 28.

92. Joint Meeting of Curriculum and Advanced Curriculum Committees with Dr. Cottrell, 3/24/52, SASS Records, Box 4.

93. Minutes, Curriculum Committee, 12/4/50, 10/23/50, 11/6/50, 12/6/50, SASS Records, Boxes 4 and 5; Minutes, Faculty Meeting, 9/10/52 and 9/22/52, SASS Records, Box 28.

94. Minutes, Faculty Meeting, 6/11/54, 11/9/56, SASS Records, Box 28. Though Sage had originally suggested that the project lead to a publication, Eaton's major projects were an article and an in-house report.

95. Coyle to Eaton, 9/24/56, Coyle Papers, Box 4; Minutes, Faculty Meeting, 11/13/53, SASS Records, Box 28.

96. Joseph Eaton, "Whence and Whither Social Work: A Sociological Analysis," Social Work, I: 11-26 (January, 1956).

97. Minutes, Curriculum Committee, 1/16/50, SASS Records, Box 4. Similarly, the University of Tennessee SSW brought in social scientists to lecture to students, but the social work faculty "really [wanted] to make all the presentations themselves." Letter from Sue Spencer to Coyle, 10/31/56. Another correspondent told Coyle of "trying desperately" to teach herself social science. Mary Lee Nicholson, Wayne State, to Coyle, 12/20/55, Coyle Papers, Box 8. Coyle's monograph was financed by Sage and published by CSWE in 1958.

98. Grace Coyle, Social Science in the Professional Education of Social Workers (New York: Russell Sage, 1958), pp. 6-7, 20-33, 50-58.

99. Ibid., pp. 3, 23-38. For examples from the social work literature, see Ernest Greenwood, "Social Science and Social Work: A Theory of Their Relationship," Social Service Review, XXIX: 20-33 (March, 1955); Kahn; Henry S. Maas, "Problems in the Use of the Behavioral Sciences in Social Work Education," CSWE APM (1957), pp. 79-91, CSWE Records, Ephemera; Herman D. Stein, "Social Science in Social Work Practice and Education," Social Casework, XXXVI: 147-55 (April, 1955); Herman D. Stein and Richard A. Cloward, Social Perspectives on Behavior (Glencoe, Ill.: Free Press, 1958); and Leonard S. Kogan, ed., Social Science Theory and Social Work Research (New York: NASW, 1960).

100. Harold Wilensky and Charles Lebeaux, Industrial Society and Social Welfare (New York: Russell Sage, 1958);

Howard Polsky, <u>Cottage Six</u> (New York: Russell Sage, 1962
Richard Cloward and Lloyd Ohlin, <u>Delinquency and Opportunity, A
Theory of Delinquent Gangs</u> (Glencoe, Ill.: Free Press, 1960).

101. Russell Sage, <u>AR</u>, 1958-59, pp. 8-13.

102. Kahn, p. 199. See also Maas, "Problems in the Use
of the Behavioral Sciences," and Coyle, <u>Social Science in
Professional Education</u>, pp. 11-15, 50-57.

103. Charlotte Towle, "Aims and Characteristics of
Advanced Education Differentiated from Master's Degree
Education," in Council on Social Work Education, <u>Social Work
Education in the Post-Master's Program</u>, no. 1 (New York: CSWE,
1953), p. 29.

104. SWRG, <u>The Function and Practice of Research in Social Work</u> (New York: SWRG, May, 1955), Foreward; Ernest
Greenwood, "Social Work Research: A Decade of Reappraisal,"
<u>Social Service Review</u>, XXXI: 311-20 (September, 1957).

105. William E. Gordon, "Scientific Training in the
Social Work Doctorate," in <u>Social Work Education in the
Post-Master's Program</u>, no. 2, p. 7. See also Gordon, "The
Function of Social Work Research," <u>Social Work</u>, III: 99-106
(October, 1958); Philip Klein, "Past and Future in Social Work
Research," <u>Social Welfare Forum</u>, Proceedings, National
Conference of Social Work (New York: Columbia University
Press, 1951), pp. 130-47; Katherine D. Lower, "Responsibilities
for Research in the Profession of Social Work," CSWE APM (1955),
CSWE Records, Ephemera; Hilde Landenberger Hochwald, "The
Function of Social Work Research," <u>Social Casework</u>, XXXIV: 29-
33 (January, 1953); Minutes, Post-Master's Committee on
Advanced Curriculum, AASSW, 11/20-22/52, CSWE Records, XXII-
236.

106. Minutes, SWRG Steering Committee, 9/13-14, 1951,
NASW Records, SWRG Supplement.

107. Letter from Katherine Kendall to Joseph Eaton,
8/1/60, CSWE Records, XXII-231. In a survey of ten doctoral
programs in 1954, Coyle found only one school with a full time
sociologist on the faculty. Coyle, "The Place of the Social
Sciences in the Doctoral Program for Social Work Students," pp.
67-81. Wisconsin and Minnesota did develop programs somewhat
similar to that of Michigan.

108. Towle, "Aims and Characteristics of Advanced
Education," pp. 15-32.

109. <u>Social Work Education in the Post-Master's Pro-
gram</u>, no. 1, pp. 9-11. The AASSW Committee on Advanced
Curriculum was set up in 1948.

110. William Gordon, "Scientific Training," p. 7.

111. Eveline Burns, pp. 59-63; Benjamin Youngdahl, "Shall We Face It?" Annual Meeting, AASSW (March, 1948), and published in Social Work Journal, XXIX: 63-69 (April, 1948).

112. Perlman's book went through eleven printings in eight years and was translated into seven languages. Her work drew heavily on ego psychology, which she felt was close to Rank's concept of the "will." She also used the sociological concept of role, and acknowledged a debt to John Dewey. Her citations included Alexander Franz, Leonard Cottrell, Anna Freud, Sigmund Freud, Clyde Kluckholn, Erik Erickson, Talcott Parsons, Otto Pollak, Fritz Redl, and Ralph Linton. Mary L. Gottesfeld and Mary E. Pharis, Profiles in Social Work (New York: Human Sciences Press, 1977), pp. 112-20; Helen Harris Perlman, Social Casework: A Problem Solving Process (Chicago: University of Chicago Press, 1957), Foreword, pp. v-xiii; Perlman, "The Casework Seminar in the Advanced Curriculum," in Social Work Education in the Post-Master's Program, no. 2, pp. 54-55.

113. Report of Curriculum Planning Committee, 1/47-1/48, CSWE Records, VII-3. The term "generic," as developed at the Milford Conference, applied to case work only. For discussion of changes in the term, see Leslie Leighninger, "The Generalist-Specialist Debate in Social Work," Social Service Review, LIV: 1-12 (March, 1980); Grace White, "Generic Education for Social Work: The Implications for Fields of Practice," Child Welfare, XXXIX: 10-16 (November, 1960).

114. Kendall, "Education for Social Work," pp. 174-75. Social science content was particularly evident in the doctoral curriculum. See Mary E. Burns, "Report on Social Science Content in Doctoral Programs in Schools of Social Work," 5/12/65, CSWE Records, XXII-237.

Attempts at Unity: Formation of the National Association of Social Workers

A wish to unify the profession was an important concern of many social workers after 1950. By then, six separate organizations provided forums for medical, psychiatric, and school social workers, group workers, social work researchers, and community organization practitioners. Alongside them was the AASW, stronger than it had been in the early forties, but still not covering all fields of practice. The Association of Schools was moving toward merger of various interests into the Council on Social Work Education. Forces were at work promoting a generic preparation for practice and a broader, more sophisticated knowledge base. As Ben Youngdahl, president of the AASSW, observed:

A certain maturity . . . has developed in our profession over the last several decades. We are rapidly passing out of the teen age into adulthood.(1)

Yet the question remained: what was the nature of that adult personality, and how well integrated would it be?

In October, 1955, six separate social work organizations joined to create the National Association of Social Workers.(2) In the next few years, the association developed a "working definition" of social case work and established a code of ethics. In 1959, it joined the CSWE in producing a massive study of the professional curriculum. These movements toward professional unity had a troubled history. In that history, impulses toward unity and a single standard of education and practice were offset by forces for separate identities and pluralistic standards.

Early attempts at unification took place during World War II. They aimed at inter-organizational cooperation in personnel planning and social policy. The War Time Committee on Personnel in the Social Services and the Interim Committee on Joint Planning for Social Work both tried to speak for social work as a whole; neither was entirely successful. Each had difficulties defining social work and developing a cohesive group which could represent the variety of interests and philosophies within the field. The personnel committee came under the AASW and later disbanded; the Interim Committee was absorbed by the National Social Welfare Assembly, which had a social welfare agency orientation rather than a professional point of view.(3)

In the postwar years, social work continued to be

organizationally fragmented. It had three well-established
practice organizations: the American Association of Medical
Social Workers (AAMSW), the American Association of Psychiatric
Social Workers (AAPSW), and the National Association of School
Social Workers (NASSW). Three newer groups were gaining
strength: the American Association of Group Workers (AAGW),
the Association for the Study of Community Organization (ASCO),
and the Social Work Research Group (SWRG). The AASW aspired to
represent the entire profession, but its selective membership
standards and focus on case work limited its ability to unify
the field.

Each of these groups had a distinctive history and perspective on the advantages and disadvantages of working toward
a common professional base. The older groups, with well-
established identities and high membership standards, had more
to lose by merger than the newer ones. Yet the newer organizations had to make significant capitulations to professional
homogeneity in order to join a comprehensive professional
organization.

The AAMSW was founded in 1918. The first social work specialty to organize, it represented a well-defined form of practice which had developed under the early leadership of Richard
Cabot, a professor of medicine at Harvard, and Ida M. Cannon, a
medical social worker. In 1905, Cabot initiated social services at Massachusetts General Hospital in order to deal with
the social consequences of illness. In the next several
decades, hospital social work differentiated itself from nursing and found a place in many large city hospitals. Its practitioners investigated the family and social conditions related
to a patient's illness. They offered a "skilled professional
service"--casework--to mobilize individual and community
resources to deal with those conditions.(4)

By 1930, over 1,500 medical social workers belonged to the
AAMSW. The association had a full-time executive secretary, a
central office in Chicago, and twelve regional chapters.
Reflecting an early interest in specialized education, the
group established a Committee on Education which approved curricula in the medical specialty within graduate schools of
social work. By 1941, the AAMSW had approved curricula in
medical social work in fourteen graduate schools. The association also had a Committee on Minimum Standards, which helped
regional chapters evaluate hospital social service departments.(5)

Stimulated by their close association with the medical
profession and their need to establish a specific identity
within the hospital setting, medical social workers were particularly interested in defining and maintaining high standards
of education and practice. By the late forties, membership
requirements for the AAMSW were among the highest within the
professional associations. Members had to have completed a
two-year graduate program, including an approved medical social
work sequence, in an accredited school of social work. Those
who had not completed a medical sequence had to substitute one
to three years of supervised experience in medical social work,
in addition to the M.S.W.(6)

Although initially one of the largest and best defined

social work specialties, medical social work began to lose
ground in the forties and fifties. Various forces contributed
to this decline--a lack of development in medical social work
theory, shifts in funding sources, and the growth of the American Association of Psychiatric Social Workers, which began as a
section of the AAMSW in 1926. The AAPSW initially represented
social workers in psychiatric hospitals and child guidance
clinics. As private agencies turned more toward counseling
services, however, many social workers sought psychiatric
skills. Psychiatric knowledge became more important than medical knowledge in social work training and practice. The
National Institute of Mental Health began providing grants for
such training in the fifties. The numbers of psychiatric
social workers increased 150 percent (from about 2,250 to over
5,000) between 1950 and 1960. Growth of medical social work
slowed to a total of 3,430 practitioners.(7)

Psychiatric social workers had their own identity problems. During the thirties and forties, members of the field
debated whether they should act like psychiatrists, social case
workers, or a sort of hybrid. The first edition of Gordon
Hamilton's text (1940) took many pages to differentiate psychoanalysis and psychiatric social work. By 1950, however, psychiatric social work was firmly established as a specialty in
its own right. Its professional association, the AAPSW, had
over 1,200 members. Like the AAMSW, it had high membership
standards: graduation from a school of social work with an
approved psychiatric social work curriculum and one year's
employment in the specialty, or an M.S.W. plus two years of psychiatric social work practice. The association employed an
educational secretary to consult with schools offering training
for the specialty. A high proportion of psychiatric social
workers--65 percent in 1950--had two years of graduate training. Relations between medical and psychiatric social workers
were sometimes strained, the former envious of the latter's
growth.(8)

School social workers had also organized early as a case
work specialty. They began as "visiting teachers" hired by
boards of education, settlements, or other organizations to
work in the public schools. Their goal was to guarantee
"adjustment of conditions in the lives of individual children,
to the end that they may make more normal . . . school
progress.(9) In 1944, school social services were operating in
266 U.S. cities. By 1950, the number of cities had jumped to
450.(10)

The National Association of Visiting Teachers, a professional organization of school social workers, was formed in
1919. Renamed the National Association of School Social Workers, the organization had 600 members in 1951. It maintained
an executive office, published a Bulletin, and consulted with
AASSW on approval of specialized training in case work in the
school setting. Unlike other fields of social work, school
social workers were affected by state and local certification
in developing their own standards of practice. Certification
criteria generally included training and/or experience in
education. Consequently, membership requirements for the
NASSW in the late forties included one year of graduate training

in social work, one year of experience in the field, and "suffi-
cient courses in education and education experience to meet
local or state requirements." Because educational authorities
defined certification standards, these requirements were
broader than those of the AAMSW or AAPSW, and less stringent in
terms of social work background.(11)

The first specialized professional groups represented
fields of practice within case work. Their differences related
to setting. Although they stressed the specific skills
demanded by a setting, they recognized case work as the generic
foundation of their practice. This approach was in line with
the Milford Conference report of 1929. The three newer specialty groups identified more with a method than with a setting.
The first of these, the AASGW, promoted group work in a variety
of settings as an alternative to case work techniques.

Group workers from various backgrounds formed the AASGW in
1936. In the next decade, members of the association struggled
with issues of identity and the degree and type of professionalism the field ought to pursue. Should group work be considered
a type of social work, or a new amalgam of social workers, recreation workers, and physical education specialists? Should
their study group become a professional organization, and if
so, which identity should it reflect? Members wavered between
the desire to join the AASW and the urge to preserve their own
organization and "the movement aspect of group work."(12)

The AASW response to the group workers' dilemma changed
over the years. When individual group workers sought AASW membership during the thirties, the AASW reaction was often
negative. West and others in the AASW leadership questioned
the level of standards in group work, particularly in education
for the field. Stringent AASW membership requirements
excluded all but a few group workers.(13)

In the forties, however, attitudes within the AASW had
begun to change. West, the advocate of homogeneity based on
standards, was no longer executive secretary. The association
wanted to expand its membership. Group workers were better
organized and had established a stronger educational base. In
1944 Clara Kaiser, a member of both AAGSW and AASW, wrote Grace
Coyle, as chair of the AASW Board of Directors, to suggest creation of a committee for group workers within the AASW. It
would, she hoped, encourage other group workers to join and it
would promote discussion of group work issues within the association. The association established such a committee in
1945.(14)

Despite increasing acceptance by the AASW, group workers
in the AAGSW were ambivalent about the direction they ought to
pursue. Closer ties with the AASW might mean less attention to
relationships with workers in recreation and education and
diluting the special identity of group workers. Yet perhaps
public recognition of that identity demanded specific standards
and a narrowing of the field. Group work educators faced a similar dilemma. Continuation of a broad membership in the Conference of Professional Schools of Recreation and Group Work
might limit the organization's ability to improve standards and
to differentiate between professional and vocational training.(15)

Some group workers, including Coyle and W. I. Newstetter, argued for continued development of a separate professional organization, which would be open to group workers with a variety of backgrounds. Yet perhaps the creation of a new all-inclusive professional field seemed too difficult a task. In 1946, when AASGW members voted to reorganize as a professional organization, they rejected the name "American Association of Education, Recreation, and Group Workers" in favor of "American Association of Group Workers." Although they maintained ties with groups such as the Society of Recreation Workers of America and the Associated Youth Serving Organizations, they came more and more to see themselves as "members of a specialization in the general field of social work." By 1950, AAGW had 1,900 members. While membership requirements gave equal recognition to graduate education in social work, education, and recreation, the group was moving toward an emphasis on social work education as the most appropriate preparation for the specialty.(16) One group work leader noted the resulting "significant and regrettable, but inevitable" loss of a number of non-social work members.(17)

Community organization practitioners likewise experienced identity problems. The Association for the Study of Community Organization was organized in 1946. Like the AASGW, it grew out of a section in the National Conference of Social Work. Its membership was open to all persons interested in the study and practice of community organization. Many had no graduate preparation in social work. The organization's first president, Arthur Dunham, acknowledged an interest in improving standards of professional practice. But, Dunham added, "We are not strictly a 'professional organization' in the sense that we limit membership to persons with specific qualifications of professional education and experience."(18)

ASCO soon developed local study groups and produced a newsletter and several monographs on community organization. By 1950, it had approximately 900 members. As it grew, the association had to resolve the question of whether its field was community organization in general, or community organization in social welfare. Members grappled with the question posed by social work educator Kenneth Pray at the 1947 NCSW, "Is community organization social work?"(19)

Increasingly, community organization practitioners answered that question in the affirmative. Although ASCO had been set up as a group with a broad focus and membership, it was coming to represent a social work orientation. Its members defined community organization as the process of "bringing about . . . an effective adjustment between social welfare resources and social welfare needs" within a community. The process, they felt, was one of the basic methods in social work. By 1953, almost 80 percent of ASCO's members had dual membership in the AASW.(20)

Like group work, community organization at first had a somewhat tenuous status in the graduate social work curriculum. By 1950, however, all AASSW member schools had at least a basic course in the area, and sixteen offered a specialization. The content of these specializations varied widely, reflecting the still evolving nature of the field.(21)

    Social work researchers enjoyed a somewhat clearer and
more prestigious position within social work, yet they too had
to define their boundaries. The Social Work Research Group
organized in 1949 "to provide a medium of communication for
social work research practitioners." The SWRG hoped to establish a permanent organizational structure which would become
part of a broader organization of professional social workers.
Although the statement of purpose suggests a definite identification with social work, SWRG membership was open to any person involved in social work research "without regard to professional social work training."(22)
    During the early years of the organization's history, mem-
bers debated whether social work training and experience were
essential to the practice of social work research. Some social
welfare research was carried out by social scientists. In
addition, since the field was new, a number of experienced
researchers lacked formal training, either in the content area
or in research methodology. In recognition of this situation,
SWRG maintained a flexible membership policy.(23)
    Definition of social work research itself was also tricky.
Was it distinguished by topic, methods, practitioners, or some
combination of these? Would its most useful ideas come from
study of social work practice or from concepts in the social
sciences? Concerned lest they remain in the shadow of the more
established scholarly disciplines, many SWRG members found it
crucial to establish a separate identity for their craft. "If
there is such a thing as social work research," wrote Philip
Klein, "it can exist only if we differentiate it from social
research in general."(24) This concern echoed that of social
work educators interested in use of the social sciences.
    In delineating their area of work, social work researchers
sought to move beyond the earlier tradition of research conducted by social agencies and settlements. This had consisted
of surveys of social conditions or simple collection of agency
statistics. The latter was no longer respectable as scientific
research; the former could best be conducted on a large scale in
the universities and social research foundations.(25)
    Defining the new social work research was not an easy task,
according to a SWRG committee set up to study the matter. After
a year's work, the committee formulated this objective for
research in social work: "to provide the body of verified
knowledge directed toward increasing . . . the effectiveness of
services to clients and community." Specific research projects included determination of need for services, evaluation
of their adequacy, and most important, inquiry into the content
and effectiveness of social work techniques and methods. The
new research thus stressed study of professional services
rather than investigation of broad social problems.(26)
    The social work research literature grew appreciably in
the early fifties. Two important works dealt with evaluating
social work processes: David French's An Approach to Measuring
Results in Social Work, and J. McVicker Hunt and Leonard Kogan's
Measuring Results in Social Casework.(27) Bradley Buell's
consulting group, Community Associates, had begun the Family
Unit Report Study in St. Paul, Minnesota, which was collecting
data on a newly discovered type of social work client, the

"multiproblem family."(28) SWRG actively publicized such
research efforts in its meetings at the NCSW, and the group published a series of abstracts on research in social work. Some
SWRG members, particularly William Gordon, began to promote a
new identity for social work researchers--that of scientist--
which transcended identification as a social worker.(29)

As they achieved greater cohesiveness as a group, social
work researchers, like group workers and community organization
specialists, had important decisions to make. Which was in
their best professional interest: pursuit of a specialist
identity or of stronger ties with the more established groups in
social work? Should they narrow their membership base and concentrate on raising standards, or should they maintain a
broader, more flexible approach to the qualifications for
practitioners in their field?

Another, more amorphous practice group--workers in the
area of corrections--faced a similar dilemma. However, the
degree of professionalization and level of training in this
field was as yet too rudimentary to permit serious consideration of their absorption into social work. In 1950, only 10
percent of probation workers had completed social work training.(30)

While separate professional groups flourished, the AASW
sought to maintain its role as the organization that united the
field. In 1950, the association had 12,000 members. About a
tenth of them also belonged to a specialized practice group.
Since the AASW continued to base membership primarily on graduate education in social work, many in the newer specialty groups
could not qualify.(31) The high standards approach thus reinforced case work as the prevailing image of professional social
work.

Under Joe Anderson's leadership, the AASW had recovered
from the internal dissension which had forced West to resign in
1942. Its objectives regarding social work remained firm:
(a) to preserve high standards of practice, based on selective
membership requirements, (b) to promote reasonable personnel
practices and standards for social work employees, and (c) to
present a coherent picture of social work goals, methods, and
views on national policy to the outside world.(32)

National and international affairs in the early fifties
were becoming increasingly worrisome to those involved in
social welfare. The outbreak of the Korean War triggered a
defense mobilization which created serious problems for individuals and families. Such mobilization was also used to support arguments to cut back on the burgeoning social welfare programs created by the New Deal, on the grounds that increased
support for defense necessitated retrenchment in social welfare. Worse still, the nation had begun to witness the witch-
hunting techniques of Senator Joseph McCarthy. From his
initial charge that there were "57 card-carrying members of the
Communist Party" in the U.S. State Department, McCarthy and his
followers moved to far-reaching denunciation of Communists in
many areas of American life. Conservative politicians used the
anti-Communist movement to attack social reform.(33) Many of
the victims of McCarthyism were liberals and former New Dealers; some were social workers.

Joe Anderson and other social work leaders sounded the alarm. In a 1951 NCSW Address, "Response of Social Work to the Present Challenge," Anderson spoke of the problems and fears of the time--the "changes in social institutions, intolerance, [and] the 'hysteria' that now prevails." He warned colleagues of "the power and cunning of the forces that would undermine, and if possible destroy, the social welfare structure in this country."(34)

McCarthyism, the outbreak of war, and an increasingly con- servative national mood contributed to growing criticisms of the social welfare system and its beneficiaries. Such criticisms had surfaced earlier in the investigations of several large city public welfare agencies in the forties. Now, citing welfare "chiselling" and fraud, a number of states pressured the federal government to change the confidentiality requirements of the Social Security Act. These states wanted to make public the names of public welfare recipients and the amounts of their payments. The resulting "Jenner Amendment" to the Revenue Act of 1951 forbade the Federal Security Adminis- tration from withholding funds from states which gave public access to information about assistance clients. The AASW called on social workers to oppose these attacks on client con- fidentiality. It called the Jenner Amendment "symptomatic of an ominously widespread attack on the public assistance pro- gram."(35)

In the 1940s, public welfare workers were under fire. During the McCarthy era, the attack spread to other social work- ers. While the profession was not affected by McCarthyism as severely as was the State Department or the media, it did have victims. In 1951, the Federal Security Administration ordered the destruction of its supply of Charlotte Towle's public assistance training pamphlet, Common Human Needs, on the grounds that it contained socialist sentiments. The move was prompted by complaints from the American Medical Association, ever sensitive to the threat of "socialized medicine." Later, Towle's passport was withheld because of suspicions of her Com- munist leanings.(36) In 1951, Marion Hathway resigned from the faculty of the University of Pittsburgh School of Social Work, following charges by some city officials that she had partici- pated in "leftist activities."(37) An invitation to Bertha Reynolds to speak at a regional conference of the American Pub- lic Welfare Association brought searing letters of complaint. The commissioner of the New York City Department of Welfare wrote the conference organizer:

We don't expect anything except fuzzy-minded cant and puerile mewling about 'freedom of speech' from many of the soft-headed gentry who wear the habit of the professional social worker . . . Bertha Reynolds [must be removed] from the program of the Swampscott Conference. She is a long time spokesman for the Commie line and should have no place on the program.(38)

Other, lesser-known social workers suffered similar har- rassment. One federal employee's loyalty was questioned because his wife had been associated with the Rank and File journal Social Work Today. Some social workers were black-

listed; others were fired.   Faculty members at certain schools
of social work were required to sign statements testifying that
they had never belonged to groups such as the League against War
and Fascism.(39)
     Social work's reactions to these attacks were angry but
confused.   Though individuals and groups wrote letters of
protest, the profession as a whole did not carry out a unified
or vigorous fight against the attacks on civil liberties and on
the social welfare system.   In 1949, the AASW membership had
approved a statement on civil liberties.   Its application was
restricted, however, to defending AASW members, and it was
given little publicity outside the association.(40)
     The association was equally cautious in protesting the
attacks on social welfare.   Shortly after Eisenhower came to
office, the new Republican secretary of health, education, and
welfare had Jane Hoey fired.   Despite the outrage of individual
social workers, the AASW decided it could not take action in a
situation involving "a particular person."(41)
     Social workers failed to make more active protests partly
because they were afraid of falling victim to an escalating public hysteria, partly because they did not have a unified profession with a strong political voice.   Some thought a larger,
more inclusive professional association might provide such a
voice.   Such an association could play a greater role in formulating legislative and administrative social policies and shaping social services "for individuals and families whose needs
are not being met."(42)
     Another compelling reason for organizational consolida-
tion was social work's age old problem of numbers.   In 1950,
there were about 75,000 social workers in the United States.
Twelve thousand of these, about 16 percent, belonged to the
AASW.   Untrained public assistance workers were the largest
group lacking professional training (40 percent of all social
workers worked in public assistance, but only about 3 percent
had graduate social work training).   Other fields presented
similar problems.   Of the almost 9,000 social workers engaged
in group services, 11 percent had an M.S.W.   Of 2,600 community
services workers, one fifth had graduate professional training.
None of these groups was well represented in the AASW.(43)
     Altogether, social work was a profession with many fields
of practice but with professional representation and education
limited largely to workers in medical social work, child welfare, psychiatric social work, and family services.   Social
work leaders were concerned about the absence "of a unified
effort to study the problems created by a large group of
untrained workers in the field."   This was a legacy of the failure to incorporate the new public welfare workers into the field
in the 1930s and 1940s.   In addition, the numbers entering
social work professional schools had begun to drop, making
recruitment to the profession even more important.(44)
     By the late forties, the idea of building a broader pro-
fessional organization was gathering strength.   A number of
arguments for this were advanced.   Social workers from various
fields were concerned about a lack of unity in the profession
and the overlapping and duplication of efforts among the different practice groups.   Within the AASW, McMillen's vision of

a broader professional association was at last beginning to
make sense. The national leadership of the association thought
that to include the specialty groups would strengthen their
organization numerically and financially. The leadership was
also reacting to grassroots pressures. Local AASW chapters had
already discovered the advantages of cooperation with representatives of specialized fields in lobbying for local and
state legislation and carrying out professional development
activities. In 1946, the AASW Delegate Conference passed a
resolution directing the association to take the initiative in
getting the various professional groups together.(45) Public
welfare workers, who did not have a professional organization
of their own, were not formally included.

        Within the Association of Schools, the movement toward a
generic content in social work education provided another reason for cooperation among the various segments in social work.
In addition, the AASSW was interested in strengthening the
relationship between the professional schools and the various
professional membership associations. Part of the impetus for
this was the desire to consolidate all accrediting activities
carried out by social work organizations.(46)

        The specialized practice organizations varied in their
assessment of the advantages of such cooperation. The AAMSW
and the AAPSW, as well-established groups, hesitated to give up
their special identities. Each association had put a good deal
of effort into articulating and defining the theory, methods,
and educational standards for their fields. The AAMSW felt a
strong claim to uniqueness and wished to maintain its status
within the profession. Psychiatric social work was growing
fast, and AAPSW members hoped to capitalize on this growth.
They were particularly concerned about continuing active participation in the implementation of the 1946 National Mental
Health Act. Both social work organizations had high membership
standards and feared the possible lowering of standards in a
new, more inclusive association.(47)

        Both organizations, however, were willing to explore some
sort of inter-association activity. If arrangements could be
made to maintain membership standards and to preserve the identity of individual groups, a larger organization would have
certain advantages. Through it, medical and psychiatric
social workers could join their colleagues in further developing personnel standards, professional education, and positions
on social policy.(48)

        The NASSW had a stronger interest in organizational merger
than either the AAPSW or the AAMSW. As a smaller specialty,
school social workers felt the need to convince the public that
they were part of a recognized professional group. In addition, their organization had financial difficulties. Merger
with other social work professional groups could bring school
social workers shared resources and a better public image.(49)

        By the late forties, the AAGW was also attracted to the
idea of an all-inclusive professional organization. Though
concerned to keep a sense of identity for their field, many AAGW
members accepted a social work orientation. Like school social
workers, group workers looked to a larger professional
organization to give them a firmer professional status. They

also noted the potential of such a group for stronger stands on
public issues.(50)

These six organizations--the AASW, AAMSW, AAPSW, NASSW,
AAGW, and the Association of Schools--came together to form the
Committee on Inter-Association Structure of Professional
Social Work Organizations in January, 1949. The move was
initiated by the AASW, acting on a resolution passed by the 1948
Delegate Conference. That resolution affirmed that all social
work stemmed from a general base. It stated that the profession had "at the present time no single organization through
which it may speak and act . . . on matters of legislation and
social planning and human welfare," and called for a meeting of
representatives of the various social work groups to explore
creation of a single professional body.(51)

The Committee on Inter-Association Structure had two major
issues to resolve. First, what form of inter-organizational
structure would be best: voluntary cooperation on particular
issues; confederation, with the identity of each group being
maintained; or a new organization in which all existing
organizations would merge? Second, if one of the more formal
structures was chosen, what sort of membership requirements
should be imposed? If a new organization were planned, would
all members of existing organizations be "blanketed in" to membership, despite different levels of education and experiences?(52) These were familiar questions for social work--how
much should a profession stress standards, and how can it accommodate to the needs of diverse groups?

The committee came to a degree of consensus early on.
After four months of meetings, its members rejected the idea of
federation because of the possible administrative and financial
difficulties involved. They instead favored creation of a
single new organization of practitioners and the dissolving of
the existing practice associations, including the AASW. The
committee recommended the blanketing in of members of the
existing groups into the new organization. The specialized
groups would have structural safeguards, probably through the
creation of divisions or sections. The new organization would
also have a number of commissions, each responsible for an area
of general professional interest: personnel practices, social
legislation, defining social work, and the like. Finally, a
tentative plan of membership classification was proposed.
This included membership classes for social workers with a B.A.
and one year of experience, workers with one year of graduate
professional education, and those with a two-year graduate
degree. The B.A. classification was suggested to accommodate
the "large numbers of people . . . entering our field without
any formal social work training"--particularly public welfare
workers--but it was limited to a five-year period.(53)

The committee's work was not without tensions. Several of
the participating organizations had severe reservations about
its recommendations. A representative of the AAMSW criticized
the group for the time spent discussing social work education
and, particularly, the current difficulties of the Association
of Schools. The AASSW's quandaries over undergraduate education and accrediting issues dominated early discussion of
inter-association work. Those objecting to this focus raised a

deeper issue: was the profession concentrating on personnel and educational matters at the expense of the study of practice? It was this study of the process and settings of practice which the specialized groups felt they had to contribute. The immediate problem of AASSW domination was resolved, however, when the committee voted to recommend continuation of a separate educational group, rather than its involvement in a merger of the practice organizations.(54) Unlike other professions, organized social work thus kept educational accreditation separate from its other professional functions.

Other problems related to concerns over membership standards and preservation of the status of particular practice groups. Both the AAPSW and AAMSW were critical of the direction in which the committee was moving. The psychiatric social workers were particularly concerned about threats to standards. They pointed out the "tremendous lowering of the professional background for membership in the proposed . . . organization."(55)

Both the medical and psychiatric groups worried whether their special interests would be adequately represented in a new organization. They distrusted AASW's motives and suspected the association of enlisting the other practice groups in a move toward increasing its own power. The AAMSW representatives were convinced that unless a truly new and different professional organization was created, "we shall simply be swallowed up within the present policies and programs of the AASW."(56)

Although the AAMSW and AAPSW representatives tried to slow the committee down, other organization members were ready to proceed toward a new single organization. A veiled threat was made that those organizations ready for a new structure would push ahead and "the others . . . could wait."(57) At the same time, two new groups, ASCO and SWRG, began to lobby for inclusion in the committee. Up until now, the committee had denied their requests for formal participation. In the case of ASCO, the denial was based on the fact that the association was a study group and not a body of practitioners, and perhaps also on hesitations about the group's professional identity. Responses to SWRG were more cordial. The research group was invited to participate in the discussions by sending a nonvoting observer. In contrast to ASCO, SWRG had moved more quickly toward a social work orientation and from its formation in 1949 had anticipated being part of a new organization of professional social workers.(58)

In its first year, the Committee on Inter-Association Structure had made some progress, but tensions remained. To continue negotiations, the committee formed a more permanent group--the Council on Temporary Inter-Association Structure (TIAC), in June, 1950. The council had four representatives from each of the five existing membership associations. The Association of Schools was excluded, as well as ASCO and SWRG. For its chair, the council chose Dora Goldstine, a medical social worker on the University of Chicago faculty and president of the AAMSW. TIAC's purpose was to consider ways and means by which the different organizations might work together towards the advancement of the profession.(59)

The new council inherited the previous committee's issues
regarding the form of a single social work organization and the
requirements for membership. Strains between the AASW and the
more autonomous specialist groups continued. At one point, the
council almost disbanded. Responding to intergroup tensions,
one AASW representative expressed concern about "a large part
of our money going to advance the program of certain specialties
which . . . happen to be organized." The AASW had been a major
force in the attempt to get unity for the profession. It would
be unfair for the specialties to "hold rigidly to maintaining
all of their own gains . . . without a primary concern for the
profession as a whole."(60)

TIAC generally accepted the importance of the whole as
opposed to the parts. It eventually authorized a plan for a new
single organization of social work. The AAMSW and the AAPSW
agreed to join the new organization rather than become isolated
groups. Yet as associations preoccupied with standards, they
contributed to the ongoing battles over the appropriate standards for membership in the new organization.(61)

TIAC now faced a major decision. Should the group accept
earlier plans for an organization with flexible membership
requirements, including accommodation for B.A. social workers?
Or should it move once and for all to make graduation from a
school of social work the minimum standard for professional
social work practice? The psychiatric social workers were the
strongest supporters of the two-year requirement. Among AASW
chapters, responses were mixed. About half favored a membership requirement of one year of graduate professional education. A quarter supported the two-year standard. AAMSW members were similarly divided. In both groups, however, many of
the supporters of a one-year requirement suggested it be raised
to two within a specified time limit. The AAGW, despite hes-
itation about its impact on group workers, generally accepted
the two-year idea. The NASSW, in line with its own membership
requirements, suggested a single year of graduate training.
Eventually, the "high standard" faction won out, and two years
of professional education was mandated for the new organization.(62) Without an adequate lobby in the group, most public
welfare workers faced continued exclusion.

The membership question was also a crucial factor in the
relationships between TIAC and the social work research and
community organization groups. In these relationships,
practitioners were forced to choose between identities as professional social workers and adherence to the goals and methods
of their own organization. In 1951, SWRG inquired about
involvement with TIAC. While the AASW was encouraging, several
of the other groups objected, particularly the AAPSW. A major
complaint was the fact that the research group had "no defined
educational base for membership." A year later, TIAC finally
admitted SWRG as a voting member, after the research group went
on record in support of a professional education requirement.(63)

This move on SWRG's part meant sacrificing a particular
image of social work research. One SWRG member spoke of "win-
ning admission to the sacred precincts of TIAC" and wondered
"whether having battered our way [in] . . ., we belonged in at

all."(64) Adherence to the two-year professional education
requirement encouraged restriction of the field of social work
research to a specific group of social work practitioners.
Some feared this would lead to sterility in the development of
knowledge.(65)
      Rather than join the new professional membership organiza-
tion, SWRG might have chosen an alternate organizational model.
One member proposed that the researchers remain a separate
interest group, cast in the form of a learned society. Social
work could then structure itself around a three-way set of
organizations: an educational group, a professional "regu-
latory organization" representing practice, and "a learned
society devoted to the promotion of social work knowledge."
Essentially, the choice seemed to lie between a basic identification with practice or with knowledge-building.(66) The
SWRG Steering Committee decided that the group could best
achieve its purpose and protect its membership through participation in the professional organization. It therefore cast its
ballot for inclusion in the new single organization of practitioners.(67) By narrowing its identity, SWRG reduced the possibility of productive interdisciplinary work within its ranks.
      Community organization practitioners went through a simi-
lar process. As late as 1953, the group had no specific
requirements for membership, other than an interest in the community organization process. TIAC members were consistently
negative about ASCO's involvement in the work of the council.
They noted the group's indecisiveness about identifying with
social welfare and accepting social work training as the best
preparation for community organization practice. The specialist groups questioned whether ASCO's organizational development had reached "the same level of professional group as the
other associations." ASCO asked angrily how a new organization
that excluded community organization could pretend to represent
the whole of social work practice.(68)
      Only after ASCO pledged adherence to the social work pro-
fession did TIAC reconsider its stand and invite the group to
join. Even then, the community organization association was to
be limited to the status of a committee in the new single
organization, with division status to be decided upon after the
organization's actual formation.(69)
      By 1954, TIAC was ready to set up the machinery for a new
professional organization. A Constitutional Convention was
held in November, 1954, to draw up bylaws for the new association. In a final move for control, the AASW National Board recommended that the Association have 50 percent of the voting
power at the convention. Yet the other groups won out, and each
participating organization had a single vote. Together, they
moved formation of a National Association of Social Workers,
with a single membership standard, divisions for the specialties, six commissions on professional and social policy issues,
and a Delegate Assembly with ultimate authority for setting the
broad policies of the association.(70)
      In the following mail ballot, members of all the organiza-
tions voted overwhelmingly in favor of the proposed NASW,
although one-tenth of the medical and psychiatric social workers who voted were opposed. The new organization blanketed in

all members of the existing practice associations. It had
20,000 members. The group chose the AASW's Joe Anderson as
executive secretary. Finally joined together, the various
groups within social work (with the exception of public welfare
and corrections workers) could now attend to a list of responsibilities proposed for the new organization: definition of the
function and scope of the social work profession, development
of sound programs of education and research, the study of practice, promotion of professional standards, and pursuit of an
effective social action program.(71)

Social work had made an impressive move toward cohesion.
Yet important issues and intergroup differences remained.
These related to ongoing questions about the purposes of a professional organization and its relation to knowledge and practice, the profession's role in social action, and the most
appropriate standards for professional identification and
training.

The Commission on Social Work Practice was the first commission activated by the new NASW. This group held great promise for those social workers, particularly from the specialized
organizations, who had earlier criticized the AASW and TIAC for
lack of attention to practice issues. These individuals sought
a balance between emphasis on professional education, personnel
matters, and practice. As the commission's new chairperson,
Harriett Bartlett, later explained, the AASW should have become
the one organization to represent all social workers,

but they didn't take in practice. They worked on personnel
problems and policy and program and a journal, and somehow they
never had the vision to . . . expand and take in all the fields
and the professional practice.(72)

Earlier, Bartlett had worked with William Gordon and Margaret
Schutz, now also members of the Practice Commission, to develop
concepts in medical social work. Out of this experience, she
had concluded that social work suffered from an overemphasis on
skill, particularly in the area of case work, and from lack of
attention to developing knowledge for practice.(73)

The new commission set out to rectify this situation.
From the first, there was a sense of challenge and opportunity.
The group had twenty-one members, representing the various
specialties. But they were committed to thinking about social
work as a whole. Bartlett reminisces about their first meeting:

It was one of the most vivid memories of my life because we were
all dedicated and here we sat in this big room . . . it was the
first time that any group had had a real opportunity to look at
the profession as a profession together . . . we were determined
not to be pulled aside to the fragmented field of interest. . .
. It was very, very exciting.(74)

One of the commission's first decisions was that it needed
to develop a working definition of social work practice before
it could proceed further. No comprehensive statement about the
nature of social work existed. William Gordon and others

devised a definition encompassing knowledge, values, purpose, sanction, and method. This formulation was approved by the majority of commission members. Bartlett then applied the definition in a monograph on Social Work Practice in the Health Field. She expected that similar studies by other fields would follow. However, Gordon's definition was not universally accepted, even within the committee that drew it up, and Bartlett's study remained one of a kind.(75)

After the first few years of work, the Practice Commission ran into difficulties. The CSWE had already embarked on a major study of the social work curriculum. The commission recommended a parallel study of social work practice, but was unable to obtain NASW approval or outside funding for such research. Then Bartlett retired from practice at about the same time that the commission was reorganized by the NASW. The new commission was a much larger group. Under the chairmanship of Alfred Kahn, it pursued the study of broad programs of social service delivery, rather than continuing the former commission's examination of practice. Thus one of the major goals of the specialist groups--the attention of the profession as a whole to issues of practice--failed to be realized.(76)

Another area of professional attention for the new organization was involvement in social policy and action. During the last year of TIAC operation, a special committee drew up a series of position statements on issues relating to public social policy and the planning and administration of health and welfare programs. The Committee on Social Policy and Action hoped these statements would provide a basis for future activity by the new professional organization. The TIAC Planning Committee recommended that the work of the proposed Commission of Social Policy and Action "be given the highest priority as the NASW comes into being." They thus reinforced the fears of some in the specialized practice groups that the new organization would attend primarily to social action and public relations rather than to practice issues.(77)

The TIAC social policy committee reaffirmed the social worker's responsibility to strengthen basic social relationships between individuals, groups, and social institutions. In the case of failures in these relationships, social workers were to report this fact "and, where appropriate, to suggest solutions to . . . policy making bodies." As part of the machinery for suggesting solutions, the committee recommended that the NASW maintain a Washington office to report on federal developments in social work and to carry out decisions of the Board of Directors regarding federal legislation. For the guidance of the new Commission on Social Policy, the committee presented its statements on social work responsibilities in areas such as health, housing, and public welfare. Yet in all but the public welfare statement, recommended actions were confined to "study" and "evaluation" rather than direct involvement in the legislation and administration of policy.(78)

The social action stance envisioned by the TIAC committee and carried out in the early years of the NASW followed a different model from that proposed by activists in the thirties and forties. Study, evaluation, and suggestion replaced more active lobbying and pressure group tactics. The use of expertise seemed more appropriate, professionally, than involvement in political organizing.

While practice specialists worried about too much attention to social policy, some social workers began to fear that the field was doing far too little. Reinforced perhaps by the complacency of the fifties, the profession as a whole seemed to be concentrating more and more on narrow practice with a middle-class clientele and on issues of internal professional development. Herbert Bisno raised the alarm in an important article, "How Social Will Social Work Be?" His claim that social work was drifting away from its commitment to social action had prophetic implications regarding events in social work in the 1960s.(79)

A final issue in social work's development--the appropriate standard for professional education and practice--seemed to have been resolved when the two-year graduate degree was accepted as the basic requirement for NASW membership. Yet members of the organization were concerned about the continued exclusion of large numbers of lesser-trained social work practitioners. The first Commission on Practice recognized this problem and had planned to study the activities of nonprofessional personnel in social work.(80) In the realm of education, the issue of the place of undergraduate social work training was also unresolved. Although the 1959 CSWE Curriculum Study marked a major step in designing a total social work curriculum, it reserved the title of "professional education" for graduate training. Herbert Bisno's volume on undergraduate education, however, held out the promise of that education for future consideration by the profession.(81)

Despite ongoing issues, however, social work achieved important milestones in the late 1950s. The NASW adopted a Code of Ethics. The organization also began work toward establishing social work certification and licensing. Definitions of social work functions and practice had been formulated by the NASW Practice Commission and the authors of the CSWE Curriculum Study. That study presented a broad picture of a social work curriculum which covered a wide range of practice. It was directed by Werner Boehm and involved consultation with individual educators, the NASW, and representatives of the various fields and methods of practice. Its thirteen-volume report included discussion of curriculum in community organization, research, the public social services, case work, group work, and social policy.(82)

By 1960, then, greater cohesion existed within the profession. Yet conflicts remained. Accommodation between the various practice interests had led to a federated NASW in which differences were preserved by sections. Forces for homogeneity in the field had prevailed in the structuring of membership requirements. The NASW requirements of a master's degree perpetuated exclusion of nonprofessionally trained workers, especially those in the public welfare services. Similarly, the Curriculum Study failed to resolve the profession's ambivalence about undergraduate social work education. Although some members of the profession pushed for greater attention to social policy and others for more focus on practice, the major purpose of the new organization was to enhance

professional status. The model chosen for social work's professional association was one stressing high standards, a
single path of training, and a cautious approach to political
involvement. Cohesion existed within a core of the profession,
but at the expense of certain groups who, often supported by
outside forces, would continue to question that core.

Notes

1. Benjamin Youngdahl, "Shall We Face It?" <u>Social</u> <u>Work</u> <u>Journal</u>, XXIX: 63-69 (April, 1948).

2. The Association for the Study of Community Organization joined the new organization in November, 1955.

3. Minutes, Interim Committee for Joint Planning in Social Work, 7/15/44, Harriett Bartlett Papers, folder 9, Social Welfare History Archives, Minneapolis, Minn.

4. The group was first called the American Association of Hospital Social Workers. Interview with Harriett Bartlett, August 20, 1979; Roy Lubove, <u>The</u> <u>Professional</u> <u>Altruist</u> (New York: Atheneum, 1969), pp. 23-35.

5. Yearly Report, Ill. District, AAHSW, 1933-34, NASW: Chicago Chapter Records, folder 12, Chicago Historical Society, Chicago, Ill.; "Outline of the Curriculum in Medical Social Work in a Professional School of Social Work," Adopted by AAMSW, 12/36, NASW Records, folder 373, Social Welfare History Archives. The first medical social work training course was a one-year program at the Boston School of Social Work, developed in 1912. The New York and Philadelphia Schools of Social Work soon followed Boston's lead. Lubove, p. 34.

6. Committee on Inter-Association Structure and Program, Temporary Inter-Agency Council, 1949, NASW Records, folder 898.

7. The National Foundation for Infantile Paralysis, which had funded medical social work, was no longer a viable source of grants after the development of the polio vaccine in the fifties. Interview with Bartlett; Harriett Bartlett Oral Memoir, NASW Oral History Project, 1980, p. 65, Social Welfare History Archives; interview with Mary Burns, April 10, 1979; U.S. Department of Health, Education, and Welfare, <u>Closing</u> <u>the</u> <u>Gap</u> <u>in</u> <u>Social</u> <u>Work</u> <u>Manpower</u> (Washington, D.C.: U.S. GPO, 1965), p. 34.

8. Chicago Round Table on Psychiatric Social Work, 12/9/31, 4/20/32, NASW: Chicago Chapter Records, folders 7 and 8; Gordon Hamilton, <u>Theory</u> <u>and</u> <u>Practice</u> <u>of</u> <u>Social</u> <u>Casework</u> (New York: Columbia University Press, 1940), pp. 345-49. Committee on Inter-Association Structure and Program, TIAC, 1949, NASW Records, folder 898; <u>Closing</u> <u>the</u> <u>Gap</u> <u>in</u> <u>Social</u> <u>Work</u> <u>Manpower</u>, p. 34 (50 percent of the medical social workers in 1950 had two years of graduate training); interview with Mary Burns; Bartlett Memoir, p. 80.

9. Harriett M. Johnson, <u>The</u> <u>Visiting</u> <u>Teacher</u> <u>in</u> <u>N.Y.C.</u> (1916), quoted in Lubove, p. 37.

10. Mildred Sikkema, "School Social Services," <u>Social</u> <u>Work</u> <u>Year</u> <u>Book</u> (1951), pp. 444-50.

11.   Ibid.; Florence Poole, "Nation-Wide Developments in School Social Work," Bulletin, NASSW, XXII: 4-8 (March, 1947).

12.   Report of the "Panel Discussion," AASGW, 5/27/37, "Is Group Work Social Work, Education, or Recreation?"; "Extract from the Report of the Chairman Before the Annual Meeting to the Association in New Orleans," AASGW, 5/42; Summary Report of Business Meetings, AASGW, 5/44, NASW Records, folder 804.

13.   Gordon Hamilton was among the minority in the AASW which urged some accommodation to group work interests. Minutes, Ad Interim Committee, AASW, 6/19/37, NASW Records, folder 22.

14.   Summary Report of Business Meetings of AAGSW, 5/44, NASW Records, folder 804; letter from Coyle to Kaiser, 8/25/44, NASW Records, folder 17; Minutes, National Board Meeting, AASW, 10/44 and 3/45, NASW Records, folder 12.

15.   Minutes,   Executive   Committee,   Conference   of Professional Schools of Recreation and Group Work, 3/15/46, Grace Coyle Papers, Box 3, 3 HC 3, Case Western Reserve University Archives, Cleveland, Ohio.

16.   Summary Report of Business Meetings of AASGW, 5/44; Minutes, Tenth Annual Business Meeting, AASGW, 5/23/46, NASW Records, folder 804; Memo, Central Committee to Members of AASGW, 2/5/46, NASW Records, folder 806; Loren Crabtree, SWHA Inventory, AAGW Records in NASW Records; Letter from Gertrude Wilson to Helen Rowe, 5/13/44, NASW Records, folder 806; Sanford Solender, "Implications of the TIAC Report for the AAGW," The Group, XIV: 24-28 (October, 1951).

17.   Saul Bernstein, Group Work Memories (Chicago: Loyola University School of Social Work, 1984), p. 8.

18.   The NCSW section was organized in 1939. Arthur Dunham to Joe Anderson, 1/6/47, NASW Records, folder 857; C. F. McNeil, "Community Organization for Social Welfare," Social Work Year Book (1951), pp. 123-28.

19.   Folder 859, "NASW:ASCO, Annual Meetings, Minutes, 1948-54,"   NASW Records; McNeil; Kenneth Pray, "When Is Community Organization Social Work Practice?" National Conference of Social Work, Proceedings (1948), pp. 194-204.

20.   Minutes, TIAC, 9/11-12/53, NASW Records, folder 904. Note that this was a community planning model of community organization, rather than the grassroots mass organizing approach.

21.   McNeil, pp. 123, 126.

22.   Statement of Organization of the Social Work Research Group, 6/16/49; Meeting of Research Workers in Social Work at NCSW, 6/16/49, NASW Records, folder 891. Note that inter-

association activity aimed at establishing a new social work organization had begun before SWRG was formed.

23. Report of the Chairman, SWRG, 4/27/50, NASW Records, folder 891.

24. William Gordon, Memo to Members of Committee on Research Function and Practice, SWRG, 1951, NASW Records, folder 892; Philip Klein, "Past and Future in Social Work Research," Social Welfare Forum, Proceedings, National Conference of Social Work (1951), pp. 130-47.

25. Russell H. Kurtz, "Research in Social Work," Social Work Year Book (1937), pp. 419-23.

26. "The Function and Practice of Research in Social Work," Report to SWRG from Committee on Research Functions and Practice, 5/17/51, NASW Records, folder 892.

27. David French, An Approach to Measuring Results in Social Work (New York: Columbia University Press, 1952); J. McVicker Hunt and Leonard Kogan, Measuring Results in Social Casework (New York: FSAA, 1950).

28. L. L. Geismer, "The Multiproblem Family: Significance of Research Findings," Social Welfare Forum (1960), pp. 166-79.

29. Program of SWRG, NCSW, 4/23-28/50, NASW Records, folder 891. William Gordon, "Professional Base of Social Work Research," Minutes, SWRG Steering Committee, 9/13-14/51, SWRG Records, NASW Supplement.

30. Irving Weisman, "Courts and Social Welfare," Social Work Year Book (1957), p. 207; see also Report of Conference with Representatives of the Fields of Group Work, Community Organization, Public Welfare, and Probation and Parole, AASW, 1/11/45, NASW Records, folder 18.

31. Helen Rowe, "A Challenging Decision for AAGW," The Group, XIV: 9-23 (October, 1951).

32. The AAGW was the most interested of the specialty groups in the social action arena. It had a legislative committee, and discussed social action at national meetings. Helen Rowe, "Report of the Central Committee," in American Association of Group Workers, Toward Professional Standards (New York: Association Press, 1947), pp. 168-73.

33. See, e.g., "The Georgia Scene," Social Work Journal, XXXII: 110, 158-59 (July, 1951); Eric Goldman, The Crucial Decade and After (New York: Vintage Books, 1960), pp. 137-46; Athan Theoharis, Seeds of Repression: Harry S. Truman and the Origins of McCarthyism (New York: Quadrangle Books, 1971), pp. 14-18.

34. Joe Anderson, "Response of Social Work to the Present Challenge," NCSW, Proceedings (1951), pp. 47-60.

35. "Confidentiality of Assistance Records" (Pamphlet, New York: AASW, 1/52), NASW Records, Ephemera; Gilbert Steiner, Social Insecurity: The Politics of Welfare (Chicago: Rand McNally, 1966), pp. 95-96.

36. During an investigation of the Baltimore public welfare department in 1948, Towle's pamphlet and one by Grace Marcus came under fire from officials hostile to "the social work theories of the Federal Administration." Marion Hathway, "Preparation for Social Responsibility," AASSW Annual Meeting, 1948, Council on Social Work Education Records, Record Group I, Box 3, Social Welfare History Archives. The order for destruction by the FSA came after charges by the President of the AMA that the book was "socialistic." Helen Harris Perlman, "Charlotte Towle: An Appreciation," in Perlman, ed., Helping; Charlotte Towle on Social Work and Social Casework (Chicago: University of Chicago Press, 1969), pp. 12-13. Towle and Hathway were labelled Communist for such things as Towle's signing a petition of clemency for the Rosenbergs and Hathway's earlier membership in the League against War and Fascism.

37. Marion Hathway Papers, Inventory, Francis X. Blouin and Susan Henderson Shreve, Social Welfare History Archives.

38. Letter from Henry L. McCarthy, Commissioner, NYC Department of Welfare, to Partick A. Tompkins, 8/21/51; Raymond Hilliard, Executive Director, Welfare Council of NYC, to Tompkins, 8/22/51; Fred Hoehler to Harry M. Carey, 9/17/51, Fred K. Hoehler Papers, folder 349, Social Welfare History Archives.

39. John R. Stockman to Fred Hoehler, 1/9/51, Hoehler Papers, folder 349; Interview with Rita Novak, May 20, 1979; Interview with Mary Burns, April 10, 1979.

40. See, e.g., "Resolution of Executive Committee," AAMSW, 5/51, NASW Records, folder 336; "The 1949 Delegate Conference," Social Work Journal, XXX: 166 (October, 1949); "Social Worker's Defense Fund," Social Work Journal, XXXII: 162 (October, 1951).

41. Minutes, Faculty Meeting, 11/13/53, School of Applied Social Sciences, Western Reserve University Records, Box 28, 28F, Case Western Reserve University Archives; The Reminiscences of Jane Hoey, Social Security Project, 1965, p. 96, Oral History Collection of Columbia Universitiy.

42. Anderson, p. 53; Report of Conference with Representatives of the Fields of Group Work, pp. 3-4; Memo, Dora Goldstine to Members of TIAC, 3/29/51, "Historical Background," NASW Records, folder 903.

43. U.S. Bureau of Labor Statistics, Social Workers in

1950: A Report on the Study of Salaries and Working Conditions in Social Work (New York: AASW, 1952); Closing the Gap
in Social Work Manpower, p. 34. It should be noted that a fair
proportion of social workers in the various fields had some
graduate training short of the M.S.W.

     44. Memo, Dora Goldstine to Members of TIAC, 3/29/51,
NASW Records, folder 903. Enrollment in social work graduate
schools peaked at 4,336 in 1950, dropped to 4,195 in 1951, and
3,694 in 1953. "Notes and Comments," Social Service Review,
XXX: 453-62 (December, 1956).

     45. See the inter-association cooperation discussed by
AASW chapters in New Jersey and Detroit, Proceedings, AASW
Delegate Conference, 1940, pp. 272-85, NASW Records, folder 77.
"Inter-Professional Association Committee," Report submitted
by Sub-Committee of Committee on Inter-Association Structure,
ca 1948, NASW Records, folder 896; Jt. Meeting of Executive
Committees of AASW, AAMSW, AAPSW, AAGW, and AASSW with Clyde
Murray, Chairman of Committee on Inter-Association Structure,
3/14/49, NASW Records, folder 897; Memo from Goldstine,
3/29/51, NASW Records, folder 903.

     46. Report of Curriculum Planning Committee, AASSW,
1/47-1/48, CSWE Records, VII-3; Report of Conference on
Proposals for Inter-Association Activities, 11/6/47, NASW
Records, folder 982. A joint AASW-AASSW Committee had been
active for some time.

     47. Interview with Mary Burns; Letter from Dora
Goldstine, AAMSW, to Mary Blanche Moss, 5/5/49, NASW Records,
folder 968; Elizabeth P. Rice to Goldstine, 1/10/50, NASW
Records, folder 971; Minutes, Joint Meeting of Representatives,
Professional Social Work Associations, 1/24/49, NASW Records,
folder 899.

     48. Minutes, Joint Meeting of Representatives of
Professional Social Work Organizations, 4/22-23/49, NASW
Records, folder 899.

     49. Minutes, Joint Meeting of Representatives of
Professional Social Work Organizations, 1/24/49, NASW Records,
folder 899; Letter from Rice to Goldstine, 1/10/50, NASW
Records, folder 971.

     50. Resolution adopted by AAGW Membership, 6/14/49, NASW
Records, folder 896.

     51. Resolutions Adopted by 1948 Delegate Conference,
AASW, April, 1948, NASW Records, folder 982.

     52. Committee on Inter-Association Structure, Local
Joint Executive Committee Meeting, St. Louis, Mo., 3/14/49,
NASW Records, folder 897.

     53. Ibid.; Report, Committee on Inter-Association

Structure, 5/15/49, NASW Records, folder 898; Minutes, Committee on Inter-Association Structure, 4/22-23/49; Summary, Meeting of Working Committee of Committee on Inter-Association Structure, 3/18/49, pp. 6-7, NASW Records, folder 899.

54. Letter from Goldstine to Grace White, President Pro-tem, Committee on Inter-Association Structure, 2/9/49; Goldstine to Pauline Ryman, 11/28/49, NASW Records, folder 986; Report, Committee on Inter-Association Structure, 5/15/49, NASW Records, folder 898; Minutes, Committee on Inter-Association Structure, 1/7-8/50, p. 5; Report of Subcommittee on Principles of Committee on Inter-Association Structure, 1/8/50, NASW Records, folder 899.

55. Letter from Rice (AAMSW) to Goldstine, 1/10/50, NASW Records, folder 971; Leon Lucas, Pres., AAPSW, to Clyde Murray, Chair, Committee on Inter-Association Structure, 3/16/50, NASW Records, folder 896.

56. Letter from Goldstine to Moss, 5/5/49, NASW Records, folder 968; Rice to Goldstine, 1/10/50, Goldstine to Moss, 2/7/50, NASW Records, folder 971.

57. Letter from Rice to Goldstine, 1/10/50, NASW Records, folder 971.

58. Proposal for Establishment of An Association of Research Workers in Social Work, 4/22/49, NASW Records, folder 891; Murray to Ann Shyne, SWRG, 1/20/50, NASW Records, folder 899; Memo to Members of ASCO from Ernest Harper, 3/30/53, NASW Records, folder 1004.

59. Minutes, Committee on Inter-Association Structure, 3/25/50, NASW Records, folder 899; TIAC By-Laws, First Draft, 10/50, NASW Records, folder 901.

60. Letter from Dorothy Hankins, AASW Representative to TIAC, to Ernest Witte, Pres., AASW, 4/25/51, NASW Records, folder 983; Report on 1951 Delegate Conference, AASW, 5/51, NASW Records, folder 982; Roberta E. Finkbinder, AASW Representative to TIAC, to Joe Anderson, 4/11/51, NASW Records, folder 983.

61. "The TIAC Report," Social Work Journal, XXXII: 111-57 (July, 1951); "Plan for a Single New Organization of Social Workers," TIAC, 12/52, NASW Records, Ephemera.

62. AASW, Committee on Inter-Association Structure Report to Executive Committee, ca 1952; Letter from Rice to Goldstine, n.d.; Resolution of AAGW Board, 12/28/51; Opal Boston (NASSW) to Goldstine, 1/12/52, NASW Records, folder 904.

63. Letter from Ethel Ginsburg (AAPSW) to Goldstine, 3/23/51; Ruth Smalley to Goldstine, 3/30/51, NASW Records, folder 905; Minutes, TIAC 2/2-3/52, NASW Records, folder 904.

64. Letter from Ann Shyne to Philip Klein, 1/17/53, SWRG Records in NASW Supplement.

65. Memo to Members of Committee on Research Function and Practice from Isaac Hoffman, SWRG, 5/52, NASW Records, folder 892; Minutes, Annual Meeting, SWRG, 6/2-4/53, NASW Records, folder 891.

66. Hoffman, Memo, 5/52, NASW Records, folder 892. See also William Gordon, "The Professional Base of Social Work Research," pp. 2-3.

67. Minutes, SWRG Steering Committee, 5/31/53, SWRG Records in NASW Supplement.

68. The AASW was at first the only group in favor of ASCO's inclusion in TIAC. ASCO was invited to join in September, 1953. Minutes, TIAC, 12/20-21/52, NASW Records, folder 904; Memo from Harper to members of ASCO, 3/30/53, NASW Records, folder 1004.

69. Letter from Merrill F. Krughoff, Pres., ASCO, to Goldstine, 7/31/53, NASW Records, folder 904; Harper, "Are Community Organization Practitioners Social Workers?" 8/30/53, NASW Records, folder 1004; Minutes, TIAC, 9/11-12/53, NASW Records, folder 904.

70. The NASW also had an Executive Board to administer the decisions of the Delegate Assembly. Minutes, TIAC, 9/11-12/53, NASW Records, folder 904; Memo to members of AASW from Joe Anderson, 3/27/53; Letter from Ruth Knee, President, AAPSW, to Goldstine, 6/11/53; Anderson to Goldstine, 6/15/53; Janet Korpola (AAGW) to Goldstine, 7/1/53, NASW Records, folder 928; Grace White to Youngdahl, Pres., AASW, 3/25/53, NASW Records, folder 986; "Plan for a New Single Organization," TIAC, 12/52, NASW Ephemera; Memo to Presidents of the Member Organizations from Sanford Solender, Chairman, TIAC, NASW Records, folder 941.

71. The vote among the other organizations was almost unanimously in favor of the new assoc+ation. Solender, memo; TIAC By-Laws, 1950 (1st Draft) and 1/1/51, NASW Records, folder 901.

72. Bartlett, Oral Memoir, pp. 62, 75-76. See also letter from Goldstine to White, 2/9/49, and Goldstine to Ryman, 11/28/49, NASW Records, folder 986.

73. Minutes, Planning Committee, Commission on Social Work Practice, 12/9-10/55, NASW Records, folder 1042.

74. Bartlett, Oral Memoir, p. 87; interview with Bartlett.

75. Interview with Bartlett; Bartlett, "Toward Clarification and Improvement of Social Work Practice," Social

Work, III: 309 (April, 1958); Bartlett, Social Work Practice
in the Health Field (New York: NASW, 1961); Report by
Commission on Soc. Work Practice to Delegate Assembly, NASW,
5/9/58, NASW Records, folder 1042; William E. Gordon, "A
Critique of the Working Definition," Social Work, VII: 3-13
(October, 1962).

    76. Memo, Policy and Planning Committee, to Commission on
Social Work Practice, 12/12/58, NASW Records, folder 1042.
Gordon was not a member of the second commission; Bartlett was a
consultant rather than an active member. Interview with
Bartlett; Bartlett, Oral Memoir, p. 210.

    77. Memos to Members of TIAC Commission on Social Policy
and Action from Joe Anderson, 1/14/55 and 4/21/55, NASW
Records, folder 951; Minutes, TIAC, 9/11-12/53, NASW Records,
folder 904.

    78. Emphasis mine. Report of TIAC Committee on Social
Policy and Action and Proposed Position Statements, 5/55, NASW
Records, folder 951.

    79. Herbert Bisno, "How Social Will Social Work Be?"
Social Work, I: 12-18 (April, 1956). See also Eveline Burns,
"Social Welfare is Our Commitment," Social Welfare Forum
(1958), pp. 3-19. This was the Presidential Address at the
1958 NCSW.

    80. Because of the commission's difficulties, that study
was not carried out. Report by Commission on Social Work
Practice to Delegate Assembly, NASW, 5/19/58, NASW Records,
folder 1042.

    81. Herbert Bisno, The Place of the Undergraduate Cur-
riculum in Social Work Education, The Comprehensive Report of
the Curriculum Study, vol. 2 (New York: CSWE, 1959).

    82. Werner Boehm, Objectives of the Social Work Cur-
riculum of the Future, The Comprehensive Report of the
Curriculum Study, vol. 1.

10
Conclusion

Social workers of the 1920s were a diverse lot. They differed among themselves in levels of skill and education, in types of work settings, and in degree of professional identity. They were a small group--some 25,000--concentrated in large cities. Their professional training varied widely. Their salaries were low, and their public image, with the exception of certain leaders, was unprepossessing.

Yet in 1929 Porter Lee could look forward in confidence to the future. Social workers had taken significant steps toward professional development. They had established a professional organization, begun to develop social case work as a distinctive skill, and set up a professional education association with rudimentary standards. Reflecting on social work's past glories as a "cause," Lee spoke confidently of the profession's "function" in a modern system of social welfare.(1)

The next thirty years witnessed significant achievements in social work's professional development. Forecast in the late twenties, these included a greater number in the field, a broader, stronger professional association, an enlarged and more consolidated system of professional education, a wider intellectual and practice base, and a more legitimized role in both the public and the private social services. Yet each area of strength brought with it unresolved issues and problems, relating to ongoing tensions within the field.

The number of social workers increased more than fivefold from 1930 to 1960. In 1960, an estimated 105,000 were employed in the field. Although social workers in private agencies worked largely in the big cities and industrialized areas, public welfare workers were spread more evenly across the country. Though the number of social workers had increased, many still lacked professional training. Of social workers employed in 1960, only about 20 percent had completed two years of graduate school. The situation was most acute in public assistance work, where just 3 percent of the personnel was professionally trained.(2)

Group workers, community organizers, and case workers had come together in a new professional association in 1955. However, only some 21 percent of employed social workers belonged to the National Association of Social Workers in 1960. This was an improvement over the 16 percent--mostly case workers--who had been part of the AASW in 1950. Yet the new association, though more diverse, could not speak confidently as repre-

sentative of the entire field. NASW membership requirements
called for the master's degree. B.S.W. social workers and public assistance workers did not have a corresponding professional group.

The NASW had inaugurated a number of steps toward strengthening the profession. It had begun to develop a working
definition of social work practice. A code of ethics had been
adopted. Association members were exploring the possibility
of certification and licensing for social work practice. The
new organization was composing statements on social policy
issues. A vanguard more than a rank and file group, the NASW
nevertheless marked an important merger of representatives of
the various fields and methods of social work.

Patterns in professional education were similar. The
massive curriculum study of 1959 raised but did not resolve the
issue of the proper place of undergraduate education within the
social work training and accreditation scheme. Undergraduate
programs received a measure of recognition through their membership in the CSWE, but exerted little influence over council
policy. At the same time, the numbers of graduate schools and
graduate students expanded slightly. In 1950-51, forty-nine
schools of social work granted 1,923 master's degrees. In
1959-60, fifty-six schools produced 2,087 graduates.(3)

The unification of practitioner groups in the NASW was paralleled in education by a growing emphasis on a common educational base for all social work practice. In 1956 the CSWE
adopted the recommendation of its Committee on Specializations
that "a school of social work be accredited for its basic
generic curriculum" rather than its specialized programs.(4)
The inclusion of the social sciences in the professional curriculum, the expansion of research efforts, and the development
of doctoral programs had all contributed to a more scholarly and
systematic education for social work practice.

Social work's public image, though still a problem, had
also improved since the days of the Depression. Greater use
was being made of social workers in state and federal welfare
programs. Salaries, though low compared to those of most other
professions, had risen dramatically in both the public and
private arenas. Median annual salaries had increased 76 percent between 1950 and 1960.(5)

Social work in the late fifties was a stronger, more consolidated profession, yet areas of conflict remained. These
conflicts could be viewed as temporary obstacles in the movement toward cohesion and unity. They could also be seen, however, as ongoing strains in the life of a professional group.
External and internal forces produce these strains. Reactions
to them shape the profession's growth.

The tensions in social work can be reduced to four major
issues: should social workers attend primarily to public service or to profession-building; how should social work relate
to a national system of public welfare; what is the appropriate
role of a profession in political activity; and should the profession's intellectual and practice base be narrowly or broadly
defined? Underlying these questions are debates over
selective versus inclusive standards and narrow versus broad
models of professionalism. These issues emerged early in

social work's development and played a major role in the field's growth from 1930 to 1960. Unresolved during that period, they continued to influence education and practice in the sixties and seventies, and indeed into the present. The following pages summarize these conflicts as they occurred in the period from 1930 to 1960 and as they are manifested in more recent developments.

The tumultuous events of the sixties and seventies brought sharp focus to the ongoing dilemmas in social work professionalism. The Kennedy era produced a rediscovery of poverty and, thanks to a growing civil rights movement, greater attention to the social and economic effects of discrimination in America. The Kennedy administration was open to fresh ideas. It welcomed changes in social welfare policy, particularly in the areas of relieving unemployment and expanding social services in public assistance. It predicated changes on a faith in rehabilitation of the poor as a way to tackle the problem of poverty.(6)

The Johnson administration inherited and strengthened the rehabilitative approach. At the same time, it developed a commitment to a broader attack on poverty, a commitment developing in the last months of the Kennedy presidency. Following the president's assassination, Johnson pledged the nation to an all-out War on Poverty. The war had conflicting ideologies from the start, and included both rehabilitative thrusts, with concomitant expansion of services, and a structuralist analysis of poverty. The structural notion held that poverty was at base an economic and political problem, not amenable to simple broadening of opportunity. It led to a discrediting of the public assistance approach and bureaucracy, including the "entrenched professionalism" in that bureaucracy. Under the new Office of Economic Opportunity, community action programs sought to include the poor as indigenous workers and also as participants in the planning process.

The Nixon presidency continued a concern for reforming welfare. The Family Allowance Plan, promising a minimum income floor for all American families, had been on the liberal agenda. Yet the plan, defeated in Congress, contained restrictive measures which forecast the conservatives' increasing stress on accountability and cutbacks in social welfare programs. By the mid-1970s, recession and conservative ideology had led to successful attacks on social welfare measures and their "vested interests," including social workers.

Both the expansion and contraction in antipoverty programs intensified social work's quandary over its major mission: dedication to public service or continued attention to professional development. The two are not necessarily opposed. Yet at times social workers have felt compelled to make a choice. Battles over membership requirements for the AASW in the twenties and thirties drew the initial lines between those attempting to reflect the existing broad range of social service practitioners and those seeking to limit the field to a smaller, more elite group of professionally trained workers. The fuller impact of this battle emerged with social welfare expansion after the New Deal. When Jane Hoey was building a systematic public social service, social work leaders balked at

incorporating lesser-trained public welfare workers into the
profession. When the National Association of Schools of Social
Service Administration spoke of undergraduate education to meet
the staffing needs of state and local welfare departments, the
professional schools worried about the impact on social work
educational standards. In both cases, despite outside pressures, the profession tended to stress maintenance of standards
at the expense of expansion to meet social welfare needs. Professional leaders promoted an exclusive, graduate school model
of legitimization of social work, thus excluding the majority
of those working in the field.

The stress on profession-building over public service,
although profoundly challenged, continued in the sixties and
seventies. Like the New Deal era, these years witnessed
expanding personnel needs in the public social services and
continued shortages of M.S.W.-trained practitioners.(7) Two
major areas of debate revolved around the growth of the paraprofessional movement and the renewed development of undergraduate
social work education. Both related to growing personnel needs
and the new philosophies of the War on Poverty.

The paraprofessional movement developed out of the OEO Community Action Programs' discovery of the potential of
indigenous workers who understood the public welfare and mental
health systems at firsthand. Residents of poor neighborhoods
were hired in both public and private agencies to advocate for
clients of these systems and to "bridge the gap" between middle-
class professionals and their clientele. The idea of a career
ladder for paraprofessionals grew, ensuring them a permanent
place in the social welfare system.(8) Although some social
workers helped plan the utilization and training of indigenous
workers, the new movement represented largely an external challenge to the field's traditional stress on professional skills
and education. While most social workers did not reject the
movement out of hand, many wondered uneasily about the appropriate role of indigenous workers and the proper relationship
between professionals and paraprofessionals in the social
agency.(9) A 1973 NASW job classification scheme included the
levels of social work aide and technician. Yet the two-year
college human services programs, developed in part to train
paraprofessionals, have never been covered by CSWE accreditation.(10)

The renewed growth of undergraduate social work training in
the sixties represented a more serious internal threat to proponents of standard-building. External forces--expansion in
public welfare jobs and the establishment of federal funding
for undergraduate training in 1967--helped spur this growth.
But as in the 1940s, undergraduate education was also championed from within the field, in part as a way to carry out a
public service commitment more effectively. Bolstered by
studies of the competence of B.A. workers in various social welfare settings, undergraduate social work educators envisioned
the graduates of their programs replacing the undifferentiated
B.A. worker in public assistance, the U.S. Veterans Association, and the expanding field of community mental health.(11)
B.A. programs expanded at a rapid rate. By 1967, there were
200, enrolling some 12,500 students. Three years later,

enrollment had jumped to 19,000.(12)

This growth was contested by the proponents of "high standards" in social work. The NASW lobbied for federal funding of
social work education throughout the sitties. Yet, although it
based its arguments on public social service needs, the association limited its campaign to expansion of training on the graduate level. The CSWE continued to accredit master's programs
only, and the NASW maintained its restrictive membership
requirements. Some arguments about the closed nature of the
profession surfaced early in the sixties during discussion of
the Academy of Certified Social Workers, a voluntary certification scheme passed by the NASW Delegate Assembly in 1960.
Since members of the academy were also required to belong to the
NASW, critics argued that the approach was a monopolistic
effort, excluding competent practitioners who did not belong to
the professional association.(13)

In contrast to the 1940s, however, the undergraduate movement of the sixties was too widespread, too much in keeping with
concurrent social welfare ideologies and with reform and expansion of the public welfare system to be submerged. In 1969, in
a major departure from previous policy, the NASW decided to open
membership to baccalaureate social workers who had graduated
from CSWE-recognized social welfare programs. Shortly afterward, CSWE inaugurated an accreditation system for these programs. The major professional associations had thus formally
recognized the B.A. as the beginning level of professional
practice. While this represented a significant victory for
proponents of undergraduate education, underlying resistance
remains. This has emerged most recently in competition between
graduate and undergraduate programs over limited educational
resources and in the rejection of the notion of a professional
B.A. level worker by a growing clinical social work movement.(14) Perhaps because they feel it does not represent
their interests, few B.A. social workers have joined the NASW.

The debate between maintaining standards and broadening
professional membership continues. From the twenties and
thirties on, an important element in this argument has been the
nature of social work's commitment to public service. Most
often this commitment has been expressed in terms of the profession's relation to a national system of public welfare. The
relation has been an ambivalent one. While Edith Abbott and
Sophonisba Breckinridge actively promoted the role of the field
in developing and supervising the public social services, their
stress on standards prevented a constructive response to public
welfare staffing needs. Jane Hoey's attempts to professionalize the public assistance program met with only partial support from the profession. Finally, graduate social workers
have generally chosen not to work in public welfare and have
consistently represented only a tiny fraction of public welfare
personnel.

Social work's relationship to public welfare reform in the
sixties followed patterns established thirty years earlier.
Leaders in the profession sought to influence the kinds of
changes proposed by presidential administrations and by Congress. They utilized the roles of expert consultant and lobbyist adopted by individual social work leaders and by the AASW

during the Great Depression. When testifying on broad social
policy matters, they promoted the strengthening and expansion
of the universal social insurance programs, which seek to correct structural inequities. Yet when they made recommendations regarding the more residual public welfare system, they
thought in terms of rehabilitation.(15) They stressed social
work's traditional concept of skilled case work services carried out by professionally trained staff, echoing the ideas of
Abbott and Breckinridge from thirty years before.

This view of public welfare and the social worker's role was
successfully promoted to President Kennedy and to Abraham
Ribicoff, his secretary of health, education, and welfare.
Ribicoff deliberately sought the advice of social workers in
planning welfare changes.(16) He was receptive to the lobbying
efforts of people like Elizabeth Wickenden, consultant for the
National Social Welfare Assembly. Together with social worker
Winifred Bell, Wickenden had published an influential report
supporting the usefulness of social services, including counseling, referral work, foster home placement, and the like, in
reducing the public welfare rolls. Other social workers echoed
their ideas.(17) The culmination of this campaign came in the
passage of the 1962 Social Security Amendments, which incorporated the idea of skilled services by professional workers
into the federal public assistance categories.

The 1962 amendments represented the height of social work's
interest and involvement in public welfare policy in the sixties and seventies.(18) In a departure from earlier periods,
the professional association, NASW, did maintain a consistent
lobbying effort regarding social welfare measures throughout
the period.(19) An important demonstration project, New York
City's Mobilization for Youth, provided inspiration for community action programs under the Office of Economic Opportunity.(20) An inner circle of social welfare advisors promoted its ideas to the Kennedy and Johnson administrations.
These consultants included Wickenden, Wilbur Cohen, who was
undersecretary and then secretary of HEW, and Fedele Fauri,
dean of the University of Michigan School of Social Work.
Beyond the 1962 amendments, however, it is arguable whether the
social work profession exerted a strong influence on public
welfare policy.

One effect of the War on Poverty had been a growing skep-
ticism about the role of the established professions in solving
social problems. This extended to a critique of the "social
work expert." Advocates of federally funded community action
programs distrusted social workers and the "dead hand of welfare bureaucracy."(21) More pointed discrediting of the field
characterized the Nixon administration, culminating in the
appointment of accountants and budget experts to important welfare posts.

Social work's declining influence in social welfare policy
stemmed also from the lack of a broad commitment to public welfare on the part of the profession's rank and file. Despite the
need for professionally trained workers to carry out the services laid out in the 1962 amendments, new M.S.W. graduates did
not flock to public welfare departments in the sixties. Neither did schools of social work significantly increase the use

of public assistance agencies as field placements. Even the
proponents of the social work initiative in public welfare had
changed. While early public welfare figures like Jane Hoey and
Harry Hopkins were professional social workers, and Abbott and
Breckinridge spanned the two worlds of academics and professional education, the inner circle of welfare advisors in
the sixties did not come from social work education backgrounds.(22)

While the NASW took a more active lobbying role during the
Kennedy era and the War on Poverty, social work remained divided
over the appropriate role of a profession in politics. One
image, carried out by the NASW and earlier by the AASW, holds
that practitioners should be expert lobbyists and objective
consultants rather than partisan actors in the creation of public policy. Another view maintains that partisan political
activity can be reconciled with, and even promote, professional
goals. The Rank and File Movement challenged social workers to
undertake broad-based political and union activity during the
Depression. Wayne McMillen, himself a candidate for political
office and the organizer of citywide protests against welfare
cuts in Chicago, urged a more politicized professional association as president of the AASW in the early forties. This stance
clashed with the professional expertise ideal held by Walter
West and others in the field.

The issue of the nature of political involvement arose
again during the War on Poverty and the Nixon administration.
In a departure from the traditional approach, the NASW joined in
coalitions with a variety of groups, including unions, in order
to protest program cutbacks and to lobby more effectively for
progressive social welfare legislation.(23) The professional
association moved beyond its lobbying, consensus model in 1972,
when it decided to permit chapters to endorse local candidates
for election. Yet the association recognized that such activity was controversial to many social workers.(24)

More serious tensions arose when social work activists,
most of them young, and many of them black, engaged in con-
frontational tactics both on the job and in professional meetings. In the 1968 and 1969 National Conferences on Social Welfare, National Welfare Rights Organization representatives,
minority social workers, and other activists conducted demon-
strations and walkouts urging involvement of welfare recipients
in direction of services and a more aggressive stance by the
National Conference on Social Welfare against poverty and racism. Similar confrontations took place at NASW and CSWE Delegate Assemblies and at meetings of the American Orthopsychi-
atric Association.(25) These challenges were spurred by the
growth of the Black Power and other liberation movements and by
the work of theorists and activists like Chicago community
organizer Saul Alinsky, and Richard Cloward and Frances Fox
Piven, authors of a major critique of the function of welfare.(26) Social work activists proposed a new role for
practitioners as grassroots organizers and catalysts for social
change.

The professional leadership, and mainstream social workers, handled these challenges largely through negotiation and
accommodation. The NASW adopted advocacy as an official pro-

fessional role in 1969. Yet, affected by the growing conservatism of the seventies, the profession soon moved from primary stress on advocacy for broad social change to emphasis on
case advocacy for individual clients caught up in the social
welfare bureaucracy.

Social work undertook new forms of political action in the
sixties and seventies, but remained most comfortable with the
expert   consultant   and   individually   focused   change-agent
approaches. Similarly, while the field encountered new
methods of practice and social and behavioral science theories
and data, it did not abandon its focus on case work and its
quest for a body of knowledge unique to social work. In earlier
years, narrow conceptions of the profession's intellectual and
practice base were opposed by the NASSA, organized group workers, social science-oriented educators like Grace Coyle, and
social workers who joined Hollis and Taylor in advocating a
generic base for practice. In the sixties, the rise of grassroots community organizing as a social work method posed similar challenges to the predominance of case work. Community
organizing specializations appeared in many graduate social
work programs. Community organization majors argued with case
work students over the most effective way to change and improve
clients' lives. At the same time, a number of evaluative
studies raised serious questions about the effectiveness of
case work as a helping process.(27) Finally, behavioral psychology, social systems theory, and an emerging radical social
science presented new sources of knowledge for practice.(28)

While these developments helped to widen social work's
intellectual   and   practice   base,   the   usual   resistances
interacted with external forces to put a brake on basic change
in social work's image. When political conservatism brought an
end to the War on Poverty's community action thrust, organizing
jobs and educational programs began to evaporate. Their departure was generally not vigorously opposed within education and
practice circles. Case work (now often called "social treatment") has since re-emerged as social work's basic core, bolstered by a revitalized clinical social work movement and by the
overwhleming preference of students for social treatment over
policy, administration, or community organizing courses in the
graduate curriculum.

Although behavioral psychology has made inroads in social
work practice, it remains a peripheral approach. Many social
work educators have adopted social systems theory as a major
theoretical framework. Yet the idea of a uniquely social work
body of research and knowledge continues to captivate the profession.(29)

The ongoing dilemma over a wide-ranging versus selective
intellectual and practice base, along with recurring debates
about public service versus profession-building and political
versus expert activity, can be summarized as the clash between a
broad and a narrow view of professionalism in social work. In
the broad model, social work as a profession includes a variety
of groups with different levels of training and expertise.
Leadership within the profession is decentralized. Political
activity and public service are seen as legitimate professional
goals. A responsibility to forces external to the profession

is acknowledged.

A more narrow image of social work's professional task emphasizes the importance of internal professional development. While this view recognizes public service and political commitment, the predominant focus is on strengthening the profession through selective standards of education and membership. A hierarchy exists in the profession, based on degree of training and expertise. Proponents of this model argue that development of a smaller, more expert professional group will lead to greater public recognition than growth of a larger, more amorphous one.

Those supporting the narrow model--the advocates of internal professional advancement--have generally held the upper hand in social work's development. This has led to serious consequences for social work's role in the organized public welfare system as well as in the larger social welfare arena. Social work's concentration on standard-building has retarded professionalization in public welfare. The profession's emphasis on a narrow model of development has resulted in avoidance of the political commitment and strategies necessary to successful involvement in policy making.

Nevertheless, the profession has been influenced and tempered by conflict with and co-optation of opposing groups. Confrontations have led to some broadening of the professional image and at least intermittent attention to a public service mission. Its ability to face division and struggle without splitting apart constitutes social work's peculiar strength. Out of continued conflict a broader professionalism may emerge.

Notes

1. Porter Lee, "Social Work as Cause and Function," National Conference of Social Work, Proceedings (1929), pp. 3, 20.

2. Mary R. Baker, "Personnel in Social Work," Encyclopedia of Social Work (New York: NASW, 1965), pp. 532-40; Ernest P. Witte, "Education for Social Work," Social Work Year Book (1960), pp. 223-40.

3. "Statistical Data in Social Work and Social Welfare," Encyclopedia of Social Work (1965), p. 898.

4. Katherine Kendall, "Education for Social Work," Social Work Year Book (1957), p. 221. See also Ruth Smalley, Specialization in Social Work Education (New York: CSWE, 1956).

5. Baker, pp. 536-37.

6. For helpful analyses of social welfare programs and ideologies in the sixties and seventies, see James T. Patterson, America's Struggle against Poverty, 1900-1980 (Cambridge, Mass.: Harvard University Press, 1981); Gilbert Y. Steiner, Social Insecurity: The Politics of Welfare (Chicago: Rand McNally, 1966); James L. Sundquist, Politics and Policy (Washington, D.C.: Brookings Institute, 1968).

7. U.S. Bureau of Labor Statistics and National Social Welfare Assembly, Salaries and Working Conditions of Social Welfare Manpower in 1960 (New York, n.d.); U.S. Department of Health, Education, and Welfare, Closing the Gap in Social Work Manpower (Washington, D.C.: U.S. GPO, 1965).

8. George Brager, "The Indigenous Worker: A New Approach to the Social Work Technician," Social Work, X: 33-40 (April, 1965); Arthur Pearl and Frank Riessman, New Careers for the Poor (New York: Free Press, 1965).

9. See, e.g. Frank M. Loewenberg, "Social Workers and Indigenous Non-professionals: Some Structural Dilemmas," Social Work, XIII: 65-71 (July, 1968); "The Nonprofessional in Clinic and Community Center," workshop summarized in American Journal of Orthopsychiatry, XXXVIII: 377 (March, 1968).

10. Standards of Social Work Manpower, NASW Policy Statement #4 (Washington, D.C.: NASW, 1973). Human services programs have recently begun their own accrediting body. A.A. human service workers are not eligible for membership in NASW.

11. A number of these studies from the mid-1960s are summarized in Robert L. Barker and Thomas L. Briggs, eds., Manpower Research on the Utilization of Baccalaureate Social Workers, vol. 2 (Washington, D.C.: U.S. GPO, 1971). This research was funded by the U.S. Veterans Administration. See

also Bernice Madison, <u>Undergraduate</u> <u>Education</u> <u>for</u> <u>Social</u>
<u>Welfare</u> (San Francisco: San Francisco State College, 1960),
pp. 1-9.

12. Sherman Merle, <u>Survey</u> <u>of</u> <u>Undergraduate</u> <u>Programs</u> <u>in</u>
<u>Social</u> <u>Welfare:</u> <u>Programs,</u> <u>Faculty,</u> <u>Students</u> (New York: CSWE,
1967); Alfred Stamm, <u>An</u> <u>Analysis</u> <u>of</u> <u>Undergraduate</u> <u>Social</u> <u>Work</u>
<u>Programs</u> <u>Approved</u> <u>By</u> <u>CSWE,</u> <u>1971</u> (New York: CSWE, 1972), p. 24.

13. William Schwartz, "On Certifying Each Other," <u>Social</u>
<u>Work</u>, VII: 21-26 (July, 1962).

14. Harold Lewis, "Social Work Education in the 80's:
What is to be Done?" CSWE Education Annual Planning Meeting,
March, 1982 (New York: Hunter College, 1982); letter from Bill
L. Jett to Estelle Gabriel, 11/8/73, printed in <u>Clinical</u> <u>Social</u>
<u>Work</u> <u>Journal</u>, II: 158-60 (Summer, 1974). See also "BSWs: Are
They on the Outside Looking In?" <u>NASW</u> <u>News</u> (February 1983).

15. Gordon Hamilton, Editorial, <u>Social</u> <u>Work</u>, VII: 2, 128
(January, 1962).

16. Abraham Ribicoff, "The New Administration Looks at
Social Welfare," <u>The</u> <u>Social</u> <u>Welfare</u> <u>Forum</u>, Proceedings,
National Conference on Social Welfare (1961), pp. 21-29.

17. Elizabeth Wickenden and Winifred Bell, <u>Public</u>
<u>Welfare:</u> <u>Time</u> <u>for</u> <u>a</u> <u>Change</u> (New York: New York School of
Social Work at Columbia University, 1961), pp. 12, 47-50; Ad Hoc
Committee on Public Welfare, "Recommendations for Public
Welfare Reorganization," 11/30/61, NASW: Washington Office
Records, Box 11, Social Welfare History Archives, Minneapolis,
Minn. This committee was appointed by Secretary Ribicoff and
included NASW and other social work leaders in its membership.

18. <u>Public</u> <u>Welfare</u> <u>Amendments</u> <u>of</u> <u>the</u> <u>House</u> <u>Committee</u> <u>on</u>
<u>Ways</u> <u>and</u> <u>Means</u> <u>on</u> <u>H.R.</u> <u>10032</u>, House Report No. 1414 (Washington,
D.C.: U.S. GPO, 1962), p. 86; Steiner, pp. 36-41; Martha
Derthick, <u>The</u> <u>Influence</u> <u>of</u> <u>Federal</u> <u>Grants:</u> <u>Public</u> <u>Assistance</u>
<u>in</u> <u>Massachusetts</u> (Cambridge, Mass.: Harvard University Press,
1970), pp. 131-33.

19. As shown in issues of NASW's <u>Washington</u> <u>Memorandum</u> in
the sixties and <u>The</u> <u>Advocate</u> <u>for</u> <u>Human</u> <u>Services</u> in the
seventies.

20. This project represented a fusion of efforts by social
workers, including Richard Cloward, and sociologists, notably
Lloyd Ohlin. Applying Ohlin's "opportunity theory" to the
problem of juvenile delinquency, it attempted to tackle the
problem through a broad program of community services, manpower
training, and antidiscrimination activities. Patterson, pp.
127, 138-39.

21. Patterson, pp. 144, 138; Aleanor Merrifield,

"Implications of the Poverty Program: The Caseworker's View," Social Service Review, XXXIX: 294-99 (September, 1965); Martha Derthick, Uncontrollable Spending for Social Services Grants (Washington, D.C.: Brookings, 1975), pp. 25-28; Interim Report to Mr. Sargent Shriver, OEO, from the NASW, 7/5/66, NASW: Washington Office Records, Box 9.

22. In addition, the leadership in public welfare concerns exercised by the Chicago School diminished abruptly when Edith Abbott retired. Letter from Charlotte Towle to Eileen Younghusband, 2/14/58, Younghusband Papers, National Institute for Social Work, London, England. A number of writers urged a "divorce" between social work and welfare. See John B. Turner, "In Response to Change: Social Work at the Cross Road," Social Work, XIII: 8-9 (July, 1968).

23. See, e.g., "Powerful New National Coalition to Fight Human Need Cutbacks," The Advocate for Human Services, NASW, II: 3 (April 31, 1973); "Social Services Bill Announced," The Advocate, III: 1-2 (October 15, 1974).

24. "Local Candidates--You Can Help Them," The Advocate for Human Services, I: 1-4 (September 30, 1972).

25. Pauline Lide, "The National Conference on Social Welfare and the Black Historical Perspective," Social Service Review, XLVII: 195-200 (June, 1973); James Dumpson, Memo, 11/25/69, CSWE Records, XV-1C, Social Welfare History Archives; letter from Arnulf Pins, Exec. Director, CSWE, to Bob Robinson, Black Students Caucus, 1/31/69, and Dumpson to Herman Gallegos, Southwest Council, La Raza, 10/5/69, CSWE Records, 10/5/69, XV-3A. Note that the National Conference on Social Welfare was formerly the National Conference of Social Work.

26. Richard Cloward and Frances Fox Piven, Regulating the Poor: The Functions of Public Welfare (New York: Random House, 1971).

27. E.g., Henry J. Meyer, Edgar Borgatta, and Wyatt C. Jones, Girls at Vocational High: An Experiment in Social Work Intervention (New York: Russell Sage, 1965); Notes and Comments, "Has Social Work Failed?" Social Service Review, XLVI: 427-31 (September, 1972); Joel Fischer, "Is Casework Effective? A Review," Social Work, XVII: 5-21 (January, 1973).

28. Robert D. Leighninger, Jr., "Systems Theory," Journal of Sociology and Social Welfare, IV: 446-66 (July, 1978).

29. The author was asked in a teaching job interview several years ago whether she was committed to "pushing back the frontiers of social work knowledge."

Bibliographical Note

The two most useful collections for the study of social work's
professional development after 1920 are the records of the
National Association of Social Workers and of the Council on
Social Work Education, both located in the Social Welfare History Archives, University of Minnesota, Minneapolis,
Minnesota. The NASW Records are a well-organized collection
documenting the development of the NASW's major predecessor,
the American Association of Social Workers. AASW records
include minutes and correspondence of the Executive, Membership, Government and Social Work, and other committees, proceedings of most of the annual meetings and delegate conferences, and reports on grievance cases. There is one important
gap in the AASW records--the minutes of the Executive Committee
from 1931 through 1934. Otherwise, this is a comprehensive
collection, which also includes the records of the five other
professional organizations (AAGW, AAMSW, APSW, NASSW, and SWRG)
which helped form the NASW in 1955, the papers of the American
Association for the Study of Community Organization, the
records of the Temporary Inter-Association Council, which
engineered the NASW's formation, and NASW papers for the period
1955 to 1969.

The Council on Social Work Education Records are extensive, but less well-organized at present. They include the
documents of the American Association of Schools of Social
Work: Executive Committee minutes and correspondence, proceedings from some annual meetings, and the reports and records
of various committees. The AASW Records in the CSWE collection
can be supplemented by material on the association in the Grace
Browning/Mary Houk Papers at the Social Welfare History
Archives. The CSWE collection also includes the records of the
council from 1952 to 1975. Several other collections at the
Social Welfare History Archives deal with the history of social
work education. The records of the Study of Social Work Education contain important material on Ernest Hollis and Alice
Taylor's 1951 study, Social Work Education in the United
States. The papers of Mattie Cal Maxted are extremely valuable
in presenting a picture of the development of the National Association of Schools of Social Administration in the 1940s. The
Maxted Papers include a good deal of correspondence among NASSA
leaders, as well as letters and reports from the Joint Accrediting Committee of state universities and land grant colleges.

The NASW and CSWE records were valuable resources for the

entire time period studied. Other sources were helpful for
particular periods and issues. The Records of the Chicago
Chapter of the NASW, located at the Chicago Historical Society,
offer an important regional perspective on AASW membership
issues and the relationship of a professional group to the
social work union movement in the 1930s. These papers contain
interesting correspondence, including a number of letters from
Sophonisba Breckinridge, as well as Executive Committee and
Membership Meeting Minutes for 1921-55. The Chicago Chapter
Records also include some records on the American Association
of Hospital Social Workers and the Chicago Round Table, an
informal branch of the American Association of Psychiatric
Social Workers.

Other sources helpful for the study of social work's relationship to politics in the 1930s include the papers of Harry
Lurie at the Social Welfare History Archives, the autobiography
of Bertha Reynolds (An Uncharted Journey), and the description
of social work political activity in general and the Rank and
File Movement in particular by one of its leaders, Jacob Fisher
(The Response of Social Work to the Depression). I also received helpful firsthand accounts of the period in interviews
with Chicago social workers Rita Novak, Paulette Kahn Hartrich,
and D. E. Mackelmann (who later became a major figure in the
Chicago Housing Authority), and with Mary Burns, recently
retired from the faculty of the Western Michigan University
School of Social Work. Leslie Alexander's dissertation,
"Organizing the Professional Social Worker: Union Development
in Voluntary Social Work, 1930-1950," is a useful and well-
documented study of professional social work involvement in the
Rank and File Movement.

A major resource for understanding the development of pub-
lic welfare on the federal level after 1935 is The Reminiscences
of Jane Hoey, an oral history which is part of the Social
Security Project at the Oral History Collection of Columbia
University. The project also includes the oral histories of
Katharine Lenroot and Charles Schottland of the U.S. Children's
Bureau. The National Archives in Washington, D.C., has the
records of the Bureau of Public Assistance of the Social
Security Administration and documents relating to the Chil-
dren's Bureau. The BPA Records are interesting but do not
appear to be extensive (some of the material relating to Jane
Hoey and the bureau is located in other parts of the Social
Security Administration collection). The oral history of
Valeska Bary, a social worker active in public welfare at both
the state and federal levels, gives another side to the story
recounted by Hoey. The Bary oral history is part of the
Suffragists Oral History Project and is located at the
University of California/Berkeley, The Bancroft Library. An
interview with Alice Taylor Davis, who was a case supervisor in
a state welfare department in the thirties, also shed light on
public welfare developments.

Edith Abbott and Sophonisba Breckinridge played key roles
in the development of social work as a profession. Lela
Costin's biography of Edith and Grace Abbott, Two Sisters for
Social Justice, gives an important context to discussion of
their influence. More such biographies of social work leaders

are needed. For further insights into the Chicago School
"point of view," I enjoyed the letters of Charlotte Towle in the
Dame Eileen Younghusband Papers, National Institute for Social
Work, London, England.
   Although the AASW records give an official account of the
Walter West/Wayne McMillen dispute in the Association in the
years 1941 to 1942, it is difficult to find more informal and
in-depth explanations of the issues involved in the conflict.
Correspondence in the Louis H. Towley Papers at the Social Wel-
fare History Archives sheds some light on the story. I was also
helped by interviews with Harriett Bartlett, Paulette Kahn
Hartrich, and Hasseltine Taylor, formerly on the faculty of the
School of Social Welfare at the University of California/
Berkeley. The Towley Papers and the interview with Mary Burns
gave a good picture of the effects of World War II on the personnel situation in social work. Thomas Olson's dissertation,
"Unfinished Business: American Social Work in Pursuit of
Reform, Community, and World Peace, 1939-1950," helps explain
social work's stance on issues of neutrality and national
defense.
   Details of the conflict between graduate social work
educators and the undergraduate social work movement are contained in the Marion Hathway Papers and the unpublished autobiography of Mildred Mudgett at the Social Welfare History
Archives, as well as in the CSWE Records and the Mattie Cal
Maxted Papers. An interview with Lucille Barber, formerly on
the social work faculty at Michigan State University, provided
firsthand impressions of people active in the NASSA and further
information on the philosophy of the undergraduate movement.
The interview with Alice Taylor Davis increased my understanding of the development of the Hollis-Taylor report (1951).
   There are a number of sources on the relation between
social work and social science in the 1950s. These include the
Grace Coyle Papers and the Records of the School of Applied
Social Sciences, Case Western Reserve University, located in
the Case Western Reserve University Archives. The Records of
the University of Michigan School of Social Work document the
development of the social work/social science doctorate under a
grant by Russell Sage. The Russell Sage Foundation Annual
Report gives details on a variety of such interdisciplinary
projects. Interviews with Henry Meyer, who directed the
University of Michigan doctoral program, provided an indispens-
able orientation to the topic. Talks with Norman Goroff,
School of Social Work, University of Connecticut, and Milton
Chernin, former Dean, School of Social Welfare, University of
California/Berkeley, yielded helpful information on curricular
issues in the fifties.
   Issues in social work practice are highlighted in the
Harriett Bartlett Papers at the Social Welfare History
Archives, the Bartlett Oral Memoir, which is part of the NASW
Oral History Project, the interviews with social work theorists
and practitioners conducted by Mary L. Gottesfeld and Mary E.
Pharis (Profiles in Social Work), and Virginia Robinson's The
Development of a Professional Self: Teaching and Learning in
Professional Helping Processes. The Grace Coyle Papers and the
SASS Records at Case Western Reserve are valuable sources on the

development of group work.

The formation of the NASW is well documented in the NASW Records. The Harriett Bartlett Papers and oral history give a firsthand account of earlier attempts at inter-organizational cooperation and of the early years of the new professional association. I was also fortunate to be able to interview Miss Bartlett on these topics.

Finally, I relied on a variety of sources for a general orientation to social work's development from 1930 to 1960. These included the published Proceedings of the National Conference of Social Work, the 1933-1960 volumes of the Social Work Year Book, and editorials and articles in social work journals: The Compass, The Family (later the Journal of Social Casework), the Social Service Review, and The Survey. I also consulted the Karl and Elizabeth de Schweinitz Papers and the Fred K. Hoehler Papers at the Social Welfare History Archives. The papers of Hathway and Mudgett touched on a number of important topics in social work history. In addition to providing information on particular issues, the people I interviewed corrected false impressions and gave a valuable personal picture of what it was like to be a social worker in the thirties, forties, and fifties.

Bibliography

Abbott, Edith. Social Welfare and Professional Education. Chicago: University of Chicago Press, 1942.

Alexander, Leslie. "Organizing the Professional Social Worker: Union Development in Voluntary Social Work, 1930-1950." Diss., Bryn Mawr College, 1977.

Allport, Gordon. The Nature of Prejudice. Cambridge, Mass.: Addison and Wesley, 1954.

Altmeyer, Arthur. The Formative Years of Social Security. Madison: University of Wisconsin Press, 1966.

American Association of Group Workers. Toward Professional Standards. New York: Association Press, 1947.

American Association of Schools of Social Work. Education for the Public Social Services. New York: AASSW, 1942.

American Association of Social Workers. Four Papers on Professional Function. New York: AASW, 1937.

. Social Casework, Generic and Specific. A Report of the Milford Conference. New York: AASW, 1929.

. This Business of Relief. New York: AASW, 1936.

Barker, Robert L., and Thomas L. Briggs, eds. Manpower Research on the Utilization of Baccalaureate Social Workers. Vol. 2. Washington, D.C.: U.S. GPO, 1971.

Bartlett, Harriett. Social Work Practice in the Health Field. New York: National Association of Social Workers, 1961.

Benedict, Ruth. The Chrysanthemum and the Sword. Boston: Houghton Mifflin, 1947.

Berlant, Jeffrey. Professions and Monopoly. Berkeley: University of California Press, 1975.

Bernstein, Saul. Group Work Memories. Loyola University School
     of Social Work, 1984.

Bisno, Herbert. The Place of the Undergraduate Curriculum in
     Social Work Education. The Comprehensive Report of the
     Curriculum Study. Vol. 2. New York: Council on Social
     Work Education, 1959.

Blum, John Morton. V was for Victory: Politics and American
     Culture during World War II. New York: Harcourt Brace
     Jovanovich, 1976.

Boehm, Werner.   Objectives of the Social Work Curriculum of
     the Future. The Comprehensive Report of the Curriculum
     Study. Vol. 1. New York: Council on Social Work
     Education, 1959.

Bogardus, Emory. Fundmentals of Social Psychology. New York:
     Appleton-Century Crofts, 1950.

Boyer, Paul S. Urban Masses and Moral Order in America,
     1820-1920. Cambridge, Mass.: Harvard University Press,
     1978.

Bremer, William W. Depression Winters: New York Social Work-
     ers and the New Deal. Philadelphia: Temple University
     Press, 1984.

Brown, Esther. Social Work as a Profession. New York: Rus-
     sell Sage, 1935.

     . Social Work as a Profession. 2nd ed. New York: Rus-
     sell Sage, 1936.

     . Social Work as a Profession. 4th ed. New York: Rus-
     sell Sage, 1942.

Brown, Josephine. Public Relief, 1929-1939. New York:
     Henry Holt, 1940.

Bruno, Frank. Trends in Social Work. New York: Columbia Uni-
     versity Press, 1948.

Bucher, Rue, and Joan G. Snelling. Becoming Professional.
     Beverly Hills, Calif.: Sage, 1977.

Burner, David. Herbert Hoover: A Public Life. New York:
     Alfred A. Knopf, 1979.

Carey, James T. Sociology and Public Affairs. Beverly Hills,
     Calif.: Sage, 1975.

Carr-Saunders, A. M., and P. A. Wilson. The Professions.
     Oxford: Clarendon Press, 1934.

Chambers, Clarke. Paul U. Kellogg and the Survey. Minneapolis:

University of Minneapolis Press, 1971.

. _Seedtime of Reform_. Ann Arbor, Mich.: Ann Arbor
Paperbacks, 1967.

Cloward, Richard, and Lloyd Ohlin. _Delinquency and Opportunity, A Theory of Delinquent Gangs_. Glencoe, Ill.:
Free Press, 1960.

Cloward, Richard, and Frances Fox Piven. _Regulating the Poor:
The Functions of Public Welfare_. New York: Random
House, 1971.

Cohen, Nathan. _Social Work in the American Tradition_. New York:
Dryden Press, 1958.

Costin, Lela. _Two Sisters for Social Justice_. Urbana: University of Illinois Press, 1983.

Council on Social Work Education. _Social Work Education in the
Post-Master's Program_. No. 1. New York: CSWE, 1953.

. _Social Work Education in the Post-Master's Program_. No.
2. New York: CSWE, 1954.

Coyle, Grace. _Group Experience and Democratic Values_. New
York: Woman's Press, 1947.

. _Group Work and American Youth_. New York: Harper, 1948.

. _Social Process in Organized Groups_. New York: Richard
R. Smith, 1930.

. _Social Science in the Professional Education of Social
Workers_. New York: Council on Social Work Education,
1958.

Davis, Allen. _American Heroine_. New York: Oxford University
Press, 1973.

Derthick, Martha. _The Influence of Federal Grants: Public
Assistance in Massachusetts_. Cambridge, Mass.: Harvard
University Press, 1970.

. _Uncontrollable Spending for Social Services Grants_.
Washington, D.C.: Brookings, 1975.

Deutsch, Morton, and Mary Evans Collins. _Interracial Housing_.
Minneapolis: University of Minnesota Press, 1951.

Eissler, K. R. _Searchlights on Delinquency_. New York: International Universities Press, 1949.

Elliot, Lula Jean. _Social Work Ethics_. New York: American
Association of Social Workers, June, 1931.

Elliott, Philip. The Sociology of the Professions. London:
    Macmillan, 1972.

Etzioni, Amitai. The Semi-Professions and Their Organiza-
    tion. New York: Free Press, 1969.

Fisher, Jacob. The Rank and File Movement in Social Work,
    1931-1936. New York: New York School of Social Work,
    1936.

    . The Response of Social Work to the Depression.
    Cambridge, Mass.: Schenkman, 1980.

Frazier, E. Franklin. The Negro in the U.S. New York:
    Macmillan, 1949.

Freidson, Eliot. The Professions and Their Prospects. Bever-
    ly Hills, Calif.: Sage, 1973.

French, David. An Approach to Measuring Results in Social
    Work. New York: Columbia University Press, 1952.

Gilb, Corinne. Hidden Hierarchies. New York: Harper, 1966.

Glenn, John M., Lilian Brandt, and F. Emerson Andrews. Russell
    Sage Foundation: 1907-1946. New York: Russell Sage,
    1947.

Goldman, Eric. The Crucial Decade and After. New York:
    Vintage Books, 1960.

Gottesfeld, Mary L., and Mary E. Pharis. Profiles in Social
    Work. New York: Human Sciences Press, 1977.

Halsey, A. H., ed. Traditions of Social Policy. Oxford:
    Blackwell, 1976.

Hamilton, Gordon. Theory and Practice of Social Case Work.
    New York: Columbia University Press, 1940.

    . Theory and Practice of Social Case Work. 2nd ed. New
    York: Columbia University Press, 1951.

Hare, A. Paul. Handbook of Small Group Research. New York:
    Free Press, 1962.

Hare, A. Paul, Edgar Borgatta, and Robert F. Bales, eds. Small
    Groups: Studies in Social Interaction. New York:
    Alfred A. Knopf, 1955.

Haskell, Thomas L. The Emergence of Professional Social Sci-
    ence. Urbana: University of Illinois Press, 1972.

Hickok, Lorena. One Third of a Nation. Edited by Richard
    Lowitt and Maurine Beasley. Urbana: University of
    Illinois Press, 1981.

Hinkle, Roscoe C., and Gisela Hinkle. The Development of
    Modern Sociology. Garden City, N.J.: Doubleday, 1954.

Hollis, Ernest V., and Alice L. Taylor. Social Work Education
    in the U.S. New York: Columbia University Press, 1951.

Hunt, J. McVicker, and Leonard Kogan. Measuring Results in
    Social Casework. New York: Family Service Association
    of America, 1950.

Johnson, Terence J. Professions and Power. New York:
    Macmillan, 1972.

Kaiser, Clara. The Group Records of Four Clubs at University
    Neighborhood Centers. Cleveland: School of Applied
    Social Sciences, Western Reserve University, 1930.

Kardiner, Abram. The Psychological Frontier of Society. New
    York: Columbia University Press, 1945.

Karpf, Maurice. Scientific Basis of Case Work. New York:
    Columbia University Press, 1931.

Kasius, Cora, ed. A Comparison of Diagnostic and Functional
    Case Work Concepts. New York: Family Service Associ-
    ation of America, 1950.

    . New Directions in Social Work. New York: Har-
    per, 1954.

Kogan, Leonard S., ed. Social Science Theory and Social Work
    Research. New York: National Association of Social
    Workers, 1960.

Konopka, Gisela. Eduard C. Lindeman and Social Work Philoso-
    phy. Minneapolis: University of Minnesota Press, 1958.

    . Therapeutic Group Work with Children. Minneapolis:
    University of Minnesota Press, 1949.

Larson, Magali Sarfatti. The Rise of Professionalism.
    Berkeley: University of California Press, 1977.

Lash, Joseph P. Eleanor and Franklin. New York: Signet
    Books, 1971.

Lasswell, Harold. Psychopathology and Politics. Chicago:
    University of Chicago Press, 1935.

Lazarsfeld, Paul F., William H. Sewell, and Harold L. Wilensky,
    eds. The Uses of Sociology. New York: Basic Books,
    1957.

Lee, Porter. Social Work as Cause and Function. New York:
    Columbia University Press, 1937.

Leiby, James. A History of Social Welfare and Social Work in
    the United States. New York: Columbia University Press,
    1978.

Linton, Ralph. The Cultural Background of Personality. New
    York: D. Appleton-Century, 1945.

Lubove, Roy. The Professional Altruist. New York: Atheneum,
    1969.

Lynd, Robert. Knowledge for What? Princeton: Princeton Uni-
    versity Press, 1946.

MacIver, Robert. The Contribution of Sociology to Social
    Work. New York: Columbia University Press, 1931.

McKinley, Charles, and Robert W. Frase. Launching Social
    Security. Madison: University of Wisconsin Press, 1970.

Madison, Bernice. Undergraduate Education for Social Wel-
    fare. San Francisco: San Francisco State College, 1960.

Marcus, Grace. The Nature of Service in Public Assistance
    Administration. Washington, D.C.: U.S. GPO, 1946.

Martin, George. Madame Secretary: Frances Perkins. Boston:
    Houghton Mifflin, 1976.

Martinez-Brawley, Emelia E. Seven Decades of Rural Social
    Work. New York: Praeger, 1981.

Meier, Elizabeth G. The New York School of Social Work. New
    York: Columbia University Press, 1954.

Melosh, Barbara. "The Physician's Hand:" Work Culture and
    Conflict in American Nursing. Philadelphia: Temple
    University Press, 1982.

Merle, Sherman. Survey of Undergraduate Programs in Social
    Welfare: Programs, Faculty, Students. New York: Coun-
    cil on Social Work Education, 1967.

Meyer, Henry, Edgar Borgatta, and Wyatt C. Jones. Girls
    at Vocational High: An Experiment in Social Work
    Intervention. New York: Russell Sage, 1965.

Moore, Wilbert E. The Professions: Roles and Rules. New York:
    Russell Sage, 1970.

Mullins, Nicholas C. Theories and Theory Groups in Contempo-
    rary American Sociology. New York: Harper and Row,
    1973.
Myrdal, Gunnar. An American Dilemma. New York: Harper,
    1944.

Newstetter, Wilbur. <u>Wawo-Kuje Camp, A Research Project in
    Group Work</u>. Cleveland: School of Applied Social
    Sciences, Western Reserve University, 1930.

Odum, Howard. <u>American Sociology</u>. New York: Longmans,
    Green, 1951.

Olson, Thomas Lyle. "Unfinished Business: American Social
    Work in Pursuit of Reform, Community and World Peace,
    1939-1950." Diss., University of Minnesota, 1972.

Ormsby, Ralph. <u>A Man of Vision: Francis H. McLean</u>. New York:
    Family Service Association, 1969.

Patterson, James T. <u>America's Struggle against Poverty,
    1900-1980</u>. Cambridge, Mass.: Harvard University Press,
    1981.

Pearl, Arthur, and Frank Riessman. <u>New Careers for the Poor</u>.
    New York: Free Press, 1965.

Perlman, Helen Harris. <u>Social Casework: A Problem Solving
    Process</u>. Chicago: University of Chicago Press, 1957.

    . <u>Helping: Charlotte Towle on Social Work and Social
    Casework</u>. Chicago: University of Chicago Press, 1969.

Perrett, Geoffrey. <u>Days of Sadness, Years of Triumph</u>. New
    York: Coward, McCann, and Geoghegan, 1973.

Pollak, Otto. <u>Social Science and Psychotherapy for Children</u>.
    New York: Russell Sage, 1952.

Polsky, Howard. <u>Cottage Six</u>. New York: Russell Sage, 1962.

Porter, Rose. <u>Organization and Administration of Public Re-
    lief Agencies</u>. New York: Family Welfare Association of
    America, 1931.

President's Research Committee on Social Trends. <u>Recent
    Social Trends in the U.S.</u> Vol. 2. New York: McGraw-
    Hill, 1933.

<u>Red Cross Service Records, Accomplishments of Seven Years:
    1939-1946</u>. Washington, D.C.: American National Red
    Cross, 1946.

Reid, Kenneth. <u>From Character Building to Social Treatment</u>.
    Westport, Conn.: Greenwood Press, 1981.

Reynolds, Bertha C. <u>An Uncharted Journey</u>. New York: Citadel
    Press, 1963.

Roberts, Robert W., and Robert H. Nee, eds. <u>Theories of Social
    Casework</u>. Chicago: University of Chicago Press, 1970.

Robinson, Virginia. A Changing Psychology in Social Case Work.
    Chapel Hill: University of North Carolina Press, 1930.

    . The Development of a Professional Self: Teaching and
    Learning in Professional Helping Processes. New York:
    AMS Press, 1978.

Sapir, Edward. Culture, Language, and Personality. Edited by
    David G. Mandelbaum. Berkeley: University of California
    Press, 1956.

Sheffield, Ada. Social Insight into Case Situations. New York:
    D. Appleton-Century, 1937.

Shils, Edward. The Present State of American Sociology. Glen-
    coe, Ill.: Free Press, 1948.

Smalley, Ruth. Specialization in Social Work Education. New
    York: Council on Social Work Education, 1956.

Social Welfare Research Group. The Function and Practice of
    Research in Social Work. New York: SWRG, May, 1955.

Socio-Cultural Elements in Casework: A Case Book of Seven
    Ethnic Case Studies. New York: Council on Social Work
    Education, 1955.

Stamm, Alfred. An Analysis of Undergraduate Social Work Pro-
    grams Approved by CSWE, 1971. New York: Council on Social
    Work Education, 1972.

Stein, Herman D., and Richard A. Cloward. Social Perspectives
    on Behavior. Glencoe, Ill.: Free Press, 1958.

Steiner, Gilbert. Social Insecurity: The Politics of Wel-
    fare. Chicago: Rand McNally, 1966.

Stott, William. Documentary Expression and Thirties America.
    New York: Oxford University Press, 1973.

Sundquist, James L. Politics and Policy. Washington, D.C.:
    Brookings Institute, 1968.

Swift, Linton. New Alignments between Public and Private
    Agencies. New York: Family Welfare Association of
    America, 1934.

Theoharis, Athan. Seeds of Repression: Harry S. Truman and
    the Origins of McCarthyism. New York: Quadrangle Books,
    1971.

Thomas, Edwin, ed. Behavioral Science for Social Workers. New
    York: Free Press, 1967.

Towle, Charlotte. Common Human Needs. Washington, D.C.: So-
    cial Security Board, 1945.

. _The Learner in Education for the Professions_. Chicago:
University of Chicago Press, 1954.

Trattner, Walter I. _Homer Folks: Pioneer in Social Welfare_.
New York: Columbia University Press, 1968.

. _Biographical Dictionary of Social Welfare in America_.
Westport, Conn.: Greenwood Press, 1986.

Trecker, Harleigh B. _Social Group Work: Principles and Prac-
tices_. New York: Woman's Press, 1948.

Trolander, Judith. _Settlement Houses and the Great Depres-
sion_. Detroit: Wayne State University Press, 1975.

Tyler, Ralph. _Basic Priciples of Curriculum and Instruction_.
Chicago: University of Chicago Press, 1950.

UNESCO. _The Contribution of Social Sciences in Social Work
Training_. New York: U.N., 1961.

U.S. Bureau of Labor Statistics. _Social Workers in 1950:
A Report on the Study of Salaries and Working Conditions in
Social Work_. New York: American Association of Social
Workers, 1952.

U.S. Department of Health, Education, and Welfare. _Closing
the Gap in Social Work Manpower_. Washington, D.C.: U.S.
GPO, 1965.

Viswanathan, Narayan. "The Role of the American Public Welfare
Association in the Formulation and Development of Public
Welfare Policies in the U.S.: 1930-1960." Diss.,
Columbia University, 1961.

Walker, Sydnor. _Social Work and the Training of Social Work-
ers_. Chapel Hill: University of North Carolina Press,
1928.

Warner, Amos Griswold, Stuart A. Queen, and Ernest Harper.
American Charities and Social Work. 4th ed. New York:
Thomas Y. Crowell, 1930.

White, R. Clyde, and M. K. White. _Research Memorandum on
Social Aspects of Relief in the Depression_. New York:
Social Science Research Council, 1937.

Wickenden, Elizabeth, and Winifred Bell. _Public Welfare: Time
for a Change_. New York: New York School of Social Work
at Columbia University, 1961.

Wilensky, Harold, and Charles Lebeaux. _Industrial Society and
Social Welfare_. New York: Russell Sage, 1958.

Wilson, Gertrude, and Gladys Ryland. _Social Group Work Practice. Boston: Houghton Mifflin, 1949.

Woodroofe, Kathleen. From Charity to Social Work. London:
    Routledge and Kegan Paul, 1968.

Young, Donald. American Minority Peoples. New York: Har-
    per, 1932.

. Research Memorandum on Minority Peoples in the
    Depression. New York: Social Science Research Council,
    1937.

Index

Abbott, Edith, 11, 15, 28, 45
n.7, 70 n.21, 79, 117, 157,
160; and professional
education for social work,
37, 79-80, 87, 125, 132,
133, 137, 146 n.29, 153,
160; and public welfare,
60, 62, 78, 79-80, 82, 84,
87, 90, 93, 94, 106, 107,
132, 215-16, 217, 222 n.22;
and social work as career
for women, 10, 79
Abbott, Grace, 55, 64, 66, 72
n.52; and Children's
Bureau, 11, 56, 84; and
politics, 56, 61; and
public welfare, 62, 78,
79-80, 84; and University
of Chicago, School of
Social Service Administration, 79-80
Academy of Certified Social
Workers, 215
Addams, Jane, 7, 10, 11, 176
n.44; and pacifism, 17, 104
Adler, Lillian, 43
Aid to dependent children,
85, 91, 93, 164
Alexander, Leslie, 171 n.5
Alinsky, Saul, 217
Allport, Gordon, 161
Altmeyer, Arthur, 66
American Association for
Organizing Family Social
Work. See Family Welfare
Association of America
American Association for
Study of Group Work. See

American Association of
Group Workers
American Association of Group
Workers (AAGW), 113, 157,
158, 186, 188; formation
of, 155, 188-89; and for-
mation of the National
Association of Social
Workers, 194-95, 197; professional identity, 188-
89, 194; professional
standards, 188; training
for group work, 188, 189;
and social action, 194-
95, 205 n.32
American Association of
Hospital Social Workers.
See American Association
of Medical Social Workers
American Association of
Medical Social Workers
(AAMSW), 13, 113-14, 185-
86, 194; formation of,
11-12, 186; and formation
of National Association
of Social Workers, 194-
97, 198; professional
standards, 186, 194, 197;
training for medical
social work, 13, 186
American Association of
Psychiatric Social Work-
ers (AAPSW), 13, 112, 113,
186, 187, 194; formation
of, 12, 187; and forma-
tion of National Associa-
tion of Social Workers,
194-97, 198; professional